SOUL FEAST

Newly Revised Edition

Marjorie J. Thompson

SOUL FEAST

Newly Revised Edition

An Invitation to the
Christian Spiritual Life

WESTMINSTER
JOHN KNOX PRESS
LOUISVILLE · KENTUCKY

© 1995, 2005, 2014 Marjorie J. Thompson
Forewords @ 1995 and 2014 Westminster John Knox Press

Newly Revised Edition
Published by Westminster John Knox Press
Louisville, Kentucky

14 15 16 17 18 19 20 21 22 23—10 9 8 7 6 5 4 3 2 1

Scripture quotations from the New Revised Standard Version of the Bible are copyright © 1989 by the Division of Christian Education of the National Council of the Churches of Christ in the U.S.A. and are used by permission. Scripture quotations marked CEB are taken from the Common English Bible, ©2011 Common English Bible. Used by permission. All rights reserved. Scripture quotations marked JB are from *The Jerusalem Bible,* copyright © 1966, 1967, 1968 by Darton, Longman & Todd, Ltd., and Doubleday & Co., Inc. Used by permission of the publishers. Scripture quotations marked KJV are taken from the King James or Authorized Version of the Bible. Scripture quotations marked RSV are from the Revised Standard Version of the Bible, copyright © 1946, 1952, 1971, and 1973 by the Division of Christian Education of the National Council of the Churches of Christ in the U.S.A., and are used by permission.

Book design by Allison Taylor
Cover design by Dilu Nicholas

Library of Congress Cataloging-in-Publication Data
Thompson, Marjorie J., 1953-
  Soul feast : an invitation to the Christian spiritual life / Marjorie J. Thompson. -- Newly Revised Edition.
    pages cm
  ISBN 978-0-664-23924-4 (alk. paper)
  1. Spiritual life--Christianity. I. Title.
  BV4501.3.T4745 2014
  248--dc23
                                                                2014008808

Most Westminster John Knox Press books are available at special quantity discounts
when purchased in bulk by corporations, organizations, and special-interest groups.
For more information, please e-mail SpecialSales@wjkbooks.com.

To John,

my dearest companion on the journey
and my intimate friend
at the Table

My soul is satisfied as with a rich feast,
and my mouth praises you with joyful lips . . .
—Psalm 63:5

Contents

Contents

New Foreword

While Marjorie Thompson and I have met just once—for as long as it took us to exchange names and shake hands—the first edition of *Soul Feast* has been on my shelf since its publication in 1995. During the years I taught at Columbia Theological Seminary, it was on the required reading list for more courses than I can count. Students who read it invoked her name with the same reverence that she and I once invoked the name of Henri Nouwen, our teacher (at different ends of the same decade) at Yale Divinity School. Now it is my privilege to introduce you to the third edition of *Soul Feast,* a book that belongs not only on your shelf but in your life, at least if you are hungry for the more abundant kind.

By way of full disclosure, I should tell you that I am slow to trust most spiritual guides. Earlier in my life I spent so many years searching for a church home, listening to so many people tell me so many contradictory truths about God that I acquired a kind of seeker's squint—a narrowing of both eye and heart designed to protect me from the next evangelist who came at me with the next plan for my salvation. As far as I can remember, not a single one of them ever asked me an open-ended question. They were in the answer business, and all they needed me to do was swallow.

Marjorie Thompson is not that kind of guide. She has so much trust in her readers that she invites us to amend her teaching based on what we already know about ourselves. To extend the metaphor of the title, she does not fill the table with a bunch of dishes and then tell you how many servings of each you must eat to have a balanced diet. Instead, she asks you to taste them, taking your time as you pay close attention to how each one affects you. If you hate beets, can you put your finger on what it is about them that you cannot stand? If you love nothing more than a plate full of mashed

potatoes, can you figure out what makes them so satisfying? All that Marjorie asks of you is to come to the table with your appetite intact, ready to discover more about what nourishes you and why. She even leaves plenty of room in the margins of this book for you to adapt the recipes to your own kitchen.

At the same time, she is very clear about the spiritual practices that have nourished many kinds of Christians for more than two millennia. Skip one of these dishes altogether and you will be missing essential vitamins, so don't blame Marjorie when your soul starts feeling puny. Fortunately, she has a gift for presenting each practice with such clear appeal that there is little danger of skipping a course. As Dietrich Bonhoeffer once told his preaching students, a truly effective sermon must be like offering a child a crisp red apple or holding out a cup of water to a thirsty person and asking, "Wouldn't you like it?" By that measure, every chapter of this book is an effective sermon, for when Marjorie holds out one of the central practices of Christian faith to her readers, the answer is, "Yes, please. I would like it very much."

Marjorie also trusts the body—both the individual and the corporate one—as the concrete locus of divine transformation. Whether she is inviting her readers to experiment with different prayer postures at home or to embody hospitality at work and school, she keeps body and soul together. She never opposes the two or makes one sound holier than the other. In this way and many others, she shows us what it means to live by faith in the incarnation. Whether you believe that the incarnation happened only once, in the body of Jesus Christ, or whether you believe that it happens every day in the body of the church, the truth is the same: God enters the world through human flesh.

From the very first page, Marjorie lets you know that she is less interested in giving you information *about* the spiritual life than she is in giving you the tools to *engage* the spiritual life—both for your health and the health of the world. While her book stimulates quite a lot of thought, making you a better thinker is not the point. The point is to offer you a map to living water, along with a packing list of what you might need and who you might invite to come along as you set off to make the journey for yourself.

At the same time, Marjorie has logged so many hours on that road with so many different kinds of people that she can almost read your mind as you think of a thousand reasons to turn back.

"But I get dizzy when I don't eat," you say to her in the chapter on fasting.

"Fine," she says. "Why don't you try fasting from social media instead?"

"But I'm too shy to talk to a spiritual director," you say to her in the chapter on spiritual guidance.

"Fine," she says. "Why don't you try a small group instead?"

Whatever excuse you come up with, Marjorie has already heard it. Whatever door you think is closed to you, she finds another one for you to try. In this way among many others, she embodies what she teaches: spiritual disciplines must be freely chosen. We choose them only if we have a strong desire to grow, and even then we cannot force them to produce fruit. In the words of Richard Foster, spiritual disciplines are "the means by which we place ourselves where [God] can bless us."[1]

So there you have it. Marjorie not only trusts us to adapt what she has offered in this book and further trusts our bodily experience to teach us what we need to know; she also trusts the Spirit of God to meet each of us where we are, both individually and in community. This makes her one of the most trustworthy guides I know, whose third *Soul Feast* promises to nourish another generation of seekers in the church and far beyond.

Barbara Brown Taylor

Notes

1. Richard Foster, *Celebration of Discipline* (New York: Harper Collins, 1998), 7.

Foreword

It is a real honour and joy for me to write this foreword to Marjorie Thompson's book *Soul Feast, An Invitation to the Christian Spiritual Life*, especially because of our long friendship and my great admiration for her person and her work. I met Marjorie for the first time in the fall of 1979 while I was on the faculty of Yale Divinity School. After having received her master's degree at McCormick Theological Seminary in Chicago, Marjorie came to Yale to focus her studies on ecumenical Christian spirituality and to become more familiar with its different practices and disciplines. Very soon I became aware that Marjorie had unique gifts of mind and heart that enabled her to make significant contributions to the spiritual life of the Christian church. Her personality, which loves order and clarity, her Presbyterian tradition that highly values the spoken and written word, and her conviction that all churches need a deeper spiritual vision enabled her to accomplish much during her time at Yale. She read widely, spoke with many people, and visited a rich variety of retreat and conference centers. After finishing her year at Yale, she joined the staff of a large East Coast Presbyterian church and developed there a fruitful ministry with a special emphasis on spiritual formation. When Marjorie moved to Nashville, Tennessee, almost four years later, she was well prepared to broaden and deepen her spiritual ministry through teaching, workshops, and retreats.

This book is the fruit of Marjorie's personal practice, her solid studies, and long experience in spiritual formation. It brings together in a clear, concise way the essence of her ministry. There are few books in which a solid biblical vision and a practical, hands-on approach are so well integrated. When you have read and lived this book, you have been in touch with the best that Christian spirituality has to offer. Marjorie's treatment of spiritual reading, praying, worship, fasting, examination of conscience, spiritual guidance, hospitality, and the development of a "rule of life" makes the spiritual life readily accessible to people from many different walks of life.

As I went through the pages of this book, I could feel the strong yet gentle guidance of its author. Marjorie is clear, specific, and direct, but she does not impose, push, or manipulate. She simply invites us to create the space where the life of God in us can be nurtured and brought to fruition.

Our busy lives make it hard for us to create free time or space for God. In fact, as Spinoza says, there is a "*horror vacui,*" a fear of empty space. *Soul Feast* shows us that the disciplines of the spiritual life are meant to offer creative boundaries to that empty space within and among us so that we can acknowledge it without fear and allow God to transform there our stony hearts into hearts of flesh. Spiritual disciplines are nothing more and nothing less than ways to create a room where Christ can invite us to feast with him at the table of abundance.

One of the most encouraging qualities of this book is its ecumenicity. The language is inclusive of all Christians. It is a book that will speak to those who sincerely seek God, irrespective of denomination or tradition. Marjorie's invitation to the spiritual life is a beautiful affirmation of the truth that, beyond dogmatic and liturgical differences, there is a place where we can experience the common Source of our sustenance. It is a place where the Spirit of Jesus wants to dwell and lead us to the freedom of the children of God.

I am convinced that for those who take this book seriously and apply it to their individual as well as communal lives, a true transformation will take place—a transformation that will affect not only their interior life but also the life of the Body of Christ, the Church.

Henri J. M. Nouwen

Acknowledgments

More than twenty years ago, the Theology and Worship Unit of the Presbyterian Church (U.S.A.) asked me to join the project of developing a written resource on Christian spirituality for beginners. I remain grateful to Dick Junkin for extending the invitation through the unit's Office of Discipleship and Spirituality and to Carol Wehrheim for working with Dick and me to discern the shape this resource should take and for asking me to be its author. Jeanette Hardy supplied able administrative help from the office in Louisville at that time.

It was an unusual privilege and unimaginable help for an untested author to have the benefit of eight readers to advise and guide the development of a book manuscript. This extraordinary benefit was provided by the Office of Discipleship and Spirituality under Dick's direction. I continue to bless Ben Campbell Johnson, Dick Junkin, Martha Jane Petersen, Loretta Ross-Gotta, Carson Salyer, Carol Wehrheim, and Ann Young, who read volumes of rough draft pages, met with me twice, and responded to my work-in-progress with insight, clarity, challenge, support, and encouragement. I owe a debt of gratitude to Dr. Anne Wimberly of the Interdenominational Theological Center in Atlanta for offering valuable insights and resources from an African American perspective. I also received encouragement along the way from Howard Rice, Ted Yaple, and Glenn Hinson.

Perhaps no single person has exerted a more profound influence on the direction of my spiritual life than Henri Nouwen. Were it not for Henri's insight, encouragement, and support, I would not have had the background to write a book such as this. Neither would I have met the man who most fully embodies the continued stretching and support of my spiritual life, with whom I share the vocation

of Christian marriage. I remain grateful beyond words for Henri's faithful friendship and for the gift of his original foreword to this book.

At the same time, I am completely delighted that Barbara Brown Taylor has graciously contributed a new foreword to mark and celebrate this newly revised edition. It is hard to imagine a fellow pastor and author whose powerfully creative voice and authenticity of spirit I more admire. For generously bringing her insight, mastery of metaphor, and sparkling wit to the feast, I bow in deep gratitude.

Of course, this work could not have been completed without the quiet and patient support of my husband, John Mogabgab. Not only did he take up the burden of many household tasks and suffer countless hours of imposed solitude while I wrote, but he generously gave his time to coach me on the mysteries of computer logic and read the entire manuscript to assure me of its value. I trust his judgment.

My profound thanks to all at Westminster John Knox Press who helped bring this work to fruition and who continue to value its contribution to church and society today. I remain indebted to Alexa Smith, who initiated the publication process; to Stephanie Egnotovich, my original editor whose premature death was a great loss to the Press and its authors; and to Nancy Roseberry for copyediting and finalizing the original manuscript. To these names I now add: Jana Reiss, who worked with me to plan expansions and revisions for a third edition; David Maxwell, whose enthusiasm kept up my courage through months of labor on revisions; Barbara Dick, whose care in copyediting has fine-tuned my words; and Julie Tonini, who has capably followed through on bringing this new edition to the light of day.

Introduction

When I agreed to write a book on Christian spiritual practices more than twenty years ago, the concept of spirituality was still relatively new in most Protestant branches of the church. People were largely unaware that Christians had their own history of meditative practice, and had very little knowledge of contemplative prayer. Seminaries and divinity schools did not typically regard even the history of Christian spirituality as appropriate to a curriculum in ministry training, believing that "prayer and devotion" should be taught at home and in church. Consequently congregational leaders, themselves uninformed and unformed, rarely instructed church members in historic spiritual practices such as fasting, self-examination, or even prayer. Until the late twentieth century, Protestant churches chiefly gave their energies to the practices of worship, Bible study, and service.

Christians worldwide had lost touch with the riches of historic spiritual practices, particularly those of a contemplative nature. This loss eventually triggered a hunger to recover them. Mid-century, Thomas Merton played a significant role in reclaiming contemplation for monks and nuns within the very monastic communities that once were guardians of the contemplative life. His prolific writings brought to light the integral connections between contemplation and action. Merton influenced a new crop of church leaders and writers from a broad spectrum of Christian traditions, including fellow Roman Catholic Henri Nouwen and the Quakers Richard Foster and Parker Palmer (representing two distinct strands of the Society of Friends). In one of the gentler ironies of history, Catholics from the ritual-rich, sacramental side of Roman Christianity and Quakers from the low-ritual, "non-sacramental" wing of the Reformation both helped to carry forward a renewed appreciation of contemplative Christianity. The reason, I believe, is fairly straightforward: Despite their many differences, each has historically valued and nurtured the central role of silence in the spiritual life. Silence, poetically described as "God's first language," is an indispensable condition for genuine spiritual transformation.

The last quarter of the twentieth century witnessed a groundswell of interest in the spiritual life, spurred by the writings of figures like Morton Kelsey, Henri Nouwen, Eugene Peterson, Kathleen Norris, Richard Foster, and Frederick Buechner. This same period saw the development of major formational programs such as the Shalem Institute, Spiritual Directors International, the Academy for Spiritual Formation, and Renovaré, alongside new journals like *Weavings* and *Presence*.

The pace of interest in things spiritual accelerated in the 1990s. Training programs in spiritual guidance gained a stronger appeal among Protestants, drawing many to locally available Roman Catholic centers. Several Protestant seminaries began initiatives in spiritual formation and guidance distinct from academic degree programs, offered to clergy and laity alike for ministry enrichment. Many pastors enrolling in Doctor of Ministry programs made spiritual formation a specialized focus of study and practice. The final decade of the twentieth century also spawned a great proliferation of books on the spiritual life, a trend that has continued unabated so far in the twenty-first century.

Soul Feast first appeared in the middle of this yeasty decade of spiritual fermentation. In the intervening years, the book has been deeply valued by individuals, small groups, church leaders, students, and professors. Its enthusiastic embrace has been genuinely humbling and gratifying to me. I receive it as answer to the prayer governing my writing over the two years in which the book took shape: that it might be of genuine help to both laity and leaders of diverse denominations. Some readers have told me it was "the right book at the right time," for them personally but also for the larger church. An author could scarcely hope for more.

Noteworthy Developments in Our Cultural Context

In the years since this book was first published, important shifts have occurred in our culture. One frequently noted with consternation is the growth of the religiously unaffiliated in the United

States. A Pew Research Center survey of the period between 2007–2012 shows an increasing movement away from traditional religious institutions. Twenty percent of American adults no longer identify with a particular tradition, and fully one third of those under the age of thirty are unaffiliated. Collectively, they have been given the moniker "Nones," so called for checking the box labeled None under the question about religious affiliation. This trend is in line with the "spiritual but not religious" phenomenon that began as early as the foundation of Alcoholics Anonymous and that has grown more visible since the 1960s.[1]

While the rise in disaffiliation is widely lamented among church leaders, it need not be seen in a wholly negative light. Phyllis Tickle, in her book *The Great Emergence*,[2] argues that we are undergoing the most recent of our every-500-year "rummage sales"—an upheaval in culture and worldview that will inevitably reshape our faith interpretations and institutions as surely as the Great Schism of the eleventh century and the Great Reformation of the sixteenth century. This tsunami of change is well under way, marked by the postmodern and post-Christian sensibilities of the millennial generation. We can perceive certain characteristics of this emerging Christianity: it is profoundly Spirit-centered, seeking discernment through deep listening; it is more concerned with right practice than right belief; it is comfortable with questions and leery of answers; it embraces the truth of paradox over the dualistic absolutes of right and wrong; it rejects hierarchical structure, welcoming shared leadership and democratic decision making; it reflects the egalitarianism of the worldwide web, the new paradigms of quantum physics, and the recasting of traditional sources of authority.

Since these changes are still in a fluid phase, their creative energies are not yet coalesced into highly recognizable structures. We cannot see clearly the shape of what will emerge into a new and stable cohesion over the course of the twenty-first century. However, Tickle assures us that, as with every previous upheaval, this one will result in both greater vitality and a wider spread of the faith than before. It will meet our growing need for a more mature and authentic expression of Christian life. Therefore we need not fear the crumbling of traditional institutional structures or the reshaping of conventional religious ideas. Old forms are dying to make room for the new, sheltered in the mind of God. Since birth pangs are already upon us, those of us embedded in more traditional structures are naturally in distress. Yet if we dwell in trust, we may be confident

Creates, Renews, + Fulfills.
What does this look like
in my life?

"Create in me a clean heart, + renew a
right spirit within me."

Introduction

Behold, I am doing a new thing;
now it springs forth, do you not
perceive it?

Isaiah 43:19 (RSV)

that the One who creates, renews, and fulfills all things will carry us through.

Rabbi Rami Shapiro, an unorthodox teacher and writer, suggests that the rapid rise of the religiously unaffiliated offers humanity a splendid opportunity. Assessing the same Pew Research Center survey noted above he observes, "Most of these so-called Nones are not dismissive of God or spirituality but simply find religious labels and affiliation too narrow and constraining."[3] Shapiro calls them the "spiritually independent," a less prejudicial name than the Nones. He is convinced that they hold the same existential questions most of us do but are unwilling to confine their search for satisfying answers to any one religion or philosophy. They gravitate toward universal themes that resonate with their internal sense of truth, which attracts them to the writings of the mystics and great teachers of every age and culture. Shapiro joins Richard Rohr and others who term such writings the "perennial wisdom."

As I noted in my prologue to the second edition of this book ten years ago, beyond the walls of the church, multitudes of people with searching hearts look for truth wherever they think they can find it. Indeed, many within the church do so as well, a pattern by no means confined to the younger postmodern generation. There has been a notable increase in the number of educated, curious church folk who read broadly in other faith traditions and find it important to grapple with where and how we find common ground among the great spiritual teachings. Given the alarming increase of violence perpetrated worldwide in the name of religion, this is surely a healthy impulse. Yet there is more to the impulse than anxiety over destructive expressions of religious fanaticism. Many are genuinely interested in understanding other faith claims and are often willing to test spiritual practices from other traditions. Yoga is widely embraced in the West for physical and mental well-being, leading some to explore the spiritual underpinnings of Hinduism as well. Mindfulness is now a familiar category in mainstream American life, adapted for use in many settings devoid of its spiritual origins. Yet Buddhist teachings about impermanence, non-attachment, and living mindfully in the present moment carry the appeal of realistic perspective for many in a world changing as rapidly as ours.

On the other side of such explorations, those outside the Christian fold often find Jesus' life and teachings deeply attractive but are not drawn to the doctrines, sacraments, or communities of the church. In the globalized world of Internet communication, with easy access to multiple cultural and religious perspectives, it is not surprising that more people are pondering and choosing their own synthesis of various spiritual traditions.

Another galloping cultural shift is the extent to which technology has reshaped almost every dimension of our lives. When *Soul Feast* was first published email did not exist! Now, as it is quicker than phone calls and can speed documents or photos halfway across the world in seconds, it has naturally become our preferred method of business correspondence. Means of personal communication are now splintered among a burgeoning buffet of social media platforms and messaging on mobile devices. Bills, banking, shopping, research, books, news, music, classes—all can now be done online. This constitutes an extraordinary shift in how we live day-to-day and foreshadows the path of our future. We have launched into a brave new world where technology impacts everything from industry, business, government, education, and medicine to the environment, the arts, civic engagement, community formation, and of course, religion.

The proliferation of communication modes alone is enough to saddle us daily with distraction. My editor recently acknowledged that he feels obliged to check six locations for messages, depending on who might be contacting him. When Facebook, Twitter, Instagram, Skype, and WhatsApp are vying for our loyalty along with phone messages and multiple email accounts, time for focused attention suffers. As the chatter of social media adds to that of TV, radio, and cell phone, reflective spiritual practice becomes more challenging to say the least. We have become masters in the art of distracting ourselves from life's depth. If we hope to penetrate the riches of our own interiority, we will need a strong intention to resist the clamoring demands of instant communication.

The Deeper Challenge

Despite our impressive technological advances, we have yet to learn how to live responsibly on this earth with the great multitude of God's creatures. We have been unwilling to face the full consequences of our increased affluence and unable to deal adequately with the toxic by-products of our way of life. The more technology is used to expand our appetite for consuming the world's shrinking resources, the less capable we will be of embracing with love and respect this astonishingly unique creation.

Nor have we learned, collectively speaking, to live responsibly and respectfully with one another. We are far from loving our neighbors as ourselves, much less loving our enemies and praying for those who persecute us (Matt. 5:43–44). This is true not only for enemies abroad but also those we view as political, economic, or religious enemies on home turf. Two thousand years after Christ's ministry on earth, we are still largely in moral, emotional, and spiritual adolescence. It therefore remains a frighteningly realistic possibility that we will, in some measure, end up destroying both human community and the planet that sustains us.

What I have observed over the past twenty years has increased my sense of urgency about the need for spiritual practice among us. If we do not learn to honor and strengthen the inner life of spirit, all the external changes in the world cannot save us. New laws, regulations, and technological fixes are all susceptible to human corruption and self-interest. If we do not know ourselves as beings created to reflect the divine image, we will lose the immense opportunity for transformation God has offered us in the gift of life itself. And if the love of God embodied in Christ cannot turn us, how shall we be turned?

I remain convinced that the way forward lies in practicing the truths we know. If the importance of spiritual practice has become more widely accepted in recent decades, their appeal lies partly in sheer practicality. Here are forms of prayer, methods of reflection, and patterns of commitment that tangibly impact our spiritual and emotional maturity. Moreover, these practices can transcend the boundaries of theologies that divide us. A common experience of fasting could serve to build bridges between Jews, Christians, and Muslims. Contemplative practices have given Christians and Buddhists ground for constructive dialogue and mutual understanding. Spiritual practices have the potential to heal wounds not only within but among us.

The term *practice* has more than one sense. It can mean preparation, as in practicing for a game. It can also mean the ongoing exercise of a profession, as in practicing medicine or law. Spiritual practices can embody both meanings but, in my view, carry more of the second sense. They are not just practice for the real game of discipleship but ways of expressing discipleship.

Spiritual practice is the heart of this book. The most basic practices of faith are relevant in every era. Prayer, meditation on sacred texts, self-examination, and hospitality never go out of style, although they go out of corporate memory at times. Even today, many Christians remain unfamiliar with the deeper patterns of spiritual discipline that root us in God's transforming love. Given what is at stake in the world, the need is greater than ever for people of faith and good will to understand, experience, and embody the great practices that bring us to mature humanity.

Most of the practices described in this book originate in the ancient Jewish faith from which Jesus' life and teachings come to us. Yet they hold broad application for people of diverse faith backgrounds. Any sincere seeker after God may find practical guidance here in ways to deepen the human spirit and strengthen a sound heart. The essence of it all is learning greater intimacy and freedom in our relationship with God. And the key is giving the Spirit time and space to rearrange our interior furniture—setting our disordered priorities and putting love of God and neighbor center stage.

Approaching This Book

In the pages that follow, I offer my own understanding of what Christian spirituality is and how it may be nurtured among active people in contemporary life. Theological assumptions and definitions are laid out in the first chapter. These are based on my reading of scripture, which remains our most fundamental and precious wellspring of guidance concerning authentic spirituality. My knowledge of scripture is informed by biblical scholarship but rooted in personal prayer, corporate worship, and those theological interpretations held in common among the great streams of historical Christianity.[4]

I was raised and educated in the Reformed theological tradition, which has taught me, among other things, the value of being ecumenical. Within the broader streams of Christian tradition I have found much that is illuminating and lifegiving. Part of the work of the Spirit among us is reclaiming timeless truths from the rich heritage of our historic tradition, just as part of that work is leading us into new understandings of truth: "I still have many things to say to you, but you cannot bear them now. When the Spirit of truth comes, he will guide you into all the truth" (John 16:12–13a).

I trust that this book will speak to the yearnings and convictions of others within the Reformed tradition, but my primary intent is to make a contribution to the wider conversation of the church on the topic of Christian spirituality. I aim to speak to the spiritual needs and concerns of the ordinary person in the pew as well as those who might never occupy a pew. Yet I know from experience that many pastors, church educators, and seminarians remain hungry as well for guidance in the spiritual life. Only over the past generation has leadership training in most Protestant institutions begun to include a full range of practices for nurturing inward faith alongside its outward expressions.

This is a book for beginners, yet the term *beginner* is deceptive and paradoxical. The more we comprehend of the spiritual life and the longer we try faithfully to live it out, the more we grasp how simple and primary its essential patterns are. There is a childlike simplicity to Christian spirituality. In a certain sense we never get past practicing the basics. This makes beginners of us all, a truth that is both humbling and freeing. The great sixteenth-century Carmelite nun Teresa of Avila captured the reality well when she wrote, "No soul on this road is such a giant that it does not often need to become a child at the breast again. . . . For there is no state of prayer, however sublime, in which it is not necessary often to go back to the beginning."[5]

Purpose and Scope

My purpose is to help people of faith understand and begin to practice some of the basic disciplines of the Christian spiritual life. Disciplines are simply practices that train us in faithfulness. I have chosen disciplines from the ecumenical tradition that have weathered the test of time, proving to be means of grace to Christians of different histories and cultures. Such practices have consistently been experienced as vehicles of God's presence, guidance, and call in the lives of faithful seekers.

In each chapter I treat one practice, offering (1) sufficient information to understand its nature, including historical, theological, and biblical references, and (2) questions and exercises of a practical nature to lead into an experiential encounter with the discipline. Because my intent is practical and experiential, the *information* in this book is offered in the service of faith *formation*. My aim is to engage mind and heart together in seeking nourishment for our spiritual hunger. The exercises suggested within each chapter are oriented to the individual reader but can be adapted for group use. (See Group Study Guide at the back of the book.)

No introductory book on the spiritual life can be comprehensive. I am keenly aware of the compromises made in treating certain topics and omitting others. For example, instead of a chapter on journal keeping, I chose to weave journaling suggestions into each chapter as it seemed appropriate. Within the limited scope of this book, the selection of topics inevitably represents my own sense of the weight of these practices relative to other possibilities.

I have tried to arrange the chapters with a meaningful flow between topics. In chapter 1, I discuss the widespread spiritual hunger of our time, suggesting where we might look for satisfaction. I introduce basic terms and perspectives concerning the Christian spiritual life. In chapter 2, I consider the practice of spiritual reading, understood primarily as meditative reading of scripture. For Protestants generally (but not exclusively), hearing and responding to God's Word alone or in a small group is a priority in the spiritual life.

The nature and practice of prayer is treated in chapter 3. The spiritual life receives its very heart and soul in prayer, a practice that for Christians is embedded in meditation on scripture. In chapter 4, I take up the role of public worship in our spiritual formation. This discussion is placed after that of spiritual reading and prayer only because personal reading and prayer immeasurably enrich our experience of corporate worship. Worship remains the foundation and context for every spiritual practice, especially those of a personal or "private" nature.

Chapter 5, new for this edition, addresses the theme of sabbath, a most critical practice to recover in our time. It follows the chapter on worship since reframing the concept of sabbath expands on an earlier understanding limited to the day for Christian worship. Fasting is closely associated with both public worship and private prayer in Christian tradition. In chapter 6, I look at fasting in the larger context of abstaining from excessive attachments and nurturing simplicity of life. Fasting and penitence are closely associated in most religious traditions, including Jewish and Christian tradition. Chapter 7 encourages us to reconsider the ancient art of self-examination and confession.

Christians historically have not understood confession to be solely a private matter between God and the individual. To examine one's heart alone can lead to despair, self-deception, or unhealthy scrupulosity. Chapter 8 is an introduction to the importance of consulting with another Christian who can act as a guide or mentor in spiritual growth.

In chapter 9, I consider the central Christian practice of hospitality. Here I move beyond disciplines that focus primarily on our relationship with God, even when they involve us with and affect others. Hospitality directly and visibly expresses our spiritual kinship with every human being and with the whole creation. It is both a *means* of God's transforming grace for us and a fruitful *expression* of the Spirit working in us for the sake of others.

In chapter 10, substantially expanded for this new edition, I consider what it might mean to devise a "rule of life" for ourselves from what we have learned by working through the preceding chapters. The connection between personal and corporate disciplines should be very clear at this point, not as a logical argument but as an experienced reality.

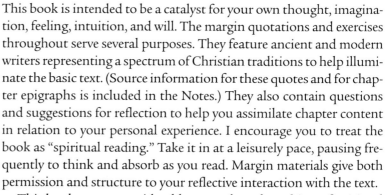

On Reading This Book

This book is intended to be a catalyst for your own thought, imagination, feeling, intuition, and will. The margin quotations and exercises throughout serve several purposes. They feature ancient and modern writers representing a spectrum of Christian traditions to help illuminate the basic text. (Source information for these quotes and for chapter epigraphs is included in the Notes.) They also contain questions and suggestions for reflection to help you assimilate chapter content in relation to your personal experience. I encourage you to treat the book as "spiritual reading." Take it in at a leisurely pace, pausing frequently to think and absorb as you read. Margin materials give both permission and structure to your reflective interaction with the text.

This book covers considerable ground on the subject of spiritual practices. You should not expect to launch into everything at once, even if you feel inspired to do so. Similarly, there is no need to be discouraged at the thought of all the things you *don't* do. My purpose is to introduce you to a variety of possibilities for enriching your spiritual life. Pay attention to what you feel especially drawn to and why. God would rather that we learn to be faithful in a few humble commitments than that we continually despair over our failures because we take on too much.

A good way to read this book is with a small community of other seekers. If you study, pray, and practice with just one chapter between gatherings, you will not run the risk of getting spiritual indigestion by trying to take it all in at once. The suggestions in the Group Study Guide will help guide your class or group through each chapter.

I trust this book will continue to add a clear voice to the ongoing conversation in our church and culture concerning how we nurture and sustain spiritual vitality in contemporary life. I hope that reading and reflecting on what follows will do more than edify—that it will draw you into a courageous and joyful exercise of those practices that may yield an experiential knowledge of God. God's own challenging guidance and providential grace are more than sufficient to satisfy the hunger in each of our lives and communities of faith. When we begin to take spiritual practices seriously, the possibilities for personal and corporate transformation are truly beyond our imagining! May grace attend your reading and reflection.

Notes

1. The growth of the religiously unaffiliated reflects more than the individualism so rampant in American society. Studies suggest that contributing factors include a strong reaction against the melding of conservative religious teachings and aggressive politics that has shaped the American landscape since the 1980s and the general secularization that marks nations with more affluent economies. See the Pew Research Religion and Public Life Project, " 'Nones' on the Rise" (Oct. 9, 2012) at pewforum.org.

2. See Phyllis Tickle, *The Great Emergence: How Christianity Is Changing and Why* (Grand Rapids, MI: Baker Books, 2008, 2012). A gifted writer with immense historical breadth, Tickle offers a condensed yet comprehensive overview of the past two millennia, drawing out the confluence of social, economic, political, religious, scientific, and technological changes shaping each era. She helpfully puts current trends into a much larger perspective than most contemporary analysts of culture.

3. *Perennial Wisdom for the Spiritually Independent*, annotation by Rami Shapiro (Woodstock, VT: Skylight Paths Publishing, 2013), xiii.

4. The three main streams are Eastern Orthodox, Roman Catholic, and Protestant. The theology they hold in common is expressed most concisely in the ecumenical creeds, particularly the Apostles' Creed and the Nicene Creed, which were adopted by the church before any major schism occurred.

5. *The Life of Teresa of Jesus: The Autobiography of St. Teresa of Avila*, trans. and ed. E. Allison Peers (Garden City, NY: Image Books, 1960), 145.

CHAPTER 1

Hunger and Thirst for the Spirit

❧

The Spiritual Yearning of Our Time

O God, you are my God, I seek you,
  my soul thirsts for you;
my flesh faints for you,
    as in a dry and weary land where there is no water.
                                            Psalm 63:1

Signs and Seasons

There is a hunger abroad in our time, haunting lives and hearts. Like an empty stomach aching beneath the sleek coat of a seemingly well-fed creature, it reveals that something is missing from the diet of our largely rational, secular, and affluent culture. If we look at the underbelly of this sleek creature, we notice ragged, unkempt fur and signs of disease. Even in communities that hold sacred values, much is awry. Both within and beyond traditional faith communities, a hunger for spiritual depth and integrity has been gaining momentum for several generations.

For some of us, the hunger is amorphous. Like free-floating anxiety, it lurks just below the surface of consciousness. Perhaps we feel an emptiness that leaves us restless for a larger meaning and purpose in life. Perhaps we sense that we are sailing through life in a rudderless ship. Something is missing. Something is out of balance. But it remains nameless.

For others of us, the hunger is recognizably spiritual. We know there is a vacuum inside us that will suck up an infinite supply of thrills, goods, and successes without satisfying the human heart. We are aware of needing a transcendent compass. Suffering has opened us to questions for which there are no easy answers—perhaps no answers at all. We have come to believe that only a power transcending this life can give meaning to our choices and circumstances.

Our suffering in developed countries is primarily psychological, relational, and addictive: the suffering of people who are comfortable on the outside but oppressed and empty within. It is a crisis of meaninglessness, which leads us to try to find meaning in possessions, perks, prestige, and power, which are always outside of the self. It doesn't finally work.

Richard Rohr

1

Yet older patterns of religious life seem increasingly antiquated and inadequate. More and more people are separating their spirituality from religion. "Institutional religion" has acquired strongly negative connotations, like the repellant end of a magnet. In line with our cultural individualism, people find it natural to devise private belief systems independent of historical faith communities or doctrines. Many seekers, especially among those who claim no religious affiliation, consider themselves spiritual but not religious.

The spiritual thirst of our time has become a traceable social phenomenon. People from all walks of life and many faiths have been searching with renewed intensity for a spiritual center. Some drink from the wells of Asian religions, Native American traditions, or New Age philosophies, and many combine the sources they draw from. Within more traditional Christian communities, increasing numbers have wholeheartedly embraced the idea of being on a "spiritual journey." Church basements have hosted AA-related "recovery spiritualities" for decades, but more are now integrating Twelve Step perspectives and practices in their sanctuaries and classrooms. As demand has increased for spaces conducive to spiritual retreat, Roman Catholic religious houses have opened their facilities to an influx of Protestants seeking experience in prayer, contemplative life, and spiritual direction. Psychotherapists note more clients asking questions of a spiritual nature, and many have learned to combine traditional therapies with spiritual guidance. Seminarians who have clamored for courses addressing their spiritual questions in a less academic way are now offered increasing options.

A sea change has been occurring whose current expressions have been building for several generations. Its pervasive character in North America suggests that what we are witnessing may surpass even the significance of the Great Awakening in the eighteenth century. Some scholars and church leaders now call it Emerging Christianity.[1] The change represents a powerful impulse toward spiritual wholeness and integration at a time of unprecedented personal and social fragmentation. The sense of restlessness and yearning is evident well beyond the boundaries of traditional faith communities.

Rhymes and Reasons

History shows that movements of religious renewal wax and wane. Why should a tide of spiritual ferment be rising in our time with such force? Many factors contribute, some cultural, some personal, and some that can qualify only as spiritual.

Cultural Factors

Four cultural factors are readily discernible. First, from the time of the Enlightenment, Western culture has been steeped in the world-view of rationalism. Rationalism makes reason the highest authority in determining what is true. Its expression in the modern scientific mind has had, until recently, little sympathy for anything that cannot be measured, quantified, or categorized. Invisible realities that do not yield to scientific inquiry have generally been dismissed from the realm of possibility. Consequently, we have suffered a loss of the sense of sacredness in life. God has no place in the assumptions of scientific rationalism. This reduction of life to narrow, mechanistic categories of reality is no longer adequate, however, even for many thoughtful scientists. Indeed, the past few decades have seen the rise of new horizons and questions within the world of science that have opened fascinating dialogues between science and religion—or perhaps, more specifically, between quantum physics and spirituality.

Second, technological advances have led to exponential change at virtually every level of our lives. The rate of development over the past century alone—in transportation, communication, industrial invention, medicine, marketing, and information—has resulted both in tremendous benefit and enormous social dislocation. In the introduction, I noted some negative effects of our electronic technologies, particularly their capacity to distract us. Unfortunately, our exploding means of communication do not necessarily lead to better or more meaningful communication. We may experience more connection with less depth of relationship. Amid these rapid and pervasive changes, many people long for some center of stability and peace.

Third, we live in a culture that glorifies superficial values. As a society, we lack a deep sense of purpose that calls us to sacrifice individual desires for the sake of a larger good. I recall a conversation with a young couple who were raising three children. Painfully aware that our cultural values made faithful living a rigorous challenge, they wanted to swim against the tide of Madison Avenue hype that seemed to be sweeping their children away in a flood of unimaginative toys, name-brand clothes, and sports idols. Twenty years after that conversation, I wish I could say that our cultural values have shifted in a more constructive direction. They have not, but that couple—now parents of well-grounded young adults—succeeded in swimming against the tide. Many faithful people continue to search for values that nourish human growth in responsible community. They know that material wealth, sexual attractiveness, physical prowess, and social status are the spiritual equivalent of empty calories. Our social order is starved for values of enduring substance.

Finally, our culture seems increasingly paralyzed by fear, shaping the way we govern and defend ourselves. The catalogue of woe is long. In this post–9/11 era, we wonder how to balance a collective desire for security with our treasured individual freedoms, including privacy. Fears concerning economic and job stability have risen sharply as a consequence of the recent worldwide recession. Optimism about secure retirement has given way to queasiness over shrinking wealth. In the face of crippling medical costs, adequate health insurance looms large for many, even as efforts to fix the system have become a political football.

Indeed, the vastly intensified polarization of our social-political life has itself become a source of grave concern for many citizens. We in the West are not the only ones suffering internal pressures from widely divergent ideologies. All over the world new conflict zones and political upheavals arise. Rightly we worry about the consequences of a widening gap between rich and poor. Fear of crime, drugs, and gang violence remains strong in much of the world, while the connection between mental illness and gun violence is of increasing concern in America.

Hanging over our collective heads is the triple-pronged scourge of nuclear, chemical, and biological weapons. More urgent still are inadequately heeded environmental warnings. Climate change is upon us, whether or not we believe in settled science. Icecaps are melting, tundra is thawing, sea levels are rising, and entire species are going extinct at alarming rates. We live in an age of high ecological anxiety, reaping the whirlwind of our two-century carbon emissions spree. As industrialization goes global, many are losing hope that we can turn around in time to curb the deadly impact of our way of life. Increasingly, we harbor deep pessimism about the ability of human beings to create just and secure orders of life. These fears contribute to both pervasive anxiety and desire for a stabilizing faith.

Personal Factors

At the personal level, three factors bear especially on our spiritual hunger. First, suffering and tragedy are powerful catalysts for moving people toward spiritual perspectives. Our rapidly changing society has brought new forms of human suffering. Painful experiences cry out for explanation. Every spiritual tradition has its theodicy, a framework for interpreting human suffering. We want to know how God is related to our pain. Suffering makes us aware of our need for a larger framework of meaning and purpose in life.

—> Need a place to put the pain.

Second, as we have noted, many people are restless and dissatisfied with church as they have experienced it. God has not come alive for them through traditional religious institutions. I know a man who has dutifully attended worship and served as a church trustee for decades. He is still mystified by the language of faith. Words about God seem mere words—beautiful and hopeful, but disconnected from the world he knows. This man would like to believe but does not experience the reality of God in his life. The faith of his friends both encourages and frustrates him by comparison. Deep inside he yearns for his faith to catch fire. Like this man, many who feel dissatisfied or empty in their faith experience continue seeking spiritual nourishment through the church. Others have chosen to look elsewhere. They share a deep hunger for direct experience of God rather than "secondhand faith."

Third, people who *have* had vivid experiences of God in their lives too often have found traditional churches inhospitable places to share them. One such person had a profound experience when she was fourteen. In a time of solitude, she heard a very clear voice that seemed startlingly more real than any human voice. The voice said, "You are my beloved child; walk with me, and you will heal my people." She felt flooded with a sense of peaceful well-being and was powerfully moved to serve God. Yet until we met, she had never felt free to share her experience with anyone. She learned early on that people who "hear voices" are considered "mental cases." This woman did not know there was a framework from her faith tradition to help her interpret what had happened. She often doubted whether her experience was real because she could not imagine anyone accepting it as real. Unless a priest, pastor, or parishioner is willing to hear and take such experiences seriously, people like this woman are left with "no basis to integrate their own experience into their faith or church life."[2]

Spiritual Factors

Beneath these cultural and personal factors lies a deeper reason for the spiritual hunger of our time. Human beings are innately religious. We harbor a bedrock desire for a transcendent wellspring of meaning and purpose in life. While sociologists may attribute the universal human religious impulse to psychosocial need, people of faith believe that we are *made* for relationship with God. Therefore until that relationship is sought and found, there will always be an existential emptiness at the core of our being. Centuries ago Saint Augustine confessed to God, "You have made us for yourself, and our heart is restless until it rests in you."[3]

Surely God is the primary factor behind the spiritual seeking of our time. It seems the Holy Spirit stirs things up when our societies and sacred institutions get complacent, corrupt, or simply fall too far behind the evolving knowledge and ethos of the times. I believe God's intentions are the most crucial force behind the sustained tide of spiritual hunger today. Without the fidelity of divine purpose, all we can hope for when the wave of hunger has crested is the frothy aftermath of a fad. But with the integrity of divine purpose, we can trust that a truer and more authentic spirituality may emerge from our restless search for soul sustenance.

You called, you cried, you shattered my deafness. You sparkled, you blazed, you drove away my blindness. You shed your fragrance, and I drew in my breath, and I pant for you. I tasted and now I hunger and thirst. You touched me, and now I burn with longing for your peace.

Saint Augustine

Approaching the Table

Before we turn to the food and drink that might satisfy our hunger and quench our thirst, I need to clarify key terms I use in this book and name my basic definitions and assumptions.

What Is Spirituality?

The term *spirituality* has gained wide currency in our cultural imagination, including our churches. Protestants are attracted to the word in part because they perceive it as fresh and open to meaning. Older terms such as "piety" or "devotion" have become weighed down with negative associations.

Piety, a word once endowed with great respect, now suggests to many a saccharin sentimentality or the delicate, easily shocked conscience of moral rigidity. Our caricature of a pious Christian has eyes rolled heavenward and hands permanently joined at the fingertips. Indeed, many would rather be taken for secular humanists than pious Christians!

The word *devotion* has suffered a similar though less damaging fate. It retains the sense of inward reflection that attracts many to the word *spiritual*. It also signifies a heart given over in love and adoration

① Excessively sweet or sentimental

to the beloved. Yet the notion of complete devotion to anyone or anything may suggest excessive emotional attachment or lack of objectivity. The term also has the ring of a potentially superficial and external exercise: "I do my five-minute devotions every morning."

In some instances, I support restoring the positive meaning of older terms. It seems clear, however, that *spirituality* has become the contemporary word of choice for expressing how we live in relation to transcendent truth. As it is now a reasonably permanent fixture in our religious vocabulary, we had best be clear what we mean when we use the term.

What does spirituality mean to you? Write out your own definition.

I prefer to begin with a more biblical phrase, "the spiritual life." Scripturally speaking, the spiritual life is simply the increasing vitality and sway of God's Spirit in us. It is a magnificent choreography of the Holy Spirit in the human spirit, moving us toward communion with both Creator and creation. The spiritual life is thus grounded in relationship. It has to do with God's way of relating to us and our way of responding to God.

In Christian theology and experience, the work of the Holy Spirit is to conform us to the image of Christ:

> Now the Lord is the Spirit, and where the Spirit of the Lord is, there is freedom. And all of us, with unveiled faces, seeing the glory of the Lord as though reflected in a mirror, are being transformed into the same image from one degree of glory to another; for this comes from the Lord, the Spirit. (2 Cor. 3:17–18)

The human creature was made in the image and likeness of God (Gen. 1:26–27), yet we obscured and distorted that likeness in the Fall. Christ is "the image of the invisible God" (Col. 1:15) in all its original purity. When we are "clothed with Christ" (see Gal. 3:27), the truth of our humanity is restored to us and the image of our Creator begins to emerge with clarity. In Christ we are reshaped according to the pattern we were created to bear.

What do you think it means for us to be made in God's image and likeness? How do you understand "the image of Christ"?

This reshaping is the basic meaning of *spiritual formation* in the Christian tradition. The term *formation* lies at the heart of words like conformation, reformation, and transformation. It invites us to consider: What or whose form are we seeking? What, in our personal or corporate lives, needs to be reformed?

The apostle Paul clearly believed that Christ could be formed in his followers: "My little children, for whom I am again in the pain of childbirth until Christ is formed in you" (Gal. 4:19). He urges, "Do not be conformed to this world, but be transformed by the renewing of your minds" (Rom. 12:2). What he means by the renewal of our minds finds expression in Philippians 2:5: "Let the same mind be in you that was in Christ Jesus." Christ is formed in us not just personally but corporately. The mind of Christ is to shape and direct the entire body of Christ. Here we receive our truest identity, meaning, and purpose. Drawing on Paul's theology, we can say that "spiritual formation" is conformation to the image of Christ by the indwelling of the Holy Spirit.

If the Christian spiritual life has to do with Christ being "formed in us," what is spirituality? In one sense spirituality is simply the capacity for a spiritual life—the universal human capacity to receive, reflect, and respond to the Spirit of God. But in a more practical sense, spirituality is the way we realize this spiritual potential. It involves conscious awareness of, and assent to, the work of the Spirit in us. Spirituality points to a path—to choices of belief, value commitments, patterns of life, and practices of faith that allow Christ to be formed in us.

The Character of the Spiritual Life

The spirituality I am describing is dynamic. God's Spirit is continually challenging, changing, and maturing us. Although we may be able to point to a single and decisive conversion experience, remaining faithful involves a journey of continual conversion. It can never be said in our lifetime that we have "arrived." The spiritual life invites a process of transformation in the life of a believer. It is a process of growing in gratitude, trust, obedience, humility, compassion, service, and joy. As we deepen our relationship with God, we begin to choose God's ways and purposes as our own.

It should be clear that Christian spirituality begins with God, depends on God, and ends in God. We owe our capacity to be spiritual to the grace of One who creates us free to share love with our living Source. The old mystics were fond of saying that we are *capax Dei*, that is, capable of receiving and embodying divine life. Paul's prayer in Ephesians 3 ends with the remarkable words, "so that you may be filled with all the fullness of God"! We are linked to the Spirit in a way that we cannot adequately conceive or describe but can experience and express in our life.

Christian spirituality is thus initiated and sustained by One who lives both within and beyond us. This means that while God chooses to be known to us in and through personal experience, the divine Being always transcends personal experience. God is mercifully free from the

What does the "capacity for a spiritual life" take? Born with or learned?

Reflect on John 21. The disciples fished all night and caught nothing. Jesus told them to cast their nets again. Does this story suggest anything to you about the relationship between human labor and divine grace?

distortions that personal experience is inevitably subject to. For example, we cannot force God to conform to our agenda for the world; we cannot manipulate God with our prayers; and we cannot achieve spiritual growth through sheer grit and willpower. The spiritual life is not a task of self-reformation. There is no fix-it-yourself kit, no manual promising "five easy steps to the complete spiritual person."

Spiritual growth is essentially a work of divine grace with which we are called to cooperate. Free and active cooperation is our share of the labor. But experience teaches that we don't cooperate with God's intentions for us easily. Opening ourselves to the work of the Spirit requires effort and discipline.

This raises a natural question about the relationship between divine grace and human free will. Is it God's work or our work that makes things happen? The answer, of course, is yes! The marvelous paradox of our relationship with God is that grace undergirds rather than undermines our free choice. So Paul can urge his flock to "work out your own salvation with fear and trembling; for it is God who is at work in you, enabling you both to will and to work for his good pleasure" (Phil. 2:12).

A metaphor from early Christian tradition may help us grasp more clearly the nature of this relationship. Observe a sailboat. It cannot move by its own power but must rely on the force of wind, over which neither sailboat nor sailor has control. Still, a sailor can shift the position of the boat by adjusting tiller and sheets so that the sails catch the wind. Free will is like the sailor. Though it is sometimes a struggle, we can choose to hold the boat of our life steady into the wind of the Spirit. Then our efforts are supported and directed by grace. One caution: Once we have opened our sails to that wind, we need to be prepared to go where the Spirit blows!

The sailboat metaphor will get leaky if we push it too far. In the end, even our ability to hold our boat steady into the wind rests on God's grace. All is grace, yet all depends on our willingness to work freely with grace. The magnificent truth of Christian faith is that the work of divine grace makes our efforts not less our own, but more.

The Role of Spiritual Disciplines

Certain practices can help us attend to the work of grace in our lives and our times. These practices—such as scriptural meditation, prayer, and discernment—are often called spiritual disciplines. What is the nature of discipline and its place in spiritual growth?

Discipline often seems a harsh word. It can conjure up images of parents punishing disobedient children or of strict teachers prowling classrooms with rulers in hand. Yet we also appreciate the value of discipline. We admire musicians, athletes, and scholars who develop their full potential through rigorous study and practice. Some of us would be happy to maintain a well-organized desk! How often I hear others echo my own struggle: our hopes for regular spiritual practice are eroded by time constraints, fatigue, or simple inertia and procrastination. Discipline does not come naturally to most of us; it must be cultivated.

I have just used the term *discipline* in two distinct ways. The first carries the sense of order imposed by an authority on someone subject to that authority. The second signifies a training regimen freely taken on for long-term personal benefit. The purpose of the second is generally mastery of a field or personal growth. Both kinds of discipline involve a "rule" or pattern of behaviors, but what motivates each is clearly different.

Spiritual disciplines are practices that help us consciously to develop the spiritual dimension of our lives. Like an artist who wishes to develop painting skills or an athlete who desires a strong and flexible body for the game, a person of faith freely chooses to adopt certain life patterns, habits, and commitments in order to grow spiritually. There is nothing externally imposed about spiritual disciplines. In adopting them, we simply recognize that our innate spiritual aptitude cannot develop fully without practice.

We will choose spiritual disciplines only if we have a strong desire to grow. If our desire to develop spiritually is not deep enough to overcome our resistances, we will find ourselves unable to maintain any discipline, however good our intentions. If this is our current state, there is no reason to berate ourselves. Desire cannot be forced or manufactured; it can be discovered only in freedom. Yet even a little desire can be encouraged to grow stronger through the practice of discipline, like a spark fanned into full flame or a seedling cultivated into full growth.

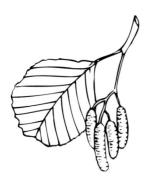

It may help to understand that spiritual disciplines are not ends in themselves. Rather, they are simply means of grace. As the Quaker writer Richard Foster puts it, "By themselves the Spiritual Disciplines can do nothing; they can only get us to the place where something can be done. . . . [They are] the means by which we place ourselves where [God] can bless us."[4]

Spiritual disciplines are like garden tools. The best spade and hoe in the world cannot guarantee a good crop; their use only makes it more likely that growth will be unobstructed. The mystery of maturation lies in the heart of the seed, and the outcome of planting depends largely on the vagaries of weather. Still, tools are important in helping to ensure that planted seeds will bear fruit. Tools can remove stones and roots, aerate the soil, weed and water the garden.

Disciplines such as contemplation, self-examination, and hospitality have the character of garden tools. They help keep the soil of our love clear of obstruction. They keep us open to the mysterious work of grace in our heart and our world. They enable us not only to receive but to respond to God's love, which in turn yields the fruit of the Spirit in our lives.

Every spiritual discipline tutors us in relationship. Our words *disciple* and *discipline* share the root meaning of being taught. Jesus' disciples were taught by his words and example in a living relationship. Our discipleship is no different. It grows in the embrace of a living relationship with the divine Spirit. What a remarkable promise it is (see John 16:12–15) that the Spirit of Jesus will be a present teacher to those who follow him with a whole heart!

Spend some time reflecting on the garden as a metaphor for the human heart. You might want to read the parable of the sower (Mark 4:1–20).

I have heard spiritual disciplines described as "windows onto grace." This lovely phrase serves also to warn us against the possible misuse of spiritual practices. As long as a discipline is like a window—transparent to God—it is a genuine means of grace. But a discipline can become opaque, reflecting only our distorted motives. For example, we might seek nothing more than a peaceful or ecstatic experience in our practice of contemplative prayer; hospitality might simply be a means of self-display, if our aim is to impress people with it. Spiritual disciplines, like all good things, can be pursued for the wrong reasons. If our motives are distorted, the practice will not yield good results.

We need to remember, of course, that our motives are almost always mixed to some extent. If we were to wait until they were completely pure before practicing a spiritual discipline, we would never get started! Better to begin practicing and pray that over time we will be given grace to live into greater purity of heart. As our own desires and intentions become aligned with God's intentions for us, we find ourselves free to follow and serve Christ. Discipline makes us disciples with a clear and joyful purpose.

It would be nice if we could simply "practice the presence of God" in all of life, without expending energy on particular exercises. But the capacity to remember and abide in God's presence comes only through steady training. If we wish to see, name, and love Christ "in the flesh" of daily existence, we will eventually need some kind of intentional practice of spiritual discipline.

Food and Drink: Finding Spiritual Nurture

Our spiritual hunger is evidence of the timeless human need for a real and abiding relationship with God. The Holy One calls us into this relationship and does everything possible to restore us when we have wriggled out of its mutual demands. God's love lies at the root of our hunger for God. Indeed, love is *God's hunger* for relationship with us! Has it ever occurred to us that God is starved for our companionship?

Years ago I was stricken by the comments of Loretta Ross, a woman of deep prayer. She was describing what she had heard in response to the question she put before Jesus each morning: What do you want me to tell the people? For many years the response she received was, "Tell the people that I love them." Then one day the reply came: "Tell the people that I miss them."[5]

Is our God a lover blinded by grief, calling out through the ache of our hunger—calling us to come home and be nourished with real life once again? Can we begin to see our hunger as a response—feeble, fitful, and fearful, but a response nonetheless? It is a response to God's anguished hunger for the creatures fashioned by divine hands for relationship with the divine heart.

We are like the prodigal son of Jesus' parable—children far from home and starving. Have we decided to go home? If so, what path will set us toward the destination of our Creator's heart? Where do we turn to find nourishment for the parched places of our souls? What food and drink will be adequate to our need? Sometimes we do not know where to look for resources, how to find others who share our yearning, or how to voice our longings.

Do the questions above fit your experience? If not, how have your experiences been different? What frustrations have you felt in seeking answers?

This book aims to help us find and partake of food and drink for the spirit. The resources we will explore are drawn from our full Christian heritage. None of the practices are new, but some have been lost to our knowledge and others require adaptation. Our current spiritual hunger is partly due to being out of touch with classic practices that could feed us. When we are severed from our roots, we are like plants without nourishment. To fruitfully appropriate classic disciplines, we need to be willing to engage "tradition" creatively. Yet each practice needs to be interpreted and tested for our time if it is to be recovered as a valuable source of spiritual nurture. Staying alert to our current context allows us to discern where the winds of the Spirit are blowing. Human beings make sense out of life by continually threading old and new together.

Tradition

Do you have ambivalent feelings about the word *tradition*? Sometimes we gaze wistfully on older traditions that seem to offer stability in a confusing world. Yet our cultural impulse is to discard the old for bright new possibilities and paradigms that would be thwarted by tradition. Many in the church today view Christian tradition as impeding creative change. Ironically, the truest aspects of Christian tradition are the most radically creative and life-changing. Indeed, tradition itself provides us with criteria for "sorting living truths from dying customs!"[6]

Just what is tradition? Scripture itself is an expression of ancient Jewish and early Christian traditions. Christian tradition came to include central creeds and confessions by which the church interpreted basic elements of the gospel theologically. The writings of great theologians, mystics, and reformers from the early church to the present also figure into tradition. For some branches of Christianity, tradition includes liturgical practices and oral legacies.

Do you remember Tevya in Fiddler on the Roof *invoking "tradition" as the reason for opposing any sort of change? What does the word evoke in your own experience?*

Tradition tracks a living faith through its history, helping us find markers that let us follow the path today. Some of those markers allow us to enter into the peculiar world of scripture so that it again becomes a vital Word for us. Some markers reveal the rich ore of contemplative prayer and meditation available for us to mine. Voices from the tradition create a kind of symphony from which we may catch a melody that moves us to sing our own praises in worship. While not all of tradition is worth preserving, there are so many riches to be recovered from its storehouse that we should be glad to sift the treasures from the sand in which they are buried!

In reappropriating the best of Christian tradition, we discover a feast for hungry hearts. Indeed, I might caution against a temptation to gluttony! The sources are rich and need to be taken in small bites. Each chapter of this book is designed to help us sample the soul feast of our historic heritage.

Hesitations about Partaking

Whenever we talk about moving closer to God, it is natural to feel certain reservations. Intimacy with the primordial Mover and Shaker of the universe can be a daunting prospect. Even while we feel drawn to our living Source through the hunger divinely implanted in our hearts, we also feel repelled at times. The reasons for this peculiar resistance are various.

Reflect on your feelings about coming closer to God. Are you aware of any anxieties? If so, try to name them and then write them down.

We may feel too small and insignificant for God to bother with or not feel at all sure that God could love us as we really are. Such feelings will make us hesitate to seek God wholeheartedly. We may be afraid of what we will encounter if we come too close to God. It is one thing to be told what God is like; it could be another thing altogether to discover the truth for ourselves! What is God really like? Can we survive contact? Perhaps we feel anxious over what God might demand of us if we get too close. Maybe God will ask us to give up certain relationships, life dreams, or things we enjoy. God might call us to do something we feel we can't do, like work with the poor or become a missionary in Borneo. Fears such as these can certainly make us hesitant to explore the deeper reaches of relationship with our Creator.

Then there are questions about the legitimacy of spirituality itself. Unhappily, our Christian tradition has fostered an unhealthy split between earth and heaven, body and spirit. Those committed to the social implications of the gospel are often concerned that spirituality is an escape from active discipleship in the world and might simply be another form of self-fulfillment that finally denies God's purposes for human community. If the spiritual life means navel gazing while human traffickers thrive, they want no part of it.

These concerns are actually easier to address than is emotional resistance to the spiritual life. The best of our faith heritage has never severed the inner from the outer or the individual from community. It has never assumed that personal experience is the ultimate measure of truth or that feelings are a finer gauge of fidelity to God than intellect. Most of us have a genuine desire for coherence between the inner and outer life. We search for unity between personal and social holiness. Horrifying breaches of justice in the world kindle in us a fire to connect prayer, compassion, and righteousness.

Let me be clear about the kind of spiritual life we will explore in this book. One of my basic assumptions is that the Spirit of God is the depth dimension of all that we know as life. The spiritual life is not one slice of existence but leaven for the whole loaf. It is the broadest, most encompassing dimension of who we are, embracing in its mystery what we call physical, mental, emotional, and volitional aspects of life. Nothing that we do, think, or imagine is without its impact on our spiritual life, and the spiritual life influences every other dimension of our being. Spirituality is naturally holistic.

The Christian spiritual life, modeled in Jesus, is thoroughly incarnate. It represents a complete unity of spiritual and physical life, including deep feeling, enjoyment of the created order, concern for the welfare of the city, and compassion for all people. Our "journey into Christ" is the lifelong process that our tradition has called *sanctification*—growth in holiness. But holiness is not some ephemeral, antiseptic state separated from family, work, or life as a public citizen. It is absolutely practical and concrete. Holy people (saints) get into the dirt and sweat of real life, where light and darkness contend with real consequences. This is where God is at work. If the Word I hear Sunday morning or during my private prayer has no bearing on the way I relate to family, friend, and foe or how I make decisions, spend my resources, and cast my vote, then my faith is fantasy.

The Spirit insists on transforming us at every level: personal, social, economic, and political. God is Lord of the *whole* of our lives. When we think of categories such as prayer and service, contemplation and action, individual and community as opposites, we create false and unnecessary divisions. Nurturing the inner life and addressing social realities are both important aspects of the Christian spiritual life. One is not more "spiritual" than the other, but either by itself is less than a full embodiment of the life we are called to in Christ.

The practices I describe in this book can help us bridge the gap. They move us from deeper personal understanding to alternative ways of being in relationship with others. It is deeply damaging to the church and its members to suppose that we can transform the world if we are unwilling to be transformed personally. What hope have we to offer, what new life do we witness to, if our own hearts are not being made new by God? Jesus' own example reveals that the clarity of a single person who is transparent to the Spirit has more impact in God's design than the best theological teachings and most ambitious social ministries. What could happen if an entire congregation or community became a faithful doorway into God's living presence?

How do you understand the connections between inward growth and outward expressions of faith? Do you believe such a connection is necessary?

I believe that life in Christ is a reality already given to us. It is ours to claim if we have the courage to enter it. And it really is new. Life in Christ is different from the patterns of the world we know so well. In place of degradation and abuse, it means reverence and respect for all of life. Instead of the politics of power, it embodies humble and joyful service. In place of retribution and revenge, it offers forgiveness and reconciliation. Beyond the forces of disease and death, it holds out healing and life. Instead of fear and anxiety, it offers trust in God. Life in the Spirit means release from idols and freedom from addictions. Christ provides realistic hope for a realistic life. He is the wellspring for our thirst, the bread for every hunger of the human heart. "O, taste and see that the LORD is good!" (Ps. 34:8). Once we have tasted living bread and drunk living water, we will be able to lead others who hunger and thirst to our common vital Source.

As for the personal anxieties or hesitance we may feel, I suggest we bring them with us into the explorations that follow. Some will evaporate as we come to recognize more about God and ourselves. Others may remain. We need to be gentle with our fears. Testing our experience over time, we can learn to trust the great love of One whose grace transforms us in ways that surpass our wildest dreams!

Notes to the Text

1. See introduction for a brief overview of this movement. Books that further illuminate Emergent Christianity include: Phyllis Tickle, *The Great Emergence* (Baker Books, 2012) and Brian McLaren, *A Generous Orthodoxy* (Zondervan, 2004).

2. Howard L. Rice, *Reformed Spirituality: An Introduction for Believers* (Louisville, KY: Westminster John Knox Press, 1991), 10.

3. *Saint Augustine: Confessions*, trans. Henry Chadwick (New York: Oxford University Press, 1991), 3.

4. Richard J. Foster, *Celebration of Discipline: The Path to Spiritual Growth* (San Francisco: Harper & Row, 1988), 7.

5. Loretta F. Ross (formerly Ross-Gotta), Presbyterian pastor, spiritual director, and executive director/founder of The Sanctuary Foundation for Prayer in Northern Kansas.

6. Avery Brooke, *Plain Prayers in a Complicated World* (Boston: Cowley Publications, 1993), 73.

Notes to the Sidebars

Richard Rohr, Franciscan friar, speaker, author, founder of the Center for Contemplation and Action, Albuquerque, NM. Adapted from *Radical Grace: Daily Meditations* (St. Anthony Messenger Press, 1995), 315.

Augustine, Bishop of Hippo, North Africa, AD 354–430. *Confessions*, X, 27. As quoted in *The Lord of the Journey: A Reader in Christian Spirituality*, ed. Roger Pooley and Philip Seddon (London: Collins, 1986), 73.

CHAPTER 2

Chewing the Bread of the Word

✣

The Nature and Practice of Spiritual Reading

The law of the LORD is perfect,
  reviving the soul;
the decrees of the LORD are sure,
  making wise the simple; . . . .
More to be desired are they than gold,
  even much fine gold;
sweeter also than honey,
  and drippings of the honeycomb.
                              Psalm 19:7, 10

Imagine for a moment that you have just received a handwritten letter from a dear friend who lives at a great distance and from whom you have not heard in a long while. What would you anticipate about this letter? Where would you like to be when you open it? Perhaps you can imagine settling into your favorite easy chair or finding a quiet and secluded spot outdoors—a place where you can set aside the unfinished tasks of your busy life and enter into the world of your friend's letter. Eagerness for news could tempt you to devour each page as quickly as possible, yet the sheer delight of spending precious time in your friend's company might compel you to slow down, savoring the words, phrases, and images written specifically for you. In them you discover how it is with one who is dear to your heart, what she or he is thinking, experiencing, and questioning. Here are words that bring a sense of your friend's presence vividly into your life.

Now imagine a different scenario. After several intensely busy days, you spy a news magazine on the coffee table and realize that you've not been keeping up with world events. You pick up the magazine and begin paging through, letting your eye rove over headlines, news photos, and captions, scanning articles that catch your interest. Perhaps you are even doing this standing up, hoping to grasp as much information as quickly as possible in order to return to those unfinished tasks.

These two examples may help us to recognize that we have different ways of reading, depending on what we expect to receive. In the case of the friend's letter, words are a means of personal relationship. In the case of the news magazine, words are a vehicle of information. We could say that our approach to the letter is basically relational while to the magazine it is functional. For some of us, this illustration will be more apt if we substitute a website newsfeed for the magazine.

The practice of "spiritual reading" has much more in common with the first example than the second. What makes our reading spiritual has as much to do with the intention, attitude, and manner we bring to the words as it does with the nature and content of those words. Spiritual reading is reflective and prayerful. It is concerned not with speed or volume but with depth and receptivity. That is because the purpose of spiritual reading is to open ourselves to how God may be speaking to us in and through any particular text.

We do not always realize what a radical suggestion it is for us to read to be formed and transformed rather than to gather information. We are information seekers. We love to cover territory.
Macrina Wiederkehr

The manner of spiritual reading is like drinking in the words of a love letter or pondering the meaning of a poem. It is not like skittering over the surface of a popular journal or plowing through a computer manual. We are seeking formation, not merely information.

Information is basically utilitarian; it is a means to some other end. We glean facts to strengthen our arguments; we garner knowledge to make our conversations convincing; we seek help with problem solving, ideas for programming, evidence for cases, and illustrations for teaching. The same information may be used for a variety of purposes. I call this approach the strip-mining method of reading; we are preoccupied with digging up little gems of wisdom from their larger contexts to apply to whatever task is at hand.

Formation, on the contrary, is generally understood as an end in itself. It has to do with the dynamics of change in the human heart, change that reshapes us into the kind of beings God intends for us to be. As this occurs, personal behavior, human relationships, and social structures will be affected quite inevitably for the better, but we do not use formative practices in order to achieve such ends.

Paul exhorts his Christian converts in Rome, "Do not be conformed to this world, but be transformed by the renewing of your minds"

(Rom. 12:2). In Paul's view, it is having the humble, love-centered "mind of Christ" in ourselves that effects this transformation (Phil. 2:1–8). The term *formation*, then, suggests being shaped ever more deeply according to the mind of Christ, who reveals and offers to us our full humanity. Spiritual reading has a formative intent. Through it we seek a living, transforming relationship with God-in-Christ.

Spiritual reading is a meditative approach to the written word. It requires unhurried time and an open heart. If the purpose of our reading is to be addressed by God, we will need to practice attentive listening and a willingness to respond to what we hear. Many kinds of literature can be read in this manner (even news magazines, if we are willing to hear what God may be saying to us through current events). But the primary focus of spiritual reading for Christians has always been scripture, with good reason. The purpose for which the scriptures were written—presenting hearers with God's Word—and the purpose of spiritual reading—allowing ourselves to be addressed by God's Word—are completely consonant. They are as suited to each other as a hand and glove.

The Nature of Scripture

It is no accident that the Bible is called God's Word, but the term may raise for us peculiar questions and tensions. We have, on the one hand, a text composed of many kinds of literature, written for various purposes and different audiences. Its words are human words, written by human beings limited in many ways by their own histories and cultures. On the other hand, we have a Bible affirmed through many centuries, and by people of vastly different histories and cultures, as authentically the Word of God for the human creation. It is a body of writings claimed to be holy scripture, inspired of God's Spirit, and cherished as a reliable guide for faith and practice.

Scripture has been compared to a lake whose depths have never been fully plumbed.[1] On the surface it looks like any other lake; that is, we see human words like those in other books. But when we jump into the lake and begin to swim downward, we may be unable to find the bottom. It is as if those human words become transparent to some mysterious and infinite depth we can never fully grasp. Perhaps that is why one writer can say, "Sounding in and through the human words of scripture, like the sea within a conch shell, is another reality, vaster than mind or imagination can compass. God has chosen to be bound to the words of scripture; in and through them, the Holy One comes near."[2]

In traditional Christian understanding, scripture is both God's Word and human word. It is part of God's chosen self-revelation, simultaneously familiar and strange. Thomas Merton, the renowned twentieth-century Trappist monk, expressed this disturbing quality of the Bible when he said that in scripture we discover "the strange and paradoxical world of meanings and experiences that are beyond us and yet often extremely and mysteriously relevant to us."[3]

If scripture truly has this character, we can expect to encounter the divine presence in its pages. It is not that the words magically or mechanically contain God's presence but that, as we allow the same Spirit through which the scriptures were written to inform our listening, the presence of God in and beyond those words becomes alive for us once more. Spiritual reading is relational in nature, a truth beautifully conveyed in the words of the twelfth-century Cistercian abbot William of St. Thierry:

> The Scriptures need to be read and understood in the same spirit in which they were written. . . . You will never understand David until by experience you have made the sentiments of the psalms your own. And that applies to all Scripture. There is the same gulf between attentive study and mere reading as there is between friendship and acquaintance with a passing guest.[4]

In a certain sense, when we are engaged in spiritual reading it is not so much we who read the Word as the Word who "reads" us! Hebrews 4:12–13 puts it in powerful, if uncomfortable, language: "Indeed, the word of God is living and active, sharper than any two-edged sword, piercing until it divides soul from spirit, joints from marrow; it is able to judge the thoughts and intentions of the heart." If we are open, God's Word will penetrate to our very depths, discerning our secret motives and intentions. As the "sword of the Spirit" (Eph. 6:17), God's Word reveals us truthfully to ourselves and lays us open to radical transformation at those points of our unlikeness to Christ. The simultaneous comfort and discomfort of this nakedness before God's discerning eye is well captured in Psalm 139:1–5, 7:

> O Lord, you have searched me and known me.
> You know when I sit down and when I rise up;
> you discern my thoughts from far away.

You search out my path and my lying down,
and are acquainted with all my ways.
Even before a word is on my tongue,
O LORD, you know it completely.
You hem me in, behind and before,
and lay your hand upon me. . . .
Where can I go from your spirit?
Or where can I flee from your presence?

Perhaps when we meditate with such a psalm we become aware that our task is not so much to master the text of scripture as to be mastered by the Source of that text. The very best historical-critical knowledge cannot give us control over interpreting the Word. Such knowledge can offer helpful parameters and guidelines, but only God's Spirit can fully interpret God's Word. To use a phrase from an old hymn, "God is his own interpreter, / and he will make it plain."[5]

We should point out here that there is an appropriate and important place for an "informational" approach to the scriptures. It involves the discipline of studying the histories, cultures, and languages through which the scriptures come to us. Thomas Merton offers a helpful perspective on the relationship between informational and formational approaches to scripture. An adequate grasp of the biblical text, he says, "requires two levels of understanding: first, a preliminary unraveling of the meaning of the texts themselves . . . which is mainly a matter of knowledge acquired by study; then a deeper level, a living insight which grows out of personal involvement and relatedness. . . . Only on this second level is the Bible really grasped."[6] For Merton, the task of acquiring information is simply the "front porch" of spiritual reading.

Understandings and perspectives gained from biblical study may greatly enrich our experience of spiritual reading of scripture, but the two are not to be confused. German theologian Dietrich Bonhoeffer, who called the practice of spiritual reading simply "biblical meditation," was very clear about the "danger of escaping from meditation to biblical scholarship."[7]

How, then, do we go about spiritual reading with scripture? How do we read in a way that allows us to be encountered by the Reality within yet beyond these familiar words? Since spiritual reading is not concerned with achieving quantity, there is no need to cover a given amount of text. Our intention is simply to sink into the words and open ourselves to their meaning in our lives. Instead of

For as God alone is a fit witness of himself in his Word, so also the Word will not find acceptance in [human] hearts before it is sealed by the inward testimony of the Spirit.

John Calvin

analyzing or judging the text, we receive it as given and attend to what may be spoken to us through it. The attitude suffusing spiritual reading is that of the boy Samuel: "Speak, Lord, your servant is listening" (1 Sam. 3:10).[8]

The art of spiritual reading as a reflective assimilation of God's Word reaches straight back into the Jewish tradition of meditation: "Happy are those . . . / [whose] delight is in the law of the LORD, / and on his law they meditate day and night" (Ps. 1:1–2). Its practice in the Christian church was refined and given special weight by Saint Benedict in the sixth century. In Benedictine tradition, spiritual reading is referred to by its Latin title, *Lectio Divina*. Both Roman Catholics and Protestants owe much of their understanding and practice of scriptural meditation to Benedict. Yet few Protestants are aware that figures such as the great Reformer John Calvin and the Puritan pastor Richard Baxter advocated a method of reflective meditation with scripture that is directly derived from Benedictine practice. Reformed adaptations of *Lectio* were common practice among the Puritans.[9] Given its significant history, it seems natural to return to the Benedictine source for clarification.[10] Perhaps if we outline the process of *Lectio Divina* as it has been classically understood and practiced for centuries, we will discover something to enliven our own way of reading scripture.

Read with a vulnerable heart. Expect to be blessed in the reading. Read as one awake, one waiting for the beloved. Read with reverence.

Macrina Wiederkehr

The Dance of *Lectio Divina*

There are four basic phases in the classic practice of spiritual reading, termed in Latin *lectio*, *meditatio*, *oratio*, and *contemplatio*. For a basic English equivalent, add the letter *n* to each. The ordering of these four phases represents a general and often natural sequence of progression not to be understood rigidly. In practice we may experience great fluidity between them, a weaving back and forth as the Spirit moves us. The image of a dance may be helpful in envisioning the movement between phases and the possibilities for changing "steps" as the "music" shifts.[11] Here, in brief, is a description of each movement.

Lectio literally means reading, from which our terms *lection* and *lectionary* are derived. It signifies the kind of reading we have been portraying: reflective, gently-paced, one-bite-at-a-time. It means reading as if you had a love letter in hand. You allow the words that are pregnant and weighty with meaning to sink in, expand, and nourish your heart. With scripture, it entails reading each sentence as if for the first time, expecting that God will address you with a direct and personal message. The message may not be comfortable. Sometimes letters from those who love us contain painful words, but they are offered out of love and may be just what we need to hear. The question behind our reading is, God, what are you saying to me just now?

Meditatio naturally translates as *meditation*. We need, however, to be clear what we mean by the term. Popular culture, both religious and secular, offers a panoply of meditation methods today. Many have their origins in Far Eastern religious traditions, where meditation involves moving beyond concepts and images to the nameless experience of divine reality. The meaning of meditation in historic Jewish and Christian practice differs in that meditation involves an active mind. The type of mental work is quite specific. It is not the critical, analytical, or formulating work of Bible study, which may inform meditation but remains distinct from it. The mind work of meditation moves us to reflection on where we are in the text. Active imagination can sometimes help us find connections between our life stories and the great story of God's redemptive work with us. Meditation engages us at the level of the "heart" in its biblical sense, where memory, experience, thoughts, feelings, hopes, desires, intuitions, and intentions are joined. This is where we are likely to discover what a given passage means in our lives personally or as a community.

In the practice of the early church, "meditation . . . was a simple repetition of the 'word' received from lectio. . . . The 'word' was repeated in the mind, or even on the lips, until it formed the heart."[12] Thus, the word received from *lectio* was to be taken up and carried in *meditatio* through the day's activities. Meditation essentially became a process of assimilating God's Word over time.

Oratio is related to terms such as *oration* and *oratory*, which most of us probably associate with spoken words. In an earlier era, they referred specifically to spoken prayer. In the context of *Lectio Divina*, it means the prayer that naturally flows out of our meditation. Here is our first response to what we have heard and assimilated in the first two phases of spiritual reading. *Oratio* is the direct cry of the heart to God that rises when we have heard ourselves personally addressed through the Word. Perhaps the Word has touched our pain, and we cry out in hurt, anger, or frustration; perhaps God has revealed our sin, and we whisper in confession and repentance;

The Word of Scripture should never stop sounding in your ears and working in you all day long, just like the words of someone you love. And just as you do not analyze the words of someone you love, but accept them as they are said to you, accept the Word of Scripture and ponder it in your heart, as Mary did. That is all. That is meditation. . . . Do not ask "How shall I pass this on?" but "What does it say to me?" Then ponder this Word long in your heart until it has gone right into you and taken possession of you.
Dietrich Bonhoeffer

perhaps the Word has evoked gratitude, and our words leap up in thanksgiving; perhaps it has sparked our joy, and we sing out adoration and praise! *Oratio* allows a full range of human responses to tumble forth in heartfelt prayer to the One for whom we were made.

Contemplatio, of course, means *contemplation*. In Christian tradition, this aspect of prayer bears more resemblance to those Eastern forms of meditation whose purpose is to move us beyond thoughts, words, and images to a kind of "emptiness" or purity of "being." Contemplation is essentially rest, play, sabbath-time in God's presence. When *oratio* has been played out in all its fury, angst, or exuberance, we come to a place of rest in God. Here there are no expectations, no demands, no need to know, no desire but to be in the divine presence, receptive to whatever God desires to do with us. Here we allow ourselves simply to be, welcoming God's own way of being with us in a "Now" that transcends time. Psalm 131 captures the essence of *contemplatio*:

> Enough for me to keep my soul tranquil and quiet
> > like a child in its mother's arms,
> as content as a child that has been weaned.
>
> > > > (v. 2, JB)

A weaned child is not seeking anything at its mother's breast; it is content to rest quietly, enjoying the simple comfort of the mother's loving presence, an image of complete peace.

Whatever pattern our steps take, and however the choreography shifts in this dance of *Lectio Divina*, our Partner remains the same—ever faithful and responsive, initiating new twists and twirls in the sacred movement of the divine-human relationship. There may be times when the dance feels expansive and delightful like a ballroom waltz; times when it seems a stormy pastiche of passion, pain, and distraction like some existential modern dance; times when it feels like the slow, gentle motion of water ballet; even times when it seems like no movement at all, unless it be the gentlest, imperceptible cradling of love. The dance of *Lectio Divina* may leave our natural energies drained or replenished; regardless, when practiced faithfully it leads to a deeper knowledge of God and ourselves in relation to God in this world.

Another rather more homely image from our tradition may help us grasp the nature of *Lectio Divina* as a whole. We are invited, by this illustration, to observe a cow. First "the cow goes out and eats some good grass (*lectio*), then she sits down under a tree and chews her cud (*meditatio*) until she extracts from her food both milk (*oratio*) and cream (*contemplatio*)."[13] The image of a cow chewing its cud is perfectly suited to the practice of meditation in the Christian tradition. We can all visualize what it looks like: processing and reprocessing food until it is fully digested! This mundane and pastoral image offers good closure on our discussion of the nature of *Lectio Divina*. It is a matter of taking in the bread of God's Word, chewing on it, and digesting it until it brings forth new life and energy that can be shared with others.

Now, if we can marry the image of the cow with that of the dance, we will have a magnificently realistic notion of the Christian spiritual life!

Invitations to Explore

When you sit down to give spiritual reading a try, you will discover that some preliminary but very practical matters need to be attended to: time, place, and text selection. It is probably clear by now that a discipline of this sort takes unhurried time. I suggest a minimum of half an hour, although more can be deeply satisfying and fruitful. I also commend the counsel of many experienced saints: give God the best time of your day, not the dregs. It is hard to listen when you are tired.

Choose a place that affords you solitude and reasonable quiet if at all possible. Do everything in your power to reduce the potential for distraction: close your door; turn off your cell phone; instruct your children, spouse, housemates, administrative assistant, or whoever may be concerned not to interrupt you except in an emergency. Give yourself permission to be unavailable to others for this time in order to be fully available to God. Some people find soft music or recordings of natural sounds a helpful backdrop to mask traffic noise or unavoidable distractions.

One easy way to select daily scripture passages is to use a lectionary.[14] If you choose this route, select one genre of reading and stick with it: Old Testament, Psalm, Gospel, or Epistle. Using a lectionary obliges you to reflect on a much wider range of texts than you might be inclined to choose on your own—a healthy discipline in and of itself. You could also base your reading on whole books or letters of the Bible, moving through them sequentially in small portions. (This approach has historically been favored in the Reformed churches in order to preserve the full context of each passage.) A third alternative is to select a passage of scripture that fits your mood or your need (not more than five to ten verses).

Begin by reaffirming that the purpose of this reading is to let yourself be addressed by the living God. Settle yourself quietly, remembering to include your body; find a position or posture that will help you to stay relaxed but alert. Be aware of your intention to listen as openly as possible to the words before you. Release your own "agenda" so you will be ready to receive whatever word the Spirit desires to offer you.

Remind yourself of God's presence with you, here and now. You may or may not sense this presence, but you can affirm through faith and trust that the Holy One is attending to you. Offer your gratitude and ask for the guidance and illumination of the Holy Spirit in your reading.

Turn to the passage and begin to read slowly, pausing between phrases and sentences. For some, silent reading allows the mind to wander, so reading aloud or whispering is preferable. Let the words echo and resonate in your mind; allow meanings to sink in, associations to arise, images to surface. If a word or phrase seems especially significant to you, remain with it, turning it over in your mind and heart. When the sense of immediacy fades, move on to another verse. If it remains meaningful for you, stay with it. Here is a word meant for your ears. Be content to listen simply and openly, like a child listening to a story.

Once you have heard a "word" that seems meant for you, start ruminating on it. Why is this a word for you? What in your life right now needs to hear this word? How is God catching your attention? If the passage is a narrative with people, it may help to imagine the setting of the story and to envision yourself within it. Who can you identify with? Why? Who do you have trouble identifying with, and why? Imagine how the characters interact, how they feel about themselves and one another. How do the dynamics of the story connect with your life experience? Is there anything you discover about yourself in this process? What does God seem to be saying to you through this word?

Let prayer emerge from your encounter with this text. How do you find yourself praying for your own needs, given what you have heard? How does this word move you to pray for others? Allow your prayer to flow spontaneously from the heart, expressing as fully as you can what surfaces out of your listening.

Finally, release all your thoughts, feelings, and intentions to God. There is no further need to listen, reflect, imagine, or respond. There is simply an invitation to return to a place of rest near the heart of God where you may be at peace. God sustains you with love every moment of your life. Delight in this gift, take comfort and joy in it!

If this part of the process seems strange or difficult, read Psalm 131. Allow yourself to be the weaned child, resting on the breast of God.

When you emerge from your contemplation, find a word, image, or phrase that carries the core message you have received. Take this with you into your daily activities and relationships. Let your reflection and prayer continue inwardly as new experiences deepen the word you hear in your spiritual reading.

Other Sources for Spiritual Reading

As I mentioned earlier, the process of spiritual reading can be applied to texts other than scripture, especially to devotional literature or good religious poetry. Great spiritual classics may be read in small portions, savored and reflected upon for personal nurture and edification. You might want to try Francis of Assisi, *The Little Flowers*; Thomas à Kempis, *The Imitation of Christ*; Brother Lawrence, *The Practice of the Presence of God*; John Woolman, *Journal*; or Thomas Kelly, *A Testament of Devotion*.

Let's try out the process of *Lectio Divina* with a passage from the seventeenth-century Carmelite Brother Lawrence, just to see how it could apply to writing other than scripture. Read the passage below at a gentle pace, absorbing the impact of the words and their meaning:

> God has infinite treasures to give us. Yet a little tangible devotion, which passes away in a moment, satisfies us. How blind we are, since in this way we tie God's hands, and we stop the abundance of His grace! But when He finds a soul penetrated with living faith, He pours out grace on it in abundance. God's grace is like a torrent. When it is stopped from taking its ordinary course, it looks for another outlet, and when it finds one, it spreads out with impetuosity and abundance.[15]

Now go back into these words with a mind seeking connections to your own life and a heart open to being addressed by God in your current condition. Pause to reflect wherever you hear something that seems especially significant. Allow questions to surface: God, do you really have infinite treasures to give me? Do you desire to pour these out into my life? Visualize what happens when a torrent of water is blocked from its normal flow. Ask yourself: What blocks do I put in the way of God's grace? Am I satisfied with too little? How do I become "a soul penetrated with living faith"?

Allow prayer to surface spontaneously from the meditations of your heart. It might be prayer for more vibrant, confident faith; prayer that blocks to faith will be healed and dissolved; prayer for those whose trust in God's grace has been depleted. Then take a few moments to rest in confidence that your desires are known and received in the heart of God. Find joy and peace in this assurance. You have just completed a process of spiritual reading.

If you find older writings difficult to grasp or relate to, begin with the works of modern interpreters of the classic spiritual tradition. Among the best known and loved of such writers are Thomas Merton, Evelyn Underhill, C. S. Lewis, Howard Thurman, Henri Nouwen, and Richard Foster.

Religious poetry, like great devotional classics, can be approached in a deeply personal and prayerful way. In addition, we have the marvelous resource of certain fiction writers whose work embodies profound spiritual insight. These are not generally read in the prayerful manner of spiritual reading per se, but can be absorbed as writings with spiritual intent that inspire deep musing.

It is the attitude we bring to spiritual reading that allows God to transform the text from interesting words to words with the power to change our very being. That attitude is an expectation that we will, through the words we read, be encountered by the loving presence and radical challenge of the living God. That attitude is a willingness to be addressed, discerned, and penetrated by the tender but decisive power of the Holy Spirit. That attitude is a desire to respond fully and freely to what is heard so that God may restore to us the wholeness of our life in Christ—the divine image obscured in our depths, yet even now being called into the light of day to reveal the glory of the children of God!

Notes to the Text

1. New Testament scholar Robert Mulholland presented this metaphor in a lecture for a session of the Academy for Spiritual Formation in Sedalia, Colorado, June 1991.

2. John S. Mogabgab, unpublished writings.

3. Thomas Merton, *Opening the Bible* (Collegeville, MN: Liturgical Press, 1970), 27.

4. *The Golden Epistle: William of St. Thierry*, trans. Theodore Berkeley (Kalamazoo, MI: Cistercian Publications, 1980), 51–52.

5. Wiliam Cowper (1731–1800), "God Moves in a Mysterious Way."

6. Merton, *Opening the Bible*, 61–62.

7. In his instructions on meditation to young pastors, Bonhoeffer says flatly, "Whatever happens, do not take the text which you are to preach next Sunday. That belongs to sermon preparation." From *Dietrich Bonhoeffer, The Way to Freedom: Letters, Lectures and Notes, 1935–1939.* See the *Collected Works of Dietrich Bonhoeffer*, Vol. II, ed. Edwin H. Robertson, trans. Edwin H. Robertson and John Bowden (London: William Collins Sons & Co., 1966), 57–61.

8. The relational character of spiritual reading is directly connected to our personal knowledge of God. Parker J. Palmer, in *To Know as We Are Known: A Spirituality of Education* (San Francisco: Harper & Row, 1983), argues eloquently for a view of truth that is personal and relational rather than objective and propositional. Knowledge, like truth, he writes, is not abstract but relational. Spiritual reading encourages this kind of knowledge.

9. Drawing on the writings of Richard Baxter, John White, and Lewis Bayly, Howard L. Rice describes the process of devotional reading used by Puritans in *Reformed Spirituality: An Introduction for Believers* (Louisville, KY: Westminster John Knox Press, 1991), chap. 4.

10. I have also drawn on insights into *Lectio* offered by Robert Mulholland, whose books *Shaped by the Word* (Nashville: The Upper Room, 1985) and *Invitation to a Journey* (Downers Grove, IL: InterVarsity Press, 1993) I commend. Some of Mulholland's ideas are woven into the fabric of this chapter.

11. The image of dance as a metaphor for the divine-human relationship has ancient roots. The early Cappadocian Fathers used the Greek term *perichoresis* (*peri*, plus *choresis*, from which our word *choreography* derives, essentially meaning "interpenetrated") to describe the mutual co-inherence of the three Persons of the Trinity. This is the very life human beings are invited to participate in, "in Christ" through the indwelling of the Holy Spirit.

12. Basil Pennington, "Lectio Divina: Receiving the Revelation," in *Living with Apocalypse*, ed. Tilden Edwards (San Francisco: Harper & Row, 1984), 68.

13. Ibid.

14. A lectionary is a systematic order of scripture readings structured to correspond to the seasons of the church year (Advent, Christmas, Epiphany, Lent, Easter, Pentecost, Ordinary Time). It traditionally offers a selection from the Old Testament, the Psalms, the Gospels, and the Epistles. Lectionaries move through the major teachings of scripture in a two- or three-year cycle.

15. *The Practice of the Presence of God*, trans. Robert J. Edmonson, ed. Hal M. Helms (Orleans, MA: Paraclete Press, 1985), 82–83.

Notes to the Sidebars

Macrina Wiederkehr, author, member of St. Scholastica Benedictine Monastery. *A Tree Full of Angels: Seeing the Holy in the Ordinary* (San Francisco: HarperSanFrancisco, 1991), 53.

John Calvin, French reformer, largely based in Geneva, 1509-1564. *Institutes of the Christian Religion*, ed. John T. McNeill (Philadelphia: Westminster Press, 1960), bk. 1, ch. 7, para.4, p. 79.

Macrina Wiederkehr, *A Tree Full of Angels*, 53.

Dietrich Bonhoeffer, German Lutheran theologian opposed to Hitler, 1906-1944. *The Way to Freedom. Letters, Lectures, and Notes 1935–1939.* In *Collected Works of Dietrich Bonhoeffer*, vol. 2, ed. Edwin H. Robertson; trans. Edwin H. Robertson and John Bowden (London: Collins, 1966), 58–59.

CHAPTER 3

Communication and Communion with God

Approaches to Prayer

All your love, your stretching out, your hope, your thirst, God is creating in you so that [God] may fill you. . . . God is on the inside of the longing.

Maria Boulding

I have said that the spiritual life has to do with how God relates to us and how we in turn relate to God. Prayer is the essential expression of this relationship. As with the spiritual life itself, prayer is initiated by God. No matter what we think about the origin of our prayers, they are all a response to the hidden workings of the Spirit within.

God's desire for us ignites the spark of our desire for God. God's guiding heart nudges forth our prayers to be led. The apostle Paul assured us that the Spirit "helps us in our weakness" and "intercedes with sighs too deep for words" (Rom. 8:26). Have you considered what an astonishing promise it is that *the Spirit prays in us*, and does so "according to the will of God" (v. 27)? Perhaps our real task in prayer is to attune ourselves to the conversation already going on deep in our hearts. Then we may align our conscious intentions with the desire of God being expressed at our core.

Prayer expresses our relationship with God. It should not surprise us that this relationship parallels in significant ways our relationships with other persons. It cannot be forced but flourishes in the soil of freedom and mutual commitment. The health and vitality of this relationship depend on clarity and frequency of communication. Like any form of intimacy, it requires time spent in each other's presence, time simply to explore and enjoy the gift of companionship.

Prayer involves freely entering a relationship of *communication* and *communion* with God, for the sake of knowledge, growth, and mutual enjoyment. I would like to look at each of these two aspects of prayer in turn.

Prayer as Communication

Most of us think of prayer as a conversation with God. This is a natural way to understand prayer and a simple way to practice it. Since the God we know in scripture is personal, we are free to speak with God heart to heart, as we might with a dear friend. The content of our conversation may cover a wide range of feelings and experiences, but we will generally express certain classic human attitudes before God: praise, adoration, thanksgiving, confession, and supplication. Our prayers are often weighted toward supplication, which includes petitions for our own needs and intercession for others.

Prayer as conversation with God can be deeply fulfilling. However, if it is the only form our prayer takes, we may begin to sense that something is missing. There are two reasons for this. First, prayer is, by nature, more than conversation. To limit its concept to dialogue is to allow some of the most profound expressions of prayer to escape our notice. Second, our "conversation" may, in practice, be less a dialogue than a monologue that borders on talking *at* God. Some of our prayers resemble "a spiritual shopping list, launched heavenward on the wings of pious words."[1] But God is not, as one author wryly notes, our "cosmic bellhop."[2]

Please understand, there is nothing wrong with supplication. Jesus encourages us to ask with open and persistent trust for what we need (Luke 11:5–13). Still, an unbalanced diet of such prayer over time will probably lead more to frustration than fulfillment. We may start to feel that our prayer is a one-way phone conversation in which all we hear is the sound of our own voice. We may wonder whether we have been heard, whether anyone is on the other end of the line, or if we are even connected!

True communication is a two-way street. Genuine dialogue asks us to listen as well as to speak, to receive in order to respond. It is the listening side of the communication loop that has been given inadequate attention in most Protestant church teachings on prayer. One of the key things we must consider, then, is how we listen to God.

I'm gonna pray now; anyone want anything?

Flip Wilson

32

In this part of the chapter I will examine the two primary expressions of prayer as communication: listening to God and speaking to God. I will also look at intercession, a particular instance of communication with God that raises its own set of questions. Finally I will invite you to explore several exercises that may help broaden your experience with prayer as communication. Then we can turn our attention to prayer as communion.

The one condition that precedes *every* kind of prayer is being present to God with conscious awareness. God is always present with us, whether or not we can feel this reality. In a very real sense, then, the foundation of all prayer is being present to the presence of God. As Quaker writer and teacher Douglas Steere points out, "in order to pray, you have to stop being 'too elsewhere' and to *be there*."[3] We have all experienced times when we are present in body but unavailable mentally to one another. When we want to communicate well, we try not to be distracted by time limits, inner thoughts, or external circumstances. The same consideration needs to be given to God. Attending to the moment of encounter is crucial. The breathing, quieting, and "centering" so frequently recommended in prayer are simply ways of helping us focus on the One we wish to be with.

When the muse comes to dine with you, you have to be at home.
Douglas V. Steere

Listening

Listening is the first expression of communication in prayer. We know that listening precedes speaking in the development of children's language skills. The same order applies to the development of our prayer life. Something in our spirit is touched by the Divine Spirit before we are drawn to speak.

But how do we listen to God? Clear communication can be very difficult between people, even with the advantage of inflection, expression, and gesture. How much more confusing it is to communicate with One who is invisible, intangible, inaudible, and inscrutable! Yet God desires to be known and has many ways of communicating with us if we are willing to listen.

As I noted in chapter 1, the place to begin is with scripture. God's self-communication is not limited to the pages of the Bible. Yet if we are open to the Spirit, we can expect to hear God speak to us through writings that are intentionally called God's Word. Through many centuries and cultures, the church has found that this Word continues to speak with contemporary wisdom and transforming power.

For some, the most natural way to listen to God is through creation. Psalm 19 acknowledges that creation speaks loudly of divine realities:

> The heavens are telling the glory of God;
> and the firmament proclaims his handiwork. . . .
> There is no speech, nor are there words; . . . .
> yet their voice goes out through all the earth .
>
> (vv. 1, 3a, 4a)

Creation has a unique language of proclamation and praise. Each part of the created order speaks eloquently of its Creator, just as consummate artistry reveals the soul of the artist.

The Creator also speaks to us through creation. All aspects of the created order can teach us about human realities and struggles. Thus, we tend to "read" the characteristics of creatures and the rhythms of nature as symbols or metaphors illuminating our spiritual lives. But God speaks to us through creation in another sense as well. Are not the distress signals of our earth and the collapse of entire ecosystems a message from God? Surely a word is being spoken to us through the earth's suffering about the urgent need for greater simplicity and more responsible stewardship in our lives. Listening to the earth can indeed be a way of listening to God.

All things are shadows of the shining true:
Sun, sea, and air . . .
Every thing holds a slender guiding clue
Back to the mighty oneness: . . .
George MacDonald

We often hear God's voice through one another. Perhaps someone who knows us well speaks just the word we need to hear in a way we can grasp. Perhaps a complete stranger appears at a crucial moment with a word of encouragement, guidance, or warning. God surrounds us with personal messengers every day, often through people who are unaware that they have become vessels of grace.

The circumstances of our lives are another medium of God's communication with us. God opens some doors and closes others. A troubling relationship may invite us to attend to something we have not fully faced in ourselves. Through the wisdom of our bodies, God tells us to slow down or reorder our priorities. The happy coincidences and frustrating impasses of daily life are laden with messages. Patient listening and the grace of the Spirit are the decoding devices of prayer. It is a good habit to ask, What is God saying to me in this situation? Listening to our lives is part of prayer and a key to authentic discernment.

In recent decades, dreams have again been recognized as potential vehicles of divine guidance. The Bible is filled with stories in which God speaks to people through dreams, yet we tend to assume this is not the case for ordinary believers today. Modern spiritual writers such as Morton Kelsey and John Sanford, building on the insights of depth psychology, have challenged that assumption. They believe the symbols of our inner life are a natural medium for spiritual insight. As the Bible richly attests, God's way of speaking to us is often mediated by symbols and images. Our dreams exist precisely in this medium. Many people of faith have found it immensely worthwhile to listen to their dreams. It takes practice to learn how to decipher the language of dreams, but persistence can yield a wealth of insight that moves us from psychological to spiritual truths.

Many seekers have discovered that journal keeping can be a way of listening to oneself and to God. Christians through the centuries have written spiritual autobiographies, personal diaries, and journals. Some were written to be read. Others were so personal and confidential that they were burned upon the writer's death. Journal keeping takes varied forms today: a prayer journal might record the insights, questions, and feelings that arise from scriptural meditation; it might be used to record and reflect upon dreams; or it might focus on life issues, struggles, and decision-making processes. One interesting technique in contemporary journal keeping is the device of dialogue with key people in our lives or with different voices inside our selves. Writing an imaginary dialogue with a biblical character can be helpful (see "Invitations to Explore," later in this chapter).

Journals give us a record of our spiritual questions, struggles, and insights over time. Reviewing them, we may start to recognize larger patterns: the characteristic marks of our journey, where we have grown and where we have gotten stuck, how we discern God's gracious presence and guidance through it all.

At times God speaks to us in more subtle and mysterious ways. They often come unbidden, amid ordinary activity or in the quiet of contemplation: a deep intuition, an acutely clear conviction, or a simple inner sense of how things are meant to be. You may be familiar with phrases such as, "Somehow I just knew this was what I had to do." Or "It suddenly became perfectly clear to me." Or "The words just came into my head."

The Quakers have a phrase for when something inside us says no: "a stop in the mind." It is a warning that we are moving in the wrong direction and normally alerts us to a selfish attitude or behavior. But there may be occasions when, in the course of a perfectly altruistic prayer, there suddenly comes "a stop in the mind." Douglas

To dream is to see love and desires transformed into symbols, words. It should not be frightening, then, that God, who is love, speaks to us through our dreams.

Rubem Alves

Steere attests to this experience.[4] It is one of God's ways of telling us not to pursue that particular prayer. Perhaps its aim contradicts the divine design; perhaps the time is not ripe; perhaps it is given to someone else to pray for this person or circumstance.

Anyone can receive such an inner "sense of things," but it becomes more likely as we learn to attune to the gentle stirrings of the Spirit within and around us. It belongs to the learning of prayer to release our own agenda and wait patiently for God's purposes to be disclosed. Solitude and inner silence provide the most promising environment for hearing the "still, small voice."

Perhaps you are starting to think that virtually anyone or anything can be a divine messenger. I suspect God is trying to get our attention through every aspect of our lives. Are we hearing? Of course, hearing clearly requires discernment as well as attentiveness. Not all the messages we hear are of divine origin. In learning to recognize what is characteristic of God and what is not, the role of a larger community seeking to be faithful to the God of scripture becomes vital.

How many ways there are to listen to God! Perhaps we can now begin to see how broad, multifaceted, and life-inclusive prayer really is.

It does not follow that because a thing is the will of God, [God] will necessarily lead you to pray for it.
James Outram Fraser

Speaking

The second primary expression of communication in prayer is speaking from the heart with unreserved honesty. This may seem self-evident. We tend to concentrate on our own words in prayer, assuming that here we are in familiar territory. We may not know what God is trying to say to us, but surely we know what we are trying to say to God! Yet the very familiarity of our thoughts and words may obscure the fact that we are not candid in what we communicate.

Many of us have absorbed tacit or explicit taboos about what we are permitted to bring into prayer. We may have learned, for instance, that doubt, anger, hatred, or despair are inappropriate to express to God. Yet we know what happens to human relationships when negative feelings are suppressed. Communication becomes artificial or breaks down; the two parties become emotionally estranged; intimacy becomes impossible. Why should we imagine it is different with God? In prayer, we need to speak whatever truth is in us: pain and grief, fear and disappointment, yearning and desire, questions and doubt, hope and faith, failure and weakness, praise and thanks, despair and sorrow, anger and, yes, even hatred.

If any of these feelings or experiences seem foreign to our prayer, we need only turn to the Psalms for help. Within their verses the whole range of human passions are expressed with magnificent candor. From them we receive permission to voice the best and worst in us; their words help us cry out to God from the depths of our human condition—both its sordidness and its glory.

It takes practice to learn not to censor prayer. But trying to keep secrets from God is like the three-year-old who covers her eyes and declares, "You can't see me." God sees into our hearts more clearly than we do. Indeed, God is the one who prompts us to look at what we have swept under the rug of our repressions and rationalizations. The Spirit awakens us to what lies hidden within—sometimes gently, sometimes with a jolt, but always so God can work with our conscious consent to free us for growth.

Stop and reflect. Are there strong feelings in your life that you are hesitant to express in prayer? Can you identify why you hold them back? How do you respond to the Psalms as a whole? What in particular attracts or repels you?

Prayers of Intercession

One way we speak to God from the heart is through intercessory prayer. Intercession is a concrete expression of the social dimension of prayer. It includes our concerns for other persons, communities, nations, the earth, and our fellow creatures.

People frequently feel confused about praying for others. Often our prayers are not answered in the way we desire or expect. We pray for healing and it does not come; we pray for peace and conflict increases. We wonder whether God does not will the good we intend by our prayers or if perhaps we are not praying rightly. We feel guilty that we do not have enough faith, and we feel angry that evil and suffering are allowed to destroy so much peace and happiness. Sometimes prayer seems to us the feeblest and least desirable option, but the only one left under the circumstances: "All I can do for you is pray."

Intercession is the most intensely social act of which the human being is capable. When carried on secretly, it is mercifully preserved from, in fact, almost immunized against, the possible corruptions to which all outer deeds of service for others are subject.
Douglas V. Steere

Views of Intercessory Prayer

In sorting out these difficult matters, it may help to identify how you understand the dynamics. What do you think you are doing and what do you think God is doing when you pray for others? Below are eight possible views of the dynamic of intercession, most of which are derived from scripture. Not all these views are mutually exclusive. Each one expresses how people actually perceive the nature and purpose of their prayer:

1. By our petitions, reasoning, or arguing, we change God's attitude and intended action in the world (see Gen. 18:22–33; Exod. 32:11–14).
2. By engaging in the struggle of prayer, we find ourselves changed, marked by our encounter with the living God (see Gen. 32:24–30).
3. In prayer we voice our desires, hopes, needs, and frustrations but cannot assume that these influence God. We are completely dependent on God's sovereign will and action in response (see Job 7:11–20; 13:3, 19:7; 42:1–6).
4. In prayer we share our positive life-energies with another person who is mystically connected with us and all other living things and who can therefore be directly influenced (no direct corollary in scripture, but a common belief in our time).
5. In prayer we join our hearts in love with the love of Christ, the great Intercessor, through the unity of the Spirit given in Baptism and sustained by the Eucharist. We give our will to the will of Christ and leave the results to him (see John 15:1–11; 17; Rom. 8:26–27; Heb. 4:14–16).
6. In prayer we become aware of God's presence with us and of the Holy Spirit already praying in us, so we do not bring specific prayers, but try to attune and entrust ourselves to that presence and inward prayer (see Ps. 139; Rom. 8:26–27).
7. When we pray, we simply trust completely that God will respond with a good and appropriate gift in God's own time and way (see Matt. 7:7, 9–11).
8. When we pray, we are cooperating with God in willing life and goodness for others, yet we remain vulnerable with God to the limits imposed by evil—limits accepted in the freedom that love creates (see Mark 14:32–36 and parallels).

Do some of the views of intercessory prayer express your understanding of intercession better than others? Which comes closest to what you think happens when we pray? Perhaps you can identify additional views.

Combining Surrender and Trust

As I consider these views, a particular question keeps asserting itself: How can I ask in simple trust for a gift to be granted and, at the same time, yield up my will to God? Jesus tells us that if we had faith the size of a mustard seed we could command and it would be accomplished. Yet when we have "mustered up" all the faith we have and still do not receive what we desire, we often try another tack. We add "if it be your will" to protect ourselves from the risk of disappointment. Then if our requests go unanswered, we can suppose it was not God's will. But what if God's desire *is* to fulfill our heartfelt prayers and other factors interfere with this intent?

First we need to examine the attitude with which we approach God in prayer. Do we come to God from within an ongoing and committed relationship or casually and at our convenience? Are we using God to fill hopes and wishes that have little to do with divine intentions and purposes for us? God will not be manipulated.

If our relationship is sincere, our prayer will basically be one of thanksgiving for grace already received. The context for "prayers of asking" is a heart offered to God in gratitude, eager to fulfill the divine intent. Jesus says, "If you abide in me, and my words abide in you, ask for whatever you wish, and it will be done for you" (John 15:7). What does it mean to "abide in Jesus"? The image is drawn from the metaphor of a vine and its branches. When we abide in the vine of Jesus' life, a single vital sap runs through us. This sap is a love that pours itself out for others. Jesus gives us everything he has and is. To abide in him is to participate in that outpouring of love.

Here is the posture from which we ask that abundant grace be given to those we pray for. We can be confident that grace will be given in a way that best expresses God's loving purpose, with which we are united. It may take time for the grace to become manifest, and perseverance is commended (Luke 18:18). The delays are due not to lack of goodwill on God's part but to various blocks on the path of grace. Some of these blocks lie within us, some are in those for whom we pray, and others have to do with the larger "powers and principalities of darkness" contending against God. Since "coercion is not an attribute of God,"[5] the Holy One must clear the path of grace in ways that do not contradict human freedom. God prefers to work through invitation and attraction, but it takes time for all the players in the delicate web of human relationships to be won over, and some may simply refuse.

Our confidence in the power of prayer is rooted in the promises that God is continually working for good in the midst of ambiguous situations and that God's purposes will prevail in the end. The divine Word does not return to God empty (Isa. 55:11). Love is the only power capable of *enduring* all things. It remains immovable after all else has fallen away. Therefore we can ask for eyes to see where God is already at work and a spirit ready to cooperate with God's activity in any given circumstance. The more fully we entrust ourselves to God, the more freely God's loving purpose can be worked out.

Here is a process that might allow your prayers of intercession to blend the simple trust that you will receive grace with offering your will to God:

- Begin with gratitude and praise, offering your whole heart to God.

- If your prayer seems good for all involved, ask boldly with as much faith as you have in you. Faith cannot be forced but can be prayed for: "I believe; help my unbelief!" (Mark 9:24).

- Wait with trust and attention for a response.

- If you receive no indication that you are *not* meant to receive what you ask for (no "stop in the mind," no closed doors), keep asking. This is not anxious repetition but trusting perseverance.

- If you receive a clear answer to your prayer, let your praise and thanksgiving be sincere and wholehearted. You may perceive that a gracious response is being given in a way you did not expect; be thankful for new insight into God's mysterious providence.

- If you see no indications of grace, ask to be shown if there is something in you that could be blocking it: lack of humility or gratitude, lack of trust, a hidden sin, or the need to forgive someone.

- If over time (perhaps several weeks or months, depending on the nature of the situation you pray for) there is no positive response, ask God to reveal to you whether another prayer is more in accord with divine intent. If the substance of your prayer is not transformed and there is still no sign of the grace asked for, God's answer may be no.

- Accept that no may be the answer to your prayer. Recognize and affirm that God's no always has a larger and better purpose than we can see.

- Seek to discover where God's grace is manifesting in the midst of this situation, even if not in the manner being asked for. Commit yourself to cooperate as fully as you can with God's work as you discern it.

You should, of course, do everything in your God-given power to bring about what you pray for. "Prayer is not a substitute for action; it is an action for which there is no substitute."[6]

Prayer is a participation in willing God's will. While God's ultimate will cannot be thwarted, the strategy God uses to reach that goal may be infinitely variable. The prayers of committed people become part of the cosmic reality God has to work with. God can use them to "tip the balance" and change the shape of distorted realities in our world.[7] It is not stretching the truth to say that God *needs* our prayers. Such is the dignity and purpose we have been given in the divine scheme of things!

More things are wrought by prayer
Than this world dreams of.
Alfred Lord Tennyson

Invitations to Explore

Would you like to try some new approaches to prayer? Here is a small sampling of possibilities. Some may be familiar; others are simply waiting to be introduced.

Imaging Intercession

Consider using your imagination rather than words as a primary avenue of prayer. Here is a simple way to pray using imaging as a vehicle for "willing God's will":

- Relax and breathe gently. Become aware of God's presence, imaging it as radiant light and warmth. Allow this *Shekinah* (glory) to fill your consciousness.

- When we are in God's presence, we are not alone. We are there with all God's children held in the divine embrace. Choose one of those children with need of healing in body, mind, or heart.

- Lift this person into God's light. Visualize divine love bathing the person and gently penetrating defenses, dissolving pain, cleansing wounds. Use any images that seem appropriate: dark becoming light, ice melting, confusion ordered.

- See the person in a state of wholeness in God's light, newly created, fresh and beautiful as seen through the eyes of divine love.

- Ask God that this beauty be fully realized according to God's design for this person.

- Thank God for whatever gift of healing is given. Release the person into divine care until you pray again.

This exercise can tutor you to use your imagination more actively in other prayers: visualize restored relationships or "see" old animosities dissolve. You are not trying to manufacture results but envisioning with God the restoration of creation.

Write Your Own Psalm

This exercise can help you become more aware of your feelings in relation to God and give you permission to express them in prayer. If you have held on to feelings such as grief, anger, or a desire for revenge, believing it would be dangerous to express them to God, try writing your own prayer in psalm form:

- Select a psalm that voices the feelings you are afraid to speak (Pss. 13, 22, 42, 77, 88, and 94 are possibilities). Ask God to help you accept the reality of your feelings.

- Get acquainted with the psalm, especially the verses that best express your attitudes.

- Lay it aside and begin to write your own psalm to God. Let it emerge from your experience, your feelings, and your faith.

- Be as honest as you can.

- If you want your feelings to change, include that desire in your psalm. If you find your feelings changing as you express them to God, include the changes of heart, too. You may end with a different perspective than you began with.

- Offer your personal psalm to God as heartfelt prayer, asking the Spirit to take your feelings in a direction that will be for your healing and God's glory.

Paraphrase a Psalm

A related exercise is to paraphrase a psalm by putting yourself into it personally. Use the psalm structure, but simplify and modify the words to express your own experience. Here is an example, based on Psalm 44 (a national lament):

> I have heard with my ears, O God,
> what deeds you performed in the days of old.
> Yet you have rejected and abased me.
> You have made me the taunt of my relatives,
> the laughingstock of my neighbors.
> All this has come upon me,
> yet I have not forgotten you.
> Why do you forget my affliction and misery?
> Come to my help, for the sake of your love!

Write a Conversation

Another helpful exercise is writing a dialogue with a person from scripture. The following example imagines Jesus as a conversation partner; the writer is identifying with Simon Peter after the miraculous catch of fish (Luke 5:1–11):

ME: Go away from me, Lord, for I am a sinful person!

JESUS: Don't be afraid; from now on you will be catching people.

ME: No, you don't understand, Lord. You are holy, pure. I'm just a common person with a lot of weaknesses. I don't belong with you.

JESUS: Remember, you didn't choose me, I chose you.

ME: But why, Lord? I'm not worthy of you!

JESUS: Did I say you had to be worthy? I only ask you to follow me in trust.

As you can see, dialogue like this goes beyond the scripture story to become part of your own faith story. You don't need to worry about whether or not it is really what Jesus would have said. The responses that come to mind as you write the dialogue become a vehicle of self-discovery in relation to God. And you may arrive at new insights into scripture as well as greater self-knowledge. This is as it should be, for prayer is a process of discovering ourselves more fully in God's love.

We have been discussing aspects of *communication* in prayer and exercises that can help us communicate more freely with God. Now it is time to look at a deeper level of prayer that I call *communion*.

Prayer as Communion

When I speak of *communion*, I mean that dimension of relationship that goes beyond words, images, or actions. Communion transcends the particularities of communication. Just as listening and speaking are the primary expressions of prayer as communication, contemplation is the foremost expression of prayer as communion.

Contemplative Prayer

A simple gaze toward One who loves us unshakably—this is contemplative prayer. It is absorption in loving God with our whole being—not strenuously, but as a spontaneous response of the heart.

Contemplative prayer is resting in God, allowing the Spirit to fill and move us as God wills. It is pure receptivity and adoration. It is quiet, tender, and sober or playful, gentle, and joyous.

Contemplative prayer has the quality of an inner sabbath. In a world driven by the need to accomplish and acquire, in a world where we judge one another on the basis of performance, God calls us to the radical trust of rest. Does the Lord require so much of us that we cannot join God in a little divine rest?

The late Russian Orthodox archbishop Anthony Bloom tells of an eighteenth-century priest who once asked an aged peasant what he was doing during the hours and hours he spent sitting in the chapel. The old man replied, "I look at Him, He looks at me, and we are happy."[8] A more homely illustration of contemplation was once recounted by a Protestant pastor who had returned from a visit to a monastery. He confessed to his son that he did not understand how the monks could sit for hours in the chapel before the Reserved Host (consecrated bread that represents the presence of Christ). His son, whose wife had just given birth to their first child, responded, "You know, Dad, I think I understand. Since our newborn arrived, I just go to her crib and look at her. She doesn't have to do a thing, she doesn't even have to be awake. I am so utterly fascinated that I don't know where the time goes!"

This new father experienced contemplation in its natural sense: total absorption in what we see, like a child wholly concentrated in play.[9] It is an experience of being present only to the moment, unconscious of time. Deep contemplation draws us momentarily into the eternal realm that transcends time.

In Christian contemplation we move from communicating with God through speech to communing with God through the gaze of love. Words fall away, and the most palpable reality is being present to the lover of our souls. When we let go of all effort to speak or even to listen, simply becoming quiet before God, the Spirit is free to work its healing mysteries in us: releasing us from bondage, energizing new patterns of life, restoring our soul's beauty. Here we allow ourselves to be loved by God into wholeness.

Such communion with God is an end in itself, not a means to another end, however good. We do not enter the prayer of rest in order to become better servants of God; that is a natural side effect. The sole purpose of contemplation is to adore and enjoy God, which glorifies divine love. The first article of the Westminster Shorter Catechism asks what our chief end as human beings is. The response is that we are to glorify and enjoy God forever! Do we ever stop to think what it means to *enjoy* God?

Why do we have such trouble believing that God longs for our companionship and delights in it, just as the Lord enjoyed "walking in the cool of the day" with Adam and Eve in a young creation (see Gen. 3:8)? What will it take to convince us that God also yearns for us to delight in the divine presence? Part of our spiritual maturation is learning to love God for who God is, not only for what God does for us.

Invitations to Explore

Perhaps it is only by giving ourselves to contemplative prayer and rest that we discover such truths for ourselves. Several pathways can open you to an experience of Christian contemplation. I focus here on three basic forms: *prayer of presence, prayer of the heart,* and *centering prayer.*

Prayer of Presence

- The first method is a simple prayer of presence: Find a posture that allows you to be relaxed and alert. It helps to have your neck and spine aligned. Close your eyes and breathe deeply several times. Consciously release any muscle tension you become aware of. Breathe in peace, breathe out tension.

- Relax your mind. If particular thoughts keep returning, gather them up and give them to God to hold for you during this time. You can take them back later if you want.

- Turn your attention to God's presence. Let yourself be fully aware of the mystery of divine love that continually surrounds and upholds all of creation, including you. God is breathing life into you at each moment; take in the gift.

- Let God's presence fill your consciousness, and simply rest in this presence—just as you might with someone you love dearly and feel no need to speak to, just to be with. Let yourself be like a child cradled in the lap of a wonderful parent or grandparent, or nestled close to Jesus' heart, or gently supported in an ocean of light, or enfolded by a peaceful warmth. Find an image that allows you to be held in God's tender embrace, then simply rest and soak up the love that holds you.

- Close your prayer by thanking God for any gifts received in this time. You can return to this communion of presence whenever you choose to receive it.

You may find it easier to try the prayer of presence with someone else guiding you through it at a gentle pace. Consider taping the instructions, timing it in a way that seems comfortable so you will be free to enter the process without having to read it. Or you may simply familiarize yourself with the content before praying at your own leisure.

If you have trouble allowing God to love you, remember this: there is nothing you can do to make God love you more, and although there are things you can do to grieve God, there is nothing you can do to make God love you less! Relax and let yourself receive the reality of God's eternal love.

Surely God's heart is comforted when we willingly receive what God longs to give us! How would a mother feel if her child resisted the overwhelming tenderness in her heart? How would a father feel if his child ran off at any sign of affection? Yet we seem so often willing to leave God lonely and disconsolate without us. Communion is *mutual* consolation and joy.

Prayer of the Heart

There is a long history of Christian prayer that aims to move us "from head to heart." Remember that this means moving from a limited and partial dimension of our lives to the center of our whole being. Prayers of the heart are typified by short phrases. They are repeated first on the lips and then in the mind, until they take on a life of their own deep within us. When such prayers become embedded in our life awareness and daily activity, they have truly become "heart prayers."

The oldest of these, known as the "Jesus Prayer," combines the prayer of the tax collector from Luke 18:13 ("God, be merciful to me, a sinner") with the earliest confession of the Christian church ("Jesus is Lord"). The long form is "Lord Jesus Christ, Son of the living God, have mercy on me, a sinner." The short form is "Lord, have mercy" (*kyrie eleison*). Consistent use of this prayer has been for many, especially in Eastern Christianity, a path to the contemplation of Christ and communion with the risen Lord.

A contemporary version of the Jesus Prayer is called "breath prayer" because the words for breath and spirit are the same in Hebrew (*ruach*) and the use of this kind of prayer over time helps us experience what it means for the Spirit to pray in us (Rom. 8:26–27). It is also a short prayer that can be said or thought in a single breath. As a prayer of the heart, it is especially easy to learn and practice. Ron DelBene, an Episcopal priest who developed this method from the older tradition, suggests that you find your own prayer of the heart.[10] Here is one way to do so:

- Visualize Jesus standing before you, asking you: "(*Your Name*), what do you want me to do for you?" Let your response surface from deep within. If more than one thing comes to mind, identify the root desire beneath all the others.

- Next, identify how you normally address God in prayer: Lord, Jesus, Holy One, Living Spirit, Eternal God? Find your name for the divine being.

Accustom yourself to walk in the presence of God. . . . To preserve this remembrance, choose a few short prayers . . . and repeat them often with appropriate thoughts and feelings.
Theophan the Recluse

46

- Combine your desire with your name for God in a single short phrase that flows easily in your mind. You may need to experiment with phrasing to find a comfortable rhythm.

- Sit quietly and repeat the phrase gently in your mind for several minutes. Take a walk, repeating your prayer while you move. Note how the prayer shapes your perceptions. You can carry this prayer with you through the day. It fits well with many solitary activities from common household chores and routine tasks to standing in line and sitting in traffic jams! It is a good companion for rhythmic exercise such as walking, jogging, or swimming as well.

Sample breath prayers:
Holy Spirit, fill me.
Give me strength, O Christ.
Father, show me your love.
Teach me patience, gracious God.
My God and my All. (from Saint Francis)
Come, Lord Jesus!

Scripture and hymn phrases can be prayed in the same way. Many of us have committed to memory a few verses of scripture that are particularly precious. We turn to them in times of special need or irrepressible joy. Simple tunes often help to carry our prayer phrase for us.

Repeated prayers tend to deepen and expand in meaning as they are used in various contexts of life. Over time, the repetition creates a space in which words fall away and we become more aware of the Presence they point to.

Simple objects or images can also be the focus of contemplative prayer. A single flower, leaf, or candle may become a pointer to divine presence. In the Eastern Orthodox Church, icons (images of Christ, Mary, and the saints) are a focus of contemplation. Henri Nouwen's book *Behold the Beauty of the Lord* is a helpful introduction to contemplation with icons.[11]

Centering Prayer

Every form of contemplative prayer aims to draw us past words and images to that mysterious place where God dwells in gracious union with the human soul. The prayer methods described above use images and words to help carry us beyond their use into a deeper experience of communion. Centering prayer specifically teaches us to let go of words, images, concepts, and emotions. The only exception is the use of a sacred word that symbolizes our intention to be inwardly receptive to divine presence and action. This word is not in any way a focus of our thoughts or feelings. It simply serves as a rudder to keep our intention directed Godward.

In contemplative prayer the Spirit places us in a position where we are at rest and disinclined to fight. . . . the Spirit heals the wounds of our fragile human nature at a level beyond our psychological perception.
Thomas Keating

Centering prayer has been enjoying a revival among Christians for at least twenty-five years, spurred largely by the writings of Thomas Keating and others in the Centering Prayer Movement he founded. This form of prayer is adapted from a fourteenth-century classic spiritual treatise, *The Cloud of Unknowing*. It aims to deepen our relationship with the living God, whose reality goes beyond our thoughts, images, and feelings yet is nearer to us than our breathing, our choosing, even our consciousness itself. In centering prayer we yield to a divine presence and action so deep within us that we cannot know or perceive what God is doing there. We simply open ourselves in trusting faith, which in itself is profoundly restful and healing.

Here are basic guidelines for this way of prayer, adapted from the Contemplative Outreach website (see http://bit.ly/Q7iHRD):

- Choose a sacred word as the symbol of your intention to consent to God's presence and action within. Select this word in a brief period of prayer, asking the Spirit to inspire you. Examples: God, Jesus, Abba, Light, Love, Peace, Be Still, Trust, Faith, Yes.

- Sitting comfortably with eyes closed, settle briefly and silently breathe your sacred word as the symbol of your consent to God's presence and action within. Introduce your word very gently, as if you were laying a feather on cotton. Let it carry you into a sense of God's real presence.

- When thoughts come, as they inevitably will, return ever-so-gently to the sacred word. "Thoughts" in this case include concepts, reflections, feelings, images, memories, plans, and sensory perceptions or body sensations. Do not try to push thoughts away, simply return your attention to the sacred word and God's presence within.

- At the end of the prayer period (20 minutes), remain in silence with eyes closed for a few minutes. You might wish to say the Lord's Prayer.

The use of a sacred word may seem similar to Eastern meditation with mantras, but the resemblance is superficial. Centering prayer has developed out of the mystical strands of Western Christianity. Although the method may seem simple, it is not easy to practice on your own. If you are unfamiliar with centering prayer, I urge you at the least to read a good book on the subject or attend an introductory centering prayer retreat.[12] For clarity and support over time, it is helpful to join a centering prayer group led by someone experienced in the method.

Contemplative prayer is not so much the absence of thoughts as detachment from them.

Thomas Keating

Practical Matters

The discussion of prayer would be incomplete without some attention to very practical matters such as time, place, and the irritation of distractions.

There is no substitute for giving time to the practice of prayer. As with most things, we learn best by doing it. But the issue of time is a formidable barrier for many of us. We live in a culture that equates constant activity with meaning. Time is often the "commodity" we are least willing to give up without tangible compensation. We all make choices about our use of time. The way we use time reveals our priorities, much as we might like to think otherwise. Were I to learn that I had only six months to live, my use of time would no doubt change significantly!

If our relationship with God is really important to us, we will make time to pray. It might mean going to bed earlier in order to get up earlier. It might mean taking a portion of the lunch hour for solitude. It could involve swapping child care with a friend for a period each day. It certainly means claiming the time that is thrust upon us when we are sick or delayed in travel. Most of us could learn to waste less time over inconsequential matters so that we have more time for what is important. Developing the habit of regular prayer is like building any new habit into our life: it takes firm commitment, creativity, and perseverance.

None of this will happen unless we *desire* a deeper relationship with God. Desire for God is fuel for prayer. When we fall in love, we readily set other things aside in order to secure coveted time to be with our beloved. It should be no different with God.

In choosing a time for prayer, it is important to take personal rhythms into account. Some of us are morning persons, some are night owls, and some experience peak energy at midday. God deserves some of the best time of our day, not the dregs.

It is easier, especially for beginners, to pay attention to God in solitude and relative quiet. For some, this poses a creative challenge. I have known people who took early morning walks in New York's Central Park for prayer. Others have learned to shut out the noise around them by entering the inner sanctuary of the heart. Some families identify a particular chair that entitles its occupant to quiet and solitude. Some have turned a spare closet into a literal "prayer closet."

When you have found your place for prayer, sanctify it through frequent use. Make it sacred space. You may want to arrange a few symbols of divine presence and beauty in it. Remember, you are not

The great thing is prayer. Prayer itself. If you want a life of prayer, the way to get it is by praying. . . . You start where you are and you deepen what you already have.

Thomas Merton

a disembodied spirit. Pay attention to your body; bring it into your prayer so it can be a support rather than a distraction. Give yourself permission to experiment with expressive postures and gestures.

Finally, there is the matter of distractions that inevitably surface in prayer. External distractions are easier to handle (see chap. 2). When the noises of civilization or nature intrude, as they invariably do despite our best efforts to find or create quiet, it is best simply to accept them and return to your prayer intentions.

Internal distractions are more difficult. Saints through the centuries have offered colorful descriptions of how the mind, left to its own devices, functions: "like monkeys jumping around in banana trees," or a "swarm of mosquitoes" buzzing in all directions. The psychological term is "free association." This is precisely why you need simple words, phrases, or images to help you focus on God's presence. Remember that certain kinds of prayer—thanksgiving, confession, or supplication—give the mind a train of thought to focus on, whereas listening prayer and contemplation tend to generate more inner distraction.

Be prepared for distractions and be patient with them. If you try to fight them head-on, the attention will make them stronger. Better to simply note that you have wandered from your focus and gently return your attention to God. Persistent thoughts may require closer examination. Do they represent something you need to confess, a person you need to be reconciled to, a situation that calls for your response? There is a Jewish tradition that "distractions in prayer are blemished deeds in our lives that push their way into prayer in expectation of the blessing that is to come."[13] Might this be true for you?

The most important thing is to keep praying, even if it feels artificial at first. Expect to learn in the process. Experiment with different forms of prayer, but keep a balance between thanksgiving and supplication, confession and intercession, speaking and listening, communication and communion. God will bless whatever offering you make from the heart with commitment and sincerity. The more you give yourself to prayer, the more life you will find in it.

I can be praying and find my mind on another matter, . . . on someone who has hurt me, on a problem coming up. This kind of distraction indicates what is . . . not integrated into my personal relationship with Jesus Christ. . . . I can put the matter into his hands, turning the distraction into a prayer.

Robert L. Faricy

Notes to the Text

1. John S. Mogabgab, unpublished writings.

2. Richard J. Foster, *Celebration of Discipline* (New York: Harper & Row, 1978), 16.

3. Douglas V. Steere, *Dimensions of Prayer* (Nashville: Upper Room Books, 1997), 13.

4. Steere, *Dimensions of Prayer*, 39.

5. From the second-century *Epistle to Diognetus*, cited in Steere's *Dimensions of Prayer*, 9.

6. Attributed to Jane Edwards; source unknown. I came upon these words in a sheaf of quotes lovingly collected, handwritten, and entrusted to me by a woman of prayer at First Presbyterian Church in Stamford, CT, where I served from 1981–1985. No clues were included as to the identity of this particular Jane Edwards.

7. These insights are borrowed from Steere, *Dimensions of Prayer*, 69.

8. Anthony Bloom, *Beginning to Pray* (New York: Paulist Press, 1970), 62.

9. I maintain a distinction between "natural contemplation," such as the complete absorption of a viewer in a glorious sunset (which may or may not be experienced as a medium of God's presence) and "Christian contemplation," which involves a direct experience of the presence of God unmediated by thoughts, images, or physical senses.

10. See any one of several short and very accessible books by Ron Del-Bene with Herb Montgomery, such as *The Breath of Life*, *The Hunger of the Heart*, and *Into the Light* (Nashville: Upper Room Books).

11. Henri J. M. Nouwen, *Behold the Beauty of the Lord* (Notre Dame, IN: Ave Maria Press, 1987).

12. I recommend Thomas Keating, *Open Mind, Open Heart* (Rockport, MA: Element, 1992), and Cynthia Bourgeault, *Centering Prayer and Inner Awakening* (Lanham, MD: Cowley Publications, 2004).

13. Steere, *Dimensions of Prayer*, 30.

Notes to the Epigraph and Sidebars

Maria Boulding, contemplative nun of Stanbrook Abbey, England 1929–2009. Epigraph from *The Coming of God* (Collegeville, MN: The Liturgical Press, 1986), 7–8.

Flip Wilson, North American comedian.

Douglas V. Steere, Quaker author and teacher, 1901–1995. *Dimensions of Prayer* (Nashville, TN: Upper Room Books, 1997), 13.

George MacDonald, Scottish clergyman, novelist, and poet, 1824–1905. *Diary of an Old Soul* (London: George Allen & Unwin Ltd., 1905), 96.

Rubem Alves, Professor of Philosophy, State University of Campinas, São Paolo, Brazil. *I Believe in the Resurrection of the Body* (Minneapolis: Fortress Press, 1986), 19.

James Outram Fraser, missionary to Lisuland, Southwest China, 1886–1938. In Mrs. Howard Taylor, *Behind the Ranges: A Biography of J. O. Fraser of Lisuland* (London: OMF, 1970), 111.

Douglas V. Steere, *Dimensions of Prayer,* 67.

Alfred Lord Tennyson, Poet Laureate of England, 1809–1892. "Idylls of the King: The Passing of Arthur," from *The Norton Anthology of English Literature*, 4th ed., vol. 2 (New York: W. W. Norton & Company, 1979), 1206.

Cynthia Bourgeault, Episcopal priest, teacher, retreat leader and author. *Centering Prayer and Inner Awakening* (Lanham, MD: Cowley Publications, 2004), 5.

Walter de la Mare, French poet, 1873–1956. "The Secret," from *The Complete Poems of Walter de la Mare* (London: Faber & Faber, 1969).

Theophan the Recluse, Russian Bishop and Staretz (elder), 1815–1894. *The Art of Prayer: An Orthodox Anthology*, compiled by Igumen Chariton of Valamo, trans. E. Kadloubovsky and E. M. Palmer (London: Faber & Faber, 1966), 109.

Thomas Keating, Trappist monk of St. Benedict's Abbey in Snowmass, CO, founder of the Centering Prayer Movement and of Contemplative Outreach. From *Open Mind, Open Heart: The Contemplative Dimension of the Gospel* (Rockport, MA: Element, Inc., 1991), 45.

Thomas Keating, Ibid., 14.

Thomas Merton, Trappist monk and eminent spiritual writer of the twentieth century, 1915–1968. From an address to nuns in California, quoted in M. Basil Pennington, *Centering Prayer* (Garden City, NY: Doubleday Image Books, 1982), 56–57.

Robert L. Faricy, American Jesuit, Emeritus Professor of Spirituality at Pontifical Gregorian University in Rome. *Praying for Inner Healing* (London: SCM, 1979), 75.

CHAPTER 4

Gathered in the Spirit

Our Common Worship

My whole heart I lay upon the altar of thy praise, an whole burnt-offering of praise I offer to thee. . . . Let the flame of thy love . . . set on fire my whole heart, let nought in me be left to myself, nought wherein I may look to myself, but may I wholly burn towards thee, wholly be on fire toward thee, wholly love thee, as though set on fire by thee.

—Saint Augustine

Christian philosopher Søren Kierkegaard developed an analogy called "the theater of worship." It invites us to see public worship as a kind of theater performance and asks us to identify the stage, actors, and audience. Based on our experience of worship, most of us would probably locate the stage in the church chancel and see worship leaders as the actors performing for a congregational audience. But Kierkegaard asks us to see the sanctuary as a stage on which the entire congregation acts, prompted by ministers and musicians. The audience is God!

The word *liturgy* comes from the Greek *leitourgia*, which simply means the service or work of the people. Worship is the work of all the faithful who gather to praise, honor, and glorify God. Have you ever thought about what kind of *service* to God a "worship service" is? Acts of service to one another have a sacrificial character. We serve God when worship expresses a spirit of sacrifice: first a sacrifice of praise and thanksgiving, then a complete self-offering—a willingness to listen for God's Word and to give ourselves wholly to God's designs in the world. We offer our will, strength, and gifts in gratitude for who God is and what God has done for us.

Of course, it is also true that in worship we are served by God. God fills us with the joy of knowing we are loved, restores our courage through forgiveness, provides the Word for hungry hearts, and fills us with the bread and wine of new life in Christ, giving new purpose to our lives. From this perspective, the stage of worship is the very kingdom of God, the prime actor is the Holy Spirit, and we—leaders and people alike—are the audience. Christian worship is paradoxical. God is both the audience and the main actor. We too are both actors and audience.

Our worship is rooted in who God is and in God's purposes. We worship because it is natural to respond to the mystery that irradiates life. We know God to be holy and pure, just and true, compassionate and loving. God is worthy to receive our praise and acclaim, worthy of our listening ears and offered hearts. The "worth-ship" of God is the origin of human worship! We also worship because we are created to reflect and glorify the One in whose image we are made. Eastern Christians believe we are most truly ourselves when we glorify God, finding our "perfection and fulfillment in worship."[1]

Worship ushers us into the presence of the living God and demands the attention, receptivity, and response of our whole being. It asks us to disengage from the nose-length focus of daily life and see below the surface to life's source. We can then reengage the realities of the world from a deeper and clearer perspective.

To worship is to quicken the conscience by the holiness of God, to feed the mind with the truth of God, to purge the imagination by the beauty of God, to open the heart to the love of God, to devote the will to the purpose of God.
William Temple

Worship from the Heart

"You shall love the Lord your God with all your heart, and with all your soul, and with all your mind, and with all your strength" (Mark 12:29–30). When Jesus identifies this great commandment, he sets worship at the center of human life. Worship, as full-hearted love of God, is meant to permeate our lives. Private or public, it is always first and foremost a matter of the heart.

We cannot realize the richness and vitality of worship until we comprehend the meaning of *heart* in the Judeo-Christian tradition. In Western culture, *head* and *heart* describe separate spheres. *Head* signifies our rational, analytic functions while *heart* represents our feeling capacities. But a purely emotional heart does not express its scriptural significance.

In the Jewish tradition, the heart is the seat and center of the whole person, the core of personal character, including thought, emotion, will, intuition, and imagination. Thoughts, both good and evil, arise from the heart; motives, desires, and intentions come from the heart. When the heart is turned toward God, one is filled with grace and truth; when the heart turns away, a person dwells in delusion. The Christian church inherited this understanding of *heart* from the Jewish tradition.

True worship from the heart, then, means responding to God's glory and love with our entire being. After all, when Spirit touches spirit, we are *moved*—in both feelings and commitments. Too many worshiping communities encourage only half-hearted worship. In churches that tend toward reason and order, many members yearn to express more fully the intuitive and feeling side of faith. In churches where intellect is less valued than emotional experiences of faith, many people are hungry for serious study and responsible action. Historically speaking, with the exception of music, Protestant churches of European background tended to neglect the body and its senses in worship, while churches with African and Hispanic roots were more likely to include the whole body in worship celebrations. This dichotomy has broken down somewhat over the past few decades as styles of worship have become less formal. Some communities have embraced diverse expressions of visual beauty along with symbolic rituals that include gestures and movement in worship. Part of the gift of our increasingly multicultural society is the opportunity to learn various styles of worship from one another and to appreciate the gifts of each tradition.

> In African American culture the emotional is not the opposite of the spiritual, nor is there any separation between the emotional and the intellectual. Both the mind and the heart are needed to grasp the truth.
>
> Jamie Phelps

Worship from the heart joins inner reality with outward expression. Reciting words and enacting rituals may be important expressions of faith but cannot by themselves finally satisfy the soul. Personal integrity demands more than external form: "these people draw near with their mouths / and honor me with their lips, / while their hearts are far from me, / and their worship of me is a human commandment learned by rote" (Isa. 29:13). Yet the integrity of lips and heart together cannot be produced by a simple act of will on our part. As author Richard Foster reminds us, "Until God touches and frees our spirit we cannot enter this realm. . . . Our spirit must be ignited by the divine fire."[2]

The Need to Gather

For many people, private worship is more attractive than public worship. Envisioning faith as a private affair reflects the individualism of our culture. Many ask why corporate worship should be so important when they can meditate on God in nature with far less distraction or why they should bother to get dressed up and go to church when they can listen to an inspiring message on radio, TV, or online.

The reasons for gathering are many and important. Whether we are alone or with others, we need to experience our Christian life as rooted in the larger community of faith. Even our most personal disciplines need to be supported, broadened, clarified, and sometimes corrected in the light of corporate theology and practice. Otherwise we become susceptible to privatized visions of spiritual truth. Moreover, we need the prayers of others as they need our prayers. The way God provides for our deepest hopes is usually through the hands and hearts of others.

Liturgy places God in the center and us in community.

John S. Mogabgab

While a worshipful attitude may permeate one's entire life, the role of common worship remains crucial. We delude ourselves if we imagine we can live the spiritual life in total isolation from Christian community, for it is impossible to be Christian in solitary splendor. To be Christian is to be joined to the body of Christ. The central and visible way in which the church expresses this reality is by gathering in the Spirit to receive and respond to God's living Word.

We gather for worship to remember who and whose we are. We come to recount the stories that shape our faith, stories that turn us from a collection of individuals into a community with a common source and vision. The church as a worshiping community carries our biblical faith and spiritual tradition down through the ages to each individual. We are joined to that community in Baptism, tutored in faith through the interpretation of scripture in preaching, and nourished at the Lord's Table *as a family of believers*. Life in the church teaches us that we are made for communion not only with God but also with one another in Christ.

Without the rites and sacraments of public worship, there would be no body of Christ. It is through the praises, prayers, sacraments, and scriptural proclamations of common worship that the church is continually given its life. In this respect, worship is the most fundamental of all Christian practices.

Common worship leads us through the seasons of Jesus' life and the life of the early church. Every time we move through Advent, Christmas, Lent, Easter, and Pentecost, we are given fresh occasion to take to heart the meaning of Jesus' life in relation to our own. Each year allows us to reexperience the coming of the Messiah, the Lord's risen presence, the birth of the church, and the energy of its mission. Such knowledge is impossible to come by on our own, even if we are steeped in the Bible. How can we comprehend the significance of Pentecost if we do not experience the grace of the Holy Spirit in a living community of faith? How can we understand the mission of the church if we are isolated from the church?

Finally, worship in community means that we can present a united front "against the cosmic powers of this present darkness" (Eph. 6:12). Biblical scholar Walter Wink argues eloquently that the powers and principalities of this world are corporate in nature.[3] It takes a *communal* witness of light, truth, and peace to overcome the corporate power of darkness, deception, and destruction in this world.

Of course, we need to keep in mind that there are faithful members of the body of Christ who are committed to the importance of common worship but are physically unable to come. Frail, elderly people and those who are homebound, the physically disabled whose churches are inaccessible, call the gathered community to accountability. Online, television or radio broadcasts of worship may be a blessing to such persons. But even more important are the ways their fellow members bring community to them in their particular circumstances. Pastors providing home Communion to shut-ins is a fairly standard practice, but greater creativity is called for in bringing community to the faithful with limited mobility. Giving homebound parishioners ways to connect with the larger community can be accomplished in several ways: for example, they can be given a special mission of prayer for the pastors and congregation; those who are able can be included in outreach through writing or craft projects; and they can form community with one another through prayer, phone calls, note cards, or emails.[4] Congregations would do well to give more attention to this matter.

Do you think forced isolation makes a person more conscious of the gift and importance of common worship? What might we learn from persons in such circumstances?

Worship as Problem

Unfortunately, many people find corporate worship a source of frustration rather than fulfillment. Our actual experience on Sunday morning may embody few of the realities I have described, even if we believe in them. We may feel that we are neither actors nor audience before God but passive (and not always happy) recipients of the limited worship forms of particular churches and their leaders.

Perhaps we come seeking a lively community of faith and find people who seem bored, preoccupied, uninterested in visitors, or eager to escape from Christian fellowship for Sunday brunch and afternoon golf. Perhaps we feel unable to penetrate the circles of people who seem to be at the heart of the church's life. We may find ourselves unaccepted for a variety of reasons, including various forms of brokenness in our personal lives. We may consistently leave worship feeling isolated and lonely.

Perhaps we come to hear a word of life in the scriptures but find ourselves instead subjected to passages rendered meaningless, dull, or exaggerated by the manner in which they are read. There may be little silence allowed for the word we *do* hear to sink in and get assimilated. Perhaps we come to receive edification in the preaching and are dished up a heavy dose of ideology, the preacher's personal views, or endless anecdotes strung together and passed off as a sermon. Maybe the preacher speaks down to us, harangues us, or fails to connect the sermon to our daily experiences of life. We become weary and angry instead of energized with good news.

Perhaps we come with an eagerness to sing the great hymns of our faith, hymns we may have known by heart from childhood. Instead we find a new hymnal with tunes that seem unsingable or familiar tunes with unfamiliar words that leave us confused and dissatisfied.

Perhaps we have been growing in our prayer life and have a strong desire to contribute our prayers to those of the gathered community. We may find no space in the service for our prayers. They may all be printed or spoken on our behalf, even if they do not express what is in our heart.

Are there aspects of your worship experience that seem consistently unsatisfying to you? If so, name them.

We may hunger for a deeper sacramental experience in our worship. Many Protestants from nonsacramental traditions (Presbyterian, Methodist, Baptist, Congregational) have begun exploring the spiritual riches of the sacramental churches (Anglican, Roman Catholic, Eastern Orthodox) through private retreats or ecumenical training programs. We may return to our churches with an acute sense of loss where the sacraments are concerned, especially Holy Communion. There is neither the frequency of celebration we may crave nor the sense of spiritual depth and mystery we have come to respect. An expectation of meeting the real presence of Christ can seem absent in our worship experience.

Other sources of dissatisfaction abound. We may yearn for greater freedom of expression in posture, gesture, and movement. We may thirst for periods of silence to balance the barrage of words. We may crave the visual blessing of beauty, light, color, and richness of symbol. We may feel that public worship has little "heart" or integrity at all. Perhaps it feels ever more rote and external each Sunday. When God seems remote, worship can feel as dry as the Sahara. We come for living water and leave with unquenched thirst. We come to be nourished and leave with a mouthful of sand.

Not everyone experiences such inadequacy in public worship, and certainly not in all these ways at once! Yet as hunger deepens for spiritual nurture, people often become more dissatisfied with the limitations they perceive in their own traditions of corporate worship. Part of the problem is that the average person in the pew has little say over how worship is planned, much less over how leaders read, preach, and pray.

How, then, are we to become lively actors in the drama of human worship before God? How can we be better attuned to God in spite of the foibles of worship leaders, the frailties of worshiping communities, and the inadequacies of our own feelings and judgments?

Worship as Promise: Practices for Deepening Our Worship

Worship need not be completely determined by the limitations of human leaders or communities. There are things we can do to help enliven our experience of common worship. We may have little power to change the external forms, but we can certainly change our way of entering into worship. We can take responsibility for our own experience in three important ways: by preparing in advance for the Sunday service; by engaging worship itself with a different quality of awareness; and by taking the initiative to speak with worship planners and leaders about how we experience worship.

Preparation

The single most important thing we can do to change our experience of public worship is to revitalize our practice of personal worship. In earlier times, the weekly prayers of the gathered community were nurtured by the daily prayers of faithful families and individuals, just as a river is fed by smaller streams. These days, I suspect that daily prayer in families is rare, while individual prayer is likely sporadic and weighted toward intercession. Electronic technology has made email prayer chains popular in many congregations, a useful prompt to regular intercession. Additionally, some spiritual life websites and blogs offer daily meditations that encourage personal prayer and reflection in the midst of online activities. While these are useful developments, I doubt that a majority of church members engage daily with such opportunities. Small wonder, then, if public worship feels spiritually dry.

When we begin to steep ourselves in scripture on a regular basis, we hear the Sunday scripture readings differently. Our own daily prayer becomes tilled soil for receiving the seed of God's Word in the liturgy. The practice of *Lectio Divina* is ideal for personal prayer, as are any of the prayer practices discussed in chapter 3. Morning and evening prayer have been the classic "daily offices" of personal and family worship in the Protestant tradition. They generally include at least a psalm, a New Testament reading, a song, and a few prayers, although the number of elements can be adapted as needed. Committing to even one such practice daily will immeasurably enrich our experience of common worship.

Christians have always known that public worship—particularly the celebration of the sacraments—requires inward preparation. It was at one time common practice to examine oneself through prayer and confession before participating in the Sunday service. If we spend half an hour assessing our lives before God, either Saturday evening or early Sunday morning, we will discover natural bridges between our personal prayer and common worship. We will find unexpected connections between our life experiences and the words of the liturgy, and we will deepen our receptivity to the grace of Word and Sacrament.

Many people have found it enriching to prepare for common worship as a group. A weekly Bible study, focusing on the passage to be preached the following Sunday, can bring the experience of worship to life in a new way. When we have studied the background of a text and reflected on how it speaks to our lives, we are likely to find connections with the sermon regardless of its quality. Such study groups are easier to maintain over time if the preaching follows a lectionary, but if the passage is known in advance, topical preaching can also allow for a useful group process.

During Worship

Many find it helpful to arrive for worship ten minutes early in order to distance themselves from last-minute rushing and prepare themselves to worship God from the heart. This is a good time for both worship leaders and worshipers to pray, asking the Spirit to be actively present and known by the gathered community and

Try out a half-hour self-examination (see chap. 6) this weekend, directing the following questions to God:

When have I been aware of your presence, guidance, or grace this week? How did I respond?

When have I been especially unaware of your presence, guidance, or grace this week? Why?

What habit of the heart do I need to acquire in order to live more faithfully?

for the faithfulness and integrity of the church in its worship and mission.

Once the service has begun, you can do several things to heighten your awareness of God's presence. First, be prepared to hear God speak—to you personally and to the whole gathering. Recognize that God can catch our attention through any part of the service, not only in the ways we expect. Pay attention to the meaning of the words in printed prayers and affirmations as you speak them. You don't have to let the congregational drone of unison reading dull your mind!

Listen to the words of hymns with an ear for the meaning of the sentences. Sometimes this meaning is obscured by musical phrases that do not correspond to the spoken phrase, and some idioms in older hymns need explanation in order to make sense. But hymns are one of the richest sources of heartfelt worship in the Protestant tradition. They allow us to express depths of joy, praise, sorrow, and yearning in music as well as words, joining emotion and thought in profound unity. Anthems serve much the same purpose. We can join our hearts in self-offering with the choir, even when we cannot join our voices. Music often carries our spirit Godward when nothing else can. It may be as much a source of inspiration as well-spoken words.

Listen carefully to any Psalm you may recite. The Psalms give us a realistic voice for praise, anguish, yearning, and confession—a way to reveal the depths of the human soul to God. If we allow it, the Psalter can school us in uninhibited prayer. Regular recitation of the Psalms gives us a repertoire of prayers known by heart that can anchor us through the gale winds of life.

If all the prayers in your service are printed or offered by worship leaders, find where you can add your inward assent or "amen!" to the words others have placed before you. Not every word will express your own heart before God, but some of them probably will. Be attentive to where the public prayers of the church stretch you to a new perception or offer to God something you had perhaps not thought important. The prayers of the church can tutor us in a richer language of personal prayer.

If you are given an opportunity to pray silently, offer to God what you discover in your heart at the time. Perhaps you are distracted by a fretful child nearby; pray for the well-being of that child and all the church's children, indeed for the children of the world. Perhaps the Gospel reading helped you see how fearful you are of people who are different; pray for those who seem most different, and pray to be

When in our music God is glorified, and adoration leaves no room for pride, it is as though the whole creation cried: Alleluia!

Fred Pratt Green

When the Rev. Benjamin Weir was held hostage for several years in Lebanon, his memory of the Psalms helped to sustain him. Do you have a reservoir of scriptural prayers that you know "by heart"? What inner resources do you draw on in trying circumstances?

released from fear so you can be free to serve. Let the themes, images, insights, and feelings from worship itself inform your prayers.

Perhaps you bring individual concerns to worship that seem only distantly related to the gathered community. If you are praying daily at home, such personal concerns will not likely prevent you from praying on behalf of the wider world. Sometimes, however, these issues are so overwhelming and immediate that our minds and hearts are completely taken over by them. Then it is well to ask for the prayers of our companions in faith, allowing the community to carry us until we find enough strength and healing to look to the needs of others again.

If certain parts of the service do not speak to you, stay focused inwardly on the parts that do. Ponder in your heart those phrases or insights that communicate the presence and grace of God to you. Let yourself respond inwardly to the gifts you *are* given in the time of worship. But remember that what speaks to you may not make you comfortable. God often communicates grace through challenge!

Claim for yourself the freedom to respond to God in worship with the fullness of your being. If tears are a natural part of your response to God's grace, or a way of communicating your need to God, let yourself cry. If you hear a word that tickles you with humor or joy, let yourself laugh! If you couldn't agree more with what the preacher says, nod your head or murmur an assent. Instead of allowing the inhibitions of others to control you, offer the example of your freedom to others. We need permission to feel and to move in our worship life.

There is nothing forbidden about using simple gestures to express what is in your heart to God. What could be more natural? We use gestures when communicating with each other, so why not with God? You may not be prepared for deep bows or even kneeling as gestures of reverence and self-offering, but smaller gestures may prove valuable aids to the integrity of your worship. Many people find that simply opening the palms of their hands in prayer, while standing, sitting, or kneeling, helps them to focus on the meaning of that prayer. I find such a gesture very unobtrusive, yet it helps me know the reality of my prayer in a deeper way. Using the body can help prayer become an expression of more than our distractible minds. The freedom we find in personal prayer to use various gestures or postures may, over time, make a significant contribution to our public worship.

Finally, we can observe and reflect upon whatever symbols of faith there may be in our places of worship. Some churches have beautiful stained glass windows with images and symbols worth pondering. Some have bright banners or wood carvings. Most churches feature

Take five minutes to try this exercise:

Sitting with your arms and legs crossed, say the Lord's Prayer silently. Then, if you are able and comfortable, try it again on your knees with the palms of your hands open before you.

Did you experience a difference in the way you prayed or how it felt? If so, describe the difference. If not, don't worry. It may be that posture and gesture do not generally affect your experience of prayer.

the central symbol of Christian faith, the cross, in a prominent place. Many also keep a traditional chalice and paten, or pitchers and plates, on the Communion table. Some have baptismal fonts in visible positions. Meditating on the meaning of these images can enrich and deepen other parts of a particular service. On those occasions when the words of worship seem dry or inaccessible, we may find our sermon in visual symbols.

The Spirit is free to speak to us in an infinite number of ways. If you do not find God's Word where you expect to, keep your ears open for the unexpected!

Beyond Worship

Although you may not be in a position to make direct decisions about how worship is planned and led, you can make your hopes and desires known to those who are. Don't be afraid to talk with your pastor or worship committee about your experience of common worship.

If you feel a need for more silent reflection time in the service, say so. You can suggest when quiet reflection would be most helpful to you: perhaps before the service, after scripture readings or sermon, during prayers of confession or intercession. If you crave more frequent celebration of the Lord's Supper, let your leadership know. There may be others like you who could form the nucleus of an early Sunday morning or weekday evening Eucharist. If you want to explore prayers for healing in your faith community, say so; there is historical precedent for services of healing prayer with the anointing of oil, commonly connected to the Eucharist, which the early church called "the medicine of immortality."

Your suggestions need not be in the form of complaint, which may elicit defensiveness on the part of decision makers. They can rather be expressed as changes you yearn for that would enrich your experience of worship.

For Worship Leaders

If you are a worship leader or planner, there are many aspects of worship that only you can affect. The overall integrity of the service is your responsibility. The ordering of parts and the thematic unity of hymns, prayers, scripture, preaching, and sacraments belong to you. You can affect elements of worship that will have a significant impact on the congregation's experience of corporate prayer and praise.

Consider, for example, where time is allowed for silent reflection in the service as a whole. Silence helps clear away the static and clutter that impede our access to deeper thought. It leaves us free to pay attention to the presence of the One we have come to encounter in worship. In the services you lead, do people have a chance to reflect on the reality of God's presence in their midst? Are they given space to assimilate the messages proclaimed in scripture and preaching? Is sufficient time offered for silent prayers of confession or intercession? A friend once told me that her son turned to her in the pew after a ten-second silence for confession and exclaimed, "I'm only seven years old and even *I* have more to say to God than that!"

Scripture reading in worship is often undervalued and one of the weakest elements of the service instead of one of the strongest. Pay attention to how Bible passages are read in your church. Does the reader convey a genuine understanding of what he or she is reading? Is the passage read without artificial emphases, sing-song phrasing, or unnatural exaggeration? Readers, including trained church professionals, could practice scripture reading in advance of a service to the benefit of all those attending worship.

Ponder the place of our physical senses in worship. Space, light, symbol, sound, fragrance, and sacred art can be powerful vehicles for the experience of the holy. Assess your sanctuary: Where does it express sensory beauty or sacred signs? Assess your worship service: How much of the whole person does it invite to participate in worship? Is there anything beyond words to encourage reflection on the goodness and beauty of God? There is a difference between simplicity and sterility.

Does the worship you plan take account of the fact that we are embodied creatures? Consider how your people participate physically in worship. What kinds of postures, gestures, or movement are encouraged? Are there occasions when the congregation can come forward to present special offerings or receive Communion in those churches that typically partake seated? Are particular gestures ever suggested for "passing the peace"? Some people are more comfortable with hand contact than hugs, but shaking hands has a formal, secular significance that feels closer to saying "Hello, how are you?" than to passing the peace of Christ. A gesture between hug and handshake is a two-handed clasp, which might be encouraged by worship leaders. Creativity and imagination are called for here. I mentioned opening the palms of the hands when saying the Lord's Prayer. Another natural opportunity for movement occurs during the opening of the Eucharistic liturgy. When the celebrant says "Lift up your hearts" and the congregation responds "We lift them up to the Lord!" both celebrant and people could lift their hands upward and outward in a simple gesture.

Consider making greater use of sung psalm responses, traditional spirituals, and simple chants or songs such as those developed in the Taizé and Iona communities. These have the quality of musical meditations and foster a reflective capacity in the congregation.

Experiencing Worship When Leading Worship

One of the most difficult aspects of leading worship is that attention to process and logistics can interfere with the ability to experience worship yourself. There is a freedom to receive and participate in the pew that worship leaders rarely share. This does not mean, however, that it is impossible to worship God while leading worship.

How can church professionals find spiritual nourishment in leading worship? The keys to meaningful worship for its leaders are essentially the same as those already suggested. The place to begin is with adequate preparation.

If you participate in a weekly lectionary study group, you will bring a wealth of fresh insight to the scripture that is read and preached Sunday morning, even if you are the reader and preacher! You will experience a different level of connection with people in the pew who have shared questions and insights with you.

Personal prayer during the week is even more critical for church leaders than for other Christians. Without it, you are truly courting the sin of works-righteousness, not to mention hypocrisy and burn-out. Meditate with scripture, listen deeply to God's Word, finding the links between it and your own life before formulating a sermon. This process will change your experience of preaching. You will discover grace in it for yourself as well as for others.

Self-examination before common worship, especially before celebrating the sacraments, is also essential for church leaders. Honest life assessment and confession is a means of grace that is as necessary to pastors and priests as to other Christians. It paves the way to forgiveness and restoration, freeing you to worship God in joy and gratitude. Self-examination allows leaders to acknowledge dependence on divine grace for all effective ministry. It can help worship leaders to relax and let the Spirit work in unplanned ways.

In one church I know of, a pastor who was not renowned for his preaching began asking one of his elders to pray for him each Sunday during the service. The elder went apart to a small room to be given entirely to prayer for the minister during this time. The results were remarkable in the worship experience of both congregation and pastor. The preaching started to "come alive" and the sense of spiritual vitality in the congregation was palpably different. Why not ask faithful lay leaders in your church to pray for you and other worship leaders during the service? They would not necessarily need to leave the sanctuary to do so.

If you are sufficiently prepared for the service in advance, you should be able to participate in worship. Take time to become aware of God's presence and sustaining grace before starting to lead worship. Keep the remembrance of God's real presence before you during the service. Cultivate this awareness, perhaps using a prayer of the heart from time to time: "Be still and know that I am God." "Worship the Lord in the beauty of holiness." "My God and my all." Let go of thoughts about how to phrase that announcement or whether you can rework a sermon illustration before the Gospel reading. Trust the Spirit to guide and direct your thoughts, words, and affections as you speak. Then you can breathe deeply and take in what is going on, even while you guide it. Enter into hymns with your whole heart and receive the anthem as a blessing. Give your attention to the meaning of what you speak. Let everything be an offering to the Holy One in your midst.

Afterward, reflect on how you experienced worship. At what points in the service were you able to be present to God and when did you become distracted or self-absorbed? If you ponder this each week, perhaps making journal entries to help you see your patterns of attitude and attention, you will gradually be able to bring more and more of the Sunday service into your actual experience of worship. Indeed, your awareness of God's presence as the source and center of worship may have a direct impact on how you design and lead the service. You will come to know more truly the difference between performing before a congregation and leading a congregation in common worship before God. We are all actors in the great drama where God is our audience!

Notes to the Text

1. Timothy Ware, *The Orthodox Church* (Baltimore: Penguin Books, 1963), 272.

2. Richard J. Foster, *Celebration of Discipline* (San Francisco: Harper & Row, 1988), 159.

3. Walter Wink, "Waging Spiritual Warfare with the Powers," *Weavings* 5, no. 2 (March–April 1990): 34–35.

4. In his book *Into the Light: A Simple Way to Pray with the Sick and Dying* (Nashville: The Upper Room, 1988), Ron DelBene has some excellent, practical suggestions about ways of calling forth the gifts of shut-ins and giving them a sense of community with one another as well as with the congregation.

Notes to the Epigraph and Sidebars

Augustine of Hippo, Epigraph from *Expositions on the Book of Psalms* (LF VI, 178) on Psalm 138:2.

William Temple, Archbishop of Canterbury, 1881–1944. Quoted in Richard J. Foster, *Celebration of Discipline*, 158, without source.

Jamie Phelps, professor of Systematic Theology at Catholic Theological Union in Chicago. From "Black Spirituality" in *Spiritual Traditions for the Contemporary Church*, ed. by Robin Maas and Gabriel O'Donnell (Nashville: Abingdon, 1990), 342.

John S. Mogabgab, founding editor of *Weavings: A Journal of the Christian Spiritual Life*. From *Weavings*, 4, no. 4 (July–August 1989): 3.

Fred Pratt Green, contemporary hymn text writer. Verse 1 of hymn, "When in Our Music." Copyright 1972, Hope Publishing Co., Carol Stream, IL. Used by permission.

CHAPTER 5

Reclaiming Sabbath Time

❧

The Sacred Art of Ceasing

Remember the sabbath day and keep it holy. Six days you shall labor and do all your work. But the seventh day is a sabbath to the LORD your God; you shall not do any work. . . . For in six days the LORD made heaven and earth, the sea, and all that is in them, but rested the seventh day; therefore the LORD blessed the sabbath day and consecrated it.

Exodus 20:8–11

Years ago, author and minister Flora Wuellner came to Upper Room Ministries as a writer in residence. As she spoke to our staff one day, a particular phrase lodged in my memory: "the beauty of the borders." Flora reminded us that landscapes are made beautiful by fences, hedges, and perimeters of flowerbeds. She pointed out that every living thing has boundaries giving it definition. Indeed, nothing can live a life of integrity or purpose without its own given form. Flora's comments were directed toward the importance of maintaining healthy psychological boundaries in our relationships with one another. But I found myself applying "the beauty of the borders" to our way of life in a broader sense.

We need to take natural human boundaries seriously simply to function as we are created to function. Yet the human mind drives toward overcoming limitations, breaking out of boundaries, exceeding ordinary functions. This aspiration toward ever-greater achievement has certainly wrought some wonderful things in human life. But it also poses great danger to the well-being of both humans and the wider creation—a truth we increasingly recognize and are beginning to respond to.

One of the natural borders we routinely disregard to our detriment is sufficient rest. Rest means stopping our ordinary work. The word *sabbath* essentially means "to cease." We are commanded to

Refraining from work on a regular basis is a way of setting limits on behavior that is perilous for both human welfare and the welfare of the earth itself.
Dorothy Bass

cease our labors one day in seven in order to honor the God who models rest after creative work. God has built a rhythm of rest into the very fabric of creation.

In his evocative book on the theme of sabbath, Wayne Muller puts an experienced finger on the pulse of contemporary culture:

> In the relentless busyness of modern life, we have lost the rhythm between work and rest. . . . Our culture supposes that action and accomplishment are better than rest, that doing something—anything—is better than doing nothing. Because of our desire to succeed, to meet the ever-growing expectations, we do not rest. Because we do not rest, we lose our way.[1]

God created a world full of natural rhythms: the cycles of the seasons and of the moon, the rhythms of day and night, the seasons of migration, and the rhythm of the tides. These boundaries are life-giving, not merely constraining. Jesus understood the necessity of such rhythms for the health of both body and soul:

> Take my yoke upon you, and learn from me;
> for I am gentle and humble in heart,
> and you will find rest for your souls.
>
> Matt. 11:29

The Lord is my shepherd,
  I shall not want.
  He makes me lie down in
    green pastures;
he leads me beside still waters;
  he restores my soul.

Psalm 23:1–2

How often do we even think of rest for the soul? When our bodies get weary from strenuous physical activity, the stress of driving in rush-hour traffic, or hours of sitting before a computer screen, we feel the need for rest. We recognize the experience of mental fatigue when dealing with ambiguities, difficult decisions, or conflicting emotions. But how do we gauge the needs of our souls? Jesus' words suggest that this inner core of our being—our very life force and vitality—also needs rest. Does he perhaps mean heart-rest, inward peace, deep joy? Surely these are the kinds of gifts Jesus offers when he says, "Come to me, all you that are weary and carrying heavy burdens, and I will give you rest" (11:28). Jesus implies that being with him is a form of sabbath. Our life in Christ is a gift of profound rest and refreshment!

The essence of sabbath is rest and renewal for the soul. In good Jewish fashion, this naturally includes our bodies and minds. Yet if rest does not reach the depth of soul it is merely vacation, not sabbath. We need time out with God, not just time off from work. In our "24/7 world" we have become electronically wired for unremitting availability to one another via cell phones, email, texting, and social media. Amid this glut of technological connectivity, we would do well to recall that Jesus was not always available to people when he walked this earth. Much to the consternation of family, disciples, crowds, and religious leaders, he simply disappeared at regular intervals to be sustained and renewed in his relationship with the One whose life he so intimately shared and from whom his power for ministry came. Jesus practiced the spiritual imperative of sabbath. He honored the beauty of the borders. He knew the sacred art of ceasing from active labor.

Sabbath as Fresh Beginning

You have surely noticed that I am speaking of sabbath in broader terms than Sunday, the traditional day associated with sabbath observance for Christians. Sunday is scarcely a day of rest for church leaders and active laity. Those who often work hardest on Sundays need to find other ways to practice the rhythm of rest that sabbath points to. Generally then, the term *sabbath* in this chapter refers to the *qualities* of sabbath time that may be sought or secured on days other than the day formally set apart by tradition.

But before exploring this broader sense of the term, I would like to suggest a deeper spiritual significance in the Christian transposition of the traditional Sabbath day. Whereas the Jewish Sabbath, adhering to the creation story in Genesis, is celebrated on the seventh day, for Christians Sabbath begins the week. Sunday is the first day, chosen to displace the historic day of Sabbath because the Resurrection of Jesus on the first day of the week inaugurates the *new creation* story. Yet what impresses me more is that the qualities of sabbath time also come first in our lives as a spiritual principle. Sabbath is the profoundly joyful refreshment from which new effort arises, the deep well from which we draw strength, the eternal newness at the root of all creativity. Therefore sabbath is a primary experience of grace—the gift that enables our human journey day upon day, week upon week.

In Jewish tradition, this principle is visible not in the weekly but rather the daily cycle. We recall how the creation story describes *day* beginning at sundown: "There was evening and there was morning, the first day. . . . There was evening and there was morning, the

It is no longer possible to prescribe one way to keep the Sabbath holy and wholly.

Don Postema

71

second day...." (see Gen. 1). Imagine starting your day with the evening meal, then getting ready for bed! The first third of your day is spent in sleep, trusting that God is at work through the night without your conscious participation. You then rise and join in God's labors with energy from rest and insight from dreams. Eugene Peterson describes it this way:

> When it is evening, 'I pray the Lord my soul to keep' and drift off into unconsciousness for the next six or eight hours, a state in which I am absolutely nonproductive and have no cash value. The Hebrew evening/morning sequence conditions us to the rhythms of grace. We go to sleep and God begins his work. We wake and are called out to participate in God's creative action. But always grace is previous. Grace is primary. We wake into a world we didn't make, into a salvation we didn't earn.[2]

The early church understood that *otium sanctum* (Latin for holy leisure) lay at the core of human life. Holy leisure was sacred time for the Spirit to convert the mind, sacred space for God in the midst of daily life. Such leisure was seen as essential to the development of our deeper humanity. It is interesting to note, then, that "the Latin word for work was *negotium*, or non-leisure. Work was thus secondary, defined as it related to leisure."[3] Our utilitarian culture has reversed this, defining leisure as non-work.

Having lost all sense of the necessity of holy leisure, we have developed a secular rhythm of life in direct contrast to the ancient sacred pattern. This *secular rhythm* begins with *work* and moves to *vacation*. It starts in a mode driven by achievement and production, moving typically to exhausted collapse or perhaps to the numbing escapes of mindless entertainment. By contrast, the *sacred rhythm* of life begins with *sabbath* and moves to *vocation*. It begins by inviting us to rest in the quiet, replenishing depths of God's presence, promise, and power; then it moves us toward a grateful, energized response. What different rhythms these are!

Ahh! The Sabbath has come. It is a time to let all the cares and tasks of the week—the drivenness of work, worries about the future—slip from our shoulders like a loosely held blanket. A day to follow a different script, to savor the givenness of life, its mystery and joy.
Martha Whitmore Hickman

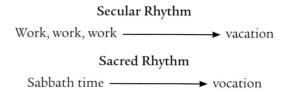

Secular Rhythm

Work, work, work ⟶ vacation

Sacred Rhythm

Sabbath time ⟶ vocation

Rest as Trust in God

Valuing and guarding the sacred rhythm of sabbath is a radical choice, particularly in a culture as devoted as ours to production and achievement. Sadly, it is even radical in most churches, which inevitably absorb and reflect cultural norms because they are made up of ordinary people like us! Most churches in the United States are so caught up with worship, classes, programs, service projects, and the demands of internal maintenance that they rarely encourage or promote real sabbath time, for either pastors or laity.

Yet of all institutions, the church ought to have something different to say about the pace of life and the value of time. It could encourage its members to float more often on the waters of grace, to practice more persistently the sacred art of ceasing. After all, to *rest* in God is implicitly to critique a culture of constant production; to *trust* in God is to undermine a culture obsessed by control; even to *enjoy* God is to play the fool in a culture that often takes itself too seriously. Sabbath values, so emblematic of divine reign, turn our world on its head:

> It is vain that you rise up early
>> and go late to rest,
> eating the bread of anxious toil;
>> for [God] gives sleep to his beloved.
>>>> Ps. 127:2

Take a few minutes to ponder this psalm verse, allowing your mind and heart to absorb its message. What is God's invitation to you in these words? Identify one practical step you could commit to in your daily life as a response. Note it down, and pray for the grace to follow through.

True sabbath has an uncomfortably subversive character for those of us formed in the Protestant work ethic. When that ethic fosters a mind-set of "bringing in God's kingdom" through tireless personal effort, it readily becomes an expression of works-righteousness. The sabbath command is a perfect antidote to works-righteousness.

Renowned Hebrew Bible scholar Walter Brueggemann suggests that the Fourth Commandment is the crux of the whole Decalogue, joining the first three commandments (concerning our relationship with God) to the last six (concerning our relationship with one another). The pivot point, in the sabbath command, is God's own rest. God is so secure about the order and goodness of creation that God can rest![4] And if God can rest, who are we to presume improving on the divine example? We do, of course, try. We imagine that we can get by without a day of deeper rest each week; we think that we do better by doing more; we squeeze in a little more productivity at the beginning

Sabbath requires surrender. . . . If we refuse rest until we are finished, we will never rest until we die. Sabbath dissolves the artificial urgency of our days, because it liberates us from the need to be finished.

>> *Wayne Muller*

and end of each day. Yet when we refuse the rhythm of grace offered to us in sabbath time, we consign ourselves to anxious lives and driven ministries. I admit that I do not care for the language of "drivenness" in recently popular books and seminars: *management-driven, excellence-driven, purpose-driven*. It seems significant that the Bible likens us to sheep, not cattle. In scripture, sheep are not driven but led.

Keeping the sabbath means putting our faith and hope in God above all else. It is a clarion call to live from a posture of profound trust. *Trust* is a small word with a high hurdle. A humorous story is told of a man named George Singer, a civic leader involved in all sorts of good works, who felt himself about to get sick. Fuming against the prospect of lost time, he fell asleep and dreamed that he saw the Lord God Almighty pacing the floor of heaven, wringing his hands and saying, "What shall I do? What shall I do? George Singer is about to get sick!"[5] Might we imagine Singer, upon waking, erupting in hearty laughter at his ludicrous image of an anxious, impotent deity? Honoring sabbath time teaches us to release our treasured illusions of being indispensable, allowing us to "let God be God."

Trust is the heartbeat of sabbath, the bedrock of soul rest. Perhaps because God knows how much we need this rest and how hard it is for us to take, sabbath is a commandment. It is probably the commandment most frequently broken by church leaders, caught up as we are in the ceaseless demands of ministry and haunted by the conviction that we can never do enough to truly satisfy others or God. What, then, is our image of the One we serve? Do we imagine that God is somehow pleased by our exhaustion or that the fewer days off we take and the busier we are, the more faithful servants we must be? And what if we are faithful only when our service is rooted in deep soul-rest? As one poet writes,

> There is time only to work slowly.
> There is no time not to love.[6]

When we neglect sabbath time as a life-sustaining rhythm, we risk great damage to ourselves and our communities as well as to our capacity for intimacy with God. Wayne Muller tells of a doctor who recognized that without sufficient rest, he needed to order more tests for patients because he was too tired to tap into his intuitive diagnostic wisdom. Muller also catalogues the tragic results of aid organizations "in a terrible hurry to do good," too impatient to attend to the actual realities of the situation and thereby

Only in stopping, really stopping, do we teach our hearts and souls that we are loved apart from what we do.
Lynne Baab

The gift of Sabbath is the gift of abundant time.
Lynne Baab

inadvertently causing more suffering.[7] He frequently notes that the most important things in life take time, especially the cultivation of relationships. And what is more central to our spirit than relationships?

Sabbath is not only a gift to nurture our relationship with God and with our deeper selves; it is centrally concerned with all human relationships. What Eugene Peterson calls "the Deuteronomy reason for Sabbath-keeping" is "that our ancestors in Egypt went four hundred years without a vacation (Deut. 5:15). Never a day off. . . . Not persons created in the image of God but equipment for making bricks and building pyramids. Humanity was defaced./ . . . The moment we begin to see others in terms of what they can *do* rather than who they *are*, we mutilate humanity and violate community. . . . Sabbath-keeping is elemental kindness."[8]

Such kindness extends, in God's sabbath command, even to domestic animals. It does not take much imagination to recognize that when we take sufficient time to cease from our obsessive use of the world's resources for our own purposes, time to open our minds and heart to the Creator of all, time to reclaim our sanity and humanity—all creatures on this earth might benefit from our keeping of the sabbath command.

Sabbath is also a celebration of deliverance from oppression . . . All are to rest, not just the rulers, the privileged few.
Martha Whitmore Hickman

Steps Toward Embracing Sabbath Time

If we hope to be faithful to the sabbath command, we will need to identify and shift certain ingrained attitudes and habits. In her fine book, *A Day of Rest*, Martha Whitmore Hickman astutely points out the following truth:

> In our harried, fragmented world, rest has to be a conscious decision . . . implemented by certain changes of mind-set and planning, or we will bring to our periods of supposed rest the same preoccupations and concerns that permeate much of our weekday activity.[9]

Shifting Our Mind-sets

Here are a few possibilities for shifting unhelpful mind-sets:

1. Acknowledge the many ways you are shaped by worldly thinking that makes productivity, achievement, and success the

In her book Keeping the Sabbath Day Wholly, *Marva Dawn expands the idea of ceasing to include ceasing work, ceasing accomplishments, ceasing worry, ceasing possessiveness, ceasing being possessed by our culture, ceasing the mundane.*

Don Postema

primary source and valuation of your identity. Embrace your deeper desire for the humility of Christ. Give yourself permission to carve out regular sabbath time from the massive over-commitment that marks most of modern life. You are aiming for a life of balance, spiritual grounding, and inward peace, emulating the life-giving rhythm Jesus himself embodied.

2. Begin to free yourself from culturally embedded patterns of people pleasing. While it is important to be cooperative, kind, and thoughtful, it is dangerous to need too much to please others. Not only can the views and demands of others be unrealistic; their desires can easily divert us from our inner truth. For example, we sometimes take on responsibilities without regard for our true gifts or God-given calling, simply to please others' hopes or expectations. This generally results in fatigue and resentment. It can also prevent us from fulfilling our deeper calling. If we can please both God and others, well and good; if not, God takes priority. Dick Wills was head pastor of a large church in Florida when he discovered the best source of freedom from people pleasing. He writes: "The more I am aware of God's love for me, the less I live my life trying to please people."[10] Here is another reason for absorbing the profound reality of God's love for you! As you invite the Spirit to help you digest this truth, you will find yourself freed for a higher obedience than that of merely pleasing others.

3. Give yourself the gift of intentional "fallow time" for mind and heart. Remember that healthy soil needs periodic rest from planting to rebuild its nutrients. Years ago a supervisor told me of a study revealing that some of the most creative and influential leaders in several fields found great value in giving their employees at least 10 percent of their work time unstructured—no assignments, meetings, appointments, or particular projects. This allowed workers to pursue deeper passions and give free reign to their imaginations; it created space to step back and see a bigger picture or a fresh angle. Such unstructured time fostered creative inspiration, innovation, and intuitive leaps that could take an idea or organization to a whole new level.[11] We know from experience that our minds are more effective when we get sufficient rest and recreation. Unstructured time is an open-spaced container for deeper reflection and new connections. It offers the same kinds of benefits that fallow time gives to the renewal and enrichment of soil.

Sabbath is a day and a time to cultivate contemplation.

Don Postema

Reshaping Attitudes and Habits

The parallel in spiritual practice is called contemplative time. Contemplative time and space are vessels of vision. Think of Elijah in his self-imposed wilderness solitude hearing "a still small voice" (see 1 Kgs. 19:12 KJV). Imagine Moses, tending sheep in remote countryside, noticing the extraordinary sight of a burning bush (Exod. 3). Isaiah was alone in the temple, tending the high altar, when he received a vision of the Lord enthroned (Isa. 6). Contemplative time offers God the opportunity to break through to us with fresh revelation, insight, and creativity. If we allow that God might be a bit more generous with the gift of unstructured time than the 10 percent enlightened businesses offer their employees, we notice that one-day-in-seven represents 14–15 percent. Is it possible that our spiritual DNA is simply wired for this basic proportion of "time out" from our busy routines to stay rooted in God's life and spirit?

I encourage you, then, to build unstructured time into your weekly calendar: no services, meetings, visits, or projects. Take time to ponder, reflect, and imagine. Pay attention to your deeper passion for life and love in the community of all creation. Listen to the Voice beyond yet also within your own voice; glimpse the uncreated Light generating your own light; feel the deep Heart sustaining your heart. Contemplative time and space are crucial for true vision and transformation.

To help us in the task of reshaping ingrained attitudes and habits, we can also make practical choices such as these:

Take time throughout the day to relax the bodily muscles, to breathe slowly and quietly, knowing that each breath is God's breath of life flowing into us. Gaze out the window at the sky, a green leaf, a bird's flight, raindrops. . . . These moments are little sabbaths, holy spaces, within our temple.
Flora Slosson Wuellner

- Keep one day a week as sacrosanct as possible. Use it for real refreshment, not merely for catching up on chores.

- Use time that is "given" to you (unexpected illness, waiting for an appointment, airport delays) to turn your mind toward God and pay attention to the gift of the moment.

- Gift yourself each year with a retreat of several days. Plan it into your calendar well in advance, giving family, friends, and colleagues ample notice. Go someplace that is genuinely restorative for your soul.

- Join a small group for your spiritual nurture. If you are a church leader, you might consider participating in an ecumenical group of faith leaders or in a group of friends from beyond your ministry setting.

- Salt your days with moments of relaxation and receptivity to grace, allowing the qualities of sabbath rest and delight to irradiate your daily life. A busy day need not be anxious!

- Begin your personal prayer time with simple adoration and praise. Linger in the exquisite gift of holy relationship before moving into prayers of petition and intercession.

Becoming Reservoirs

Because it requires us to create space in our over-extended lives, sabbath is a central practice that makes room for other practices we may yearn to give time to. One or two of the following might serve as vehicles for reflective rest or communal refreshment: prayer, spiritual reading, worship, journaling, hospitality, physical recreation, acts of compassion, or creativity. But please, don't turn sabbath time into a spiritual form of achievement! It shines with the qualities of freedom and leisure. Sabbath is God's gift of time, freely returned to God for divine purposes. It lies at the core of both faith and fidelity. Nothing else nurtures the human soul with such depth; nothing carries us so simply to the heart of God; nothing so adequately waters our spiritual thirst or empowers us to live faithfully in this world as this one command: keep a sabbath; keep it as sacred and holy time. For Christians, this is the central way we come to Jesus and find in him rest for our souls.

The great twelfth-century Cistercian Abbott, Bernard of Clairvaux, once wrote these words of counsel:

> If you are wise therefore you will show yourself a reservoir and not a canal. For a canal pours out as fast as it takes in; but a reservoir waits till it is full before it overflows, and so communicates its surplus. . . . We have all too few such reservoirs in the Church at present, though we have canals in plenty. . . . [T]hey [canals] desire to pour out when they themselves are not yet inpoured; they are readier to speak than to listen, eager to teach that which they do not know, and most anxious to exercise authority on others, although they have not learnt to rule themselves. . . . Let the reservoir of which we spoke just now take pattern from the spring; for the spring does not form a stream or spread into a lake until it is brimful. . . . Be filled thyself, then, but discreetly, mind, pour out thy fullness. . . . Out of thy fullness help me if thou canst; and, if not, spare thyself.[12]

The sabbath . . . convinces us of the goodness of God. The more we practice it, the greater privilege it becomes, the more essential it feels, the deeper it connects us to the river of life that provides fruit in all seasons.

Lynne Baab

In the sacred art of ceasing, sabbath time enables us to become such reservoirs. May God grant it!

Notes to the Text

1. Wayne Muller, *Sabbath: Restoring the Sacred Rhythm of Rest* (New York: Bantam Books, 1999), 1.

2. Abridged from "Rhythms of Grace," *Weavings* 8, no. 2 (March–April 1993): 16.

3. Tim Hansel, *When I Relax I Feel Guilty* (Colorado Springs: David C. Cook Publishing Co., 1979), 30.

4. Walter Brueggemann, *Journal for Preachers* 10, no. 2 (Lent 1987): 19.

5. A paraphrased version of the story recounted in Martha Whitmore Hickman's book, *A Day of Rest: Creating Spiritual Space in Your Week* (New York: Avon Books, 1999), 71.

6. From a Deena Metzger poem. See www.goodreads.com/author/quotes/135522.Deena-Metzger.

7. Muller, *Sabbath: Restoring the Sacred Rhythm of Rest*. For the story of the doctor, see pages 5–6; for illustrations of impatient service, see the chapter "Doing Good Badly" (157–62).

8. See "Rhythms of Grace," *Weavings*, 17–18.

9. Martha Whitmore Hickman, *A Day of Rest: Creating a Spiritual Space in Your Week* (New York: Avon Books, 1999), 69.

10. Dick Wills, *Waking to God's Dream* (Nashville: Abingdon Press, 1999), 66.

11. See Deb Gallagher, "Why Giving Employees Paid, Unstructured Time Pays Off," MIT Sloan Management Review (blog), June 13, 2011, http://sloanreview.mit.edu/article/why-giving-employees-paid-unstructured-time-pays-off/.

12. Extract from *Great Devotional Classics: Selections from the Writings of Bernard of Clairvaux*, ed. Douglas Steere (Nashville: The Upper Room, 1961), 24–25.

Notes to the Sidebars

Dorothy Bass, director of the Valparaiso Project on the Education and Formation of People in Faith, "Keeping Sabbath" in *Practicing Our Faith*, ed. by Dorothy Bass (San Francisco: Jossey-Bass, 1997), 88.

Don Postema, pastor of the Christian Reformed Church with a ministry of spiritual formation. From *Catch Your Breath: God's Invitation to Sabbath Rest* (Grand Rapids, MI: CRC Publications, 1997), 25.

Martha Whitmore Hickman, author of books for children and adults. From *A Day of Rest: Creating a Spiritual Space in Your Week* (New York: Avon Books, 1999), 48.

Wayne Muller, leadership mentor, therapist, minister, community advocate, and author. From *Sabbath: Restoring the Sacred Rhythm of Rest* (New York: Bantam Books, 1999), 82–83.

Lynne M. Baab, Presbyterian minister and author. From *Sabbath Keeping: Finding Freedom in the Rhythms of Rest* (Downer's Grove, IL: Intervarsity Press, 2005), 17–18.

Lynne Baab, *Sabbath Keeping*, 13.

Martha Whitmore Hickman, *A Day of Rest*, 50.

Don Postema, *Catch Your Breath*, 33.

Don Postema, Ibid., 55.

Flora Slosson Wuellner, retired UCC pastor and author. From *Beyond Death: What Jesus Revealed about Eternal Life* (Nashville: Upper Room Books, 2014), 102.

Lynne Baab, *Sabbath Keeping*, 17.

CHAPTER 6

The Practice of Self-Emptying

Rediscovering the Fast

[God] humbled you by letting you hunger, then by feeding you with manna, with which neither you nor your ancestors were acquainted, in order to make you understand that one does not live by bread alone, but by every word that comes from the mouth of the Lord.

Deuteronomy 8:3

Fasting may seem a peculiar discipline to commend to contemporary Christians. It is vaguely repellent to our modern sensibilities. If images of ascetic abuse linger in our historical memory, we may have shoved fasting into that mental closet with hair shirts, chastity belts, and self-flagellation whips. Why, we wonder, should we turn back to a pinched, life-denying spirituality that glories in restricting the body? Why not glorify God by enjoying the blessings of creation?

Some of us, no doubt, would be relieved to see the long-revered tradition of fasting fade into oblivion. Yet fasting has been a significant spiritual practice in virtually every religion, and there is good reason to take a fresh look at its purpose and power. The practical rationales for fasting that our culture still accepts, such as health benefits or political clout, do not express the deeper spiritual significance of a fast. I believe we need to recover the spiritual purpose of fasting precisely because of the character of contemporary culture.

What are your general reactions to the idea of fasting? Identify your feelings and reservations before you read this chapter. Then comment again when you've finished the chapter.

In ancient Jewish tradition, fasting had two primary purposes. The first was to express personal or national repentance for sin; fasting was a form of humble supplication before God in the face of imminent destruction or calamity (see Joel 2; Jonah 3; Esth. 4). The second purpose of a fast was to prepare inwardly for receiving the necessary strength and grace to complete a mission of faithful service in God's name. Primary examples are the forty-day wilderness fasts of Moses, Elijah, and Jesus (Exod. 24; 34; 1 Kgs. 19; Matt. 4). The fast prepares each one to become a personal bearer of God's saving acts to the people.

Jesus combined prayer and fasting to overcome his temptations in the desert. The early church followed this practice at critical points in its life to discern how God was leading them and to empower their ministry (Acts 13; 14). Some ancient manuscripts indicate that Jesus' cure of an epileptic boy (Mark 9:14–29) was possible only "by prayer and fasting." These examples suggest that the combination of prayer and fasting invites a greater measure of God's power to be released through us than might be possible through prayer alone.

In Jesus' time, regular fasting was a normal part of Jewish piety (Luke 18:12; Matt. 6:16). Its practice was viewed as normal in the life of Christians until quite recently, and it is still seriously practiced in Eastern Orthodox and Roman Catholic churches. Protestants, however, largely seem to have forgotten that their greatest leaders—figures such as Luther, Calvin, Wesley, and Edwards—were strong advocates of this discipline. Wesley prescribed regular fasting on Wednesdays and Fridays. Calvin commended it to (1) subdue the needless desires of "the flesh"; (2) prepare for prayer and meditation; and (3) express humility before God in confession.[1]

Take a few minutes to stop and reflect: How do you think prayer and fasting might be connected?

While Christian history reveals that at times fasting has been taken to unhealthy extremes, very sane perspectives also emerge from within the tradition:

> Abba Joseph asked Abba Poemen, "How should one fast?" Abba Poemen said to him, "For my part, I think it better that one should eat every day, but only a little, so as not to be satisfied."[2]

An "ascetical fast" of this kind serves to remind us of our dependence on God. Even with my limited experience of fasting, I am convinced that "rather than weakening us [it] makes us light, concentrated, sober, joyful, pure. One receives food as a real gift of God. One is constantly directed at that inner world which inexplicably becomes a kind of food in its own right."[3]

Some of our suspicions about fasting may simply be a rationale to cover deeper anxieties. In a land where food is so abundant that we can both glorify and trivialize it, we have developed a horror of being without it. Advertisements bombard us with images of food. The underlying message seems to be, "Eat! Food is good and good for you. You should never be hungry. But if you are, the remedy is no farther than your friendly pizza delivery service!" Like the noise we have become accustomed to or the frenetic busyness of our schedules, food is taken for granted as a constant in our lives. The very idea of intentionally being without it for even a day may threaten some of the unconscious assumptions on which our lives are built.

This is precisely why fasting remains so relevant for people of faith today. In a more tangible, visceral way than any other spiritual discipline, fasting reveals our excessive attachments and the assumptions that lie behind them. Food is necessary to life, but we have made it more necessary than God. How often have we neglected to remember God's presence when we would never consider neglecting to eat! Fasting brings us face to face with how we put the material world ahead of its spiritual Source.

Jesus tells us that his "bread" is to do the will of the One who sent him (John 4:31–34). He calls himself "the bread of life" (John 6:35). Are we aware of how much sustains our life apart from physical food? Do we have an inner conviction that *Christ* is our life? We will comprehend little of how we are nourished by Christ until we have emptied ourselves of the kinds of sustenance that keep us content to live at life's surface.

Persons well used to fasting as a systematic practice will have a clear and constant sense of their resources in God.

Dallas Willard

A Look at Lent

One of the best ways to explore the meaning and practice of fasting is to examine how Lent has been understood in the church. Lent is the traditional season of prayer and fasting in preparation for the great "Feast of feasts," Easter. Right away we can see that the church year has been characterized by *rhythms* of feasting and fasting. What real significance can Easter have if we do not know the experience of Lent? The joy and delight of a feast is proportional to the deprivation of a fast. Have we lost the art of true feasting through rejection of the fast?

Lent is the great fast of the church year. It is a season that reveals and magnifies our understanding of spiritual discipline. When I was growing up, Protestants knew little of liturgical seasons; their impressions of Lent came mainly from Roman Catholic friends. The impressions consisted largely of restriction, regulation, and penitence. As Protestants began to recover church seasons, many took on the tradition of "giving things up" for Lent—dessert, chocolate, popcorn, chewing gum, or other food frivolities. What we have participated in and witnessed is the trivialization of a very profound discipline.

We trivialize spiritual disciplines when we lose sight of their real purpose. Lent is not a six-week inconvenience in an otherwise abundant year, during which we somehow please God with voluntary if minor suffering. Lent is not a testing ground for the true grit of our willpower. It is certainly not a "spiritual" rationale for losing ten pounds before venturing to the beach in a bathing suit. Do you see how easy it is to twist a practice such as fasting into a means to accomplish our own ends? The question we need to ask with any spiritual discipline is, What does God want to accomplish in me through this practice?

For the early church, Lent was just the opposite of a dreary season of restriction and self-torture. It was understood as an opportunity to return to normal human life—the life of natural communion with God that was lost to us in the Fall. This perspective is clearly expressed in Eastern Orthodox liturgy and theology:

> In the Orthodox teaching . . . the world was given to [Adam and Eve] by God as "food"—as means of life. . . . In food itself God . . . was the principle of life. Thus to eat, to be alive, to know God and be in communion with Him were one and the same thing. The unfathomable tragedy of Adam is that . . . he ate "apart" from God in order to be independent of Him . . . because he believed that food had life in itself and that he, by partaking of that food, could be like God, i.e., have life in himself.[4]

In Eden, God gave Adam and Eve every fruit of the garden but one. That one fruit, out of a world of variety, indicated a limit to human freedom. Accepting that limit was the single abstinence required by God. It was a way of recognizing that human beings are dependent on God for life. But Adam and Eve allowed themselves to be seduced by the serpent (a figure of God's enemy, Satan). The serpent's question inverts the reality of the situation: "Did God say, 'You shall not eat of *any* tree of the garden'?" (Gen. 3:1, emphasis added). Instead of a prohibition against one fruit, God's warning is presented as a prohibition against all fruit. The temptation, it seems, is to see a single boundary as so restrictive that it negates the good of all other freedoms. Adam and Eve took the bait. Metaphorically, they "broke the fast," transgressing the one limit required of them. In refusing to accept the natural bounds of their creaturehood, they reached for the very place of God. They wanted it all.[5]

The fallen human now lives as if there are no legitimate limits. While we bow temporarily to practical limitations, limits are to be assaulted through the powers of intelligence and technology until they yield to human ingenuity and control. The appetites are given free rein. It is considered a God-given right to use every resource and creature on earth for personal enjoyment or gain. The goal of human life is to acquire more, to experience more, to stimulate every sense to capacity and beyond.

A life that recognizes no limits cannot recognize the sovereignty of God. When created things have become an end in themselves instead of a means of divine grace, they can no longer offer real life. Death and suffering entered into creation because our human forbears could not "keep the fast."

Did you know that *Lent* is derived from a Saxon word meaning "spring"? In the early church, Lent was viewed as a spiritual spring, a time of light and joy in the renewal of the soul's life. It represented a return to the "fast" that Adam and Eve broke: a life in which God was once more center and source and the material world was again received as a means of communion with God. This return to authentic human life was made possible by the Incarnation.

The early church found the reversal of Adam's sin in Christ. After his Baptism, Jesus began the work of redemption by keeping a forty-day fast in the wilderness. When he became hungry, he refused the lie that life depends on bread alone and reaffirmed that human beings depend in all things on God for life. He said no to the limitless, self-referential power Satan tempted him with. Every temptation—to self-sufficiency, to self-display, to power at the price of integrity—would have placed Jesus at center stage instead of God. Throughout his life Jesus consistently pointed to *God's* authority, power, and will in him. Jesus "kept the fast," abstaining not only from food but also from the illegitimate exercise of power. He accepted his limits, living within the normal constraints of human life and accepting a human death. Jesus lived out God's deepest intention for human beings in the created order. Through him, we too begin to live as a "new creation." The possibility of genuine communion with God in and through creation is restored.

Perhaps we can see, then, that the discipline of fasting—as with keeping Sabbath—has to do with the critical dynamic of *accepting those limits that are life-restoring.* Our culture would seduce us into

Fasting is not a renunciation of life; it is a means by which new life is released within us.

James Earl Massey

believing that we can have it all, do it all, and (even more preposterous!) that we deserve it all. Yet in refusing to accept limits on our consumption or activity, we perpetuate a death-dealing dynamic in the world. That is why the discipline of fasting is so profoundly important today.

Food Fasting

Abstaining from food is the original meaning and most basic expression of a fast. It is the core reality from which analogous forms of abstinence derive. If we are to recapture the practice of such fasting as a spiritual discipline, we need to know how to go about it. Ignorance of basic rules can be dangerous, but if we follow a few simple guidelines there is little danger and much to be gained.

Russian Orthodox theologian Alexander Schmemann reminds us that first we must prepare spiritually before fasting.[6] Depending on the shifting sands of personal willpower results only in frustration and harm. A fast for spiritual purposes must be centered on God and can be so only if we ask God's help. We need to recover both a reverence for our bodies as temples of the Holy Spirit and a genuine respect for food as God's gift. Such inner preparation will give us a vision of the spiritual dimension of fasting and arm us with the weapons we will need when temptations and difficulties arise.

Richard Foster distinguishes between a normal fast, a partial fast, and an absolute fast. The normal fast "involves abstaining from all food, solid or liquid, but not from water." A partial fast involves "a restriction of the diet but not total abstention." And an absolute fast means "abstaining from both food and water."[7] The first rule of fasting is not to practice it if sick, traveling, or under unusual stress. If you suffer from any debilitating physical condition or illness, consider a fast only under the strict supervision of a physician. Because a fast depletes your normal energy reserves, it is important to reduce your normal activity while fasting.

Beyond these considerations, if you are a beginner or have not fasted in a long time, start with a partial fast of not more than twenty-four hours, not more than once a week. Restricting your intake to fresh fruit juices is a good way to engage in a partial fast. For many, it is helpful to begin after the evening meal, fasting until the next day's evening meal, so that only two meals are missed. Some prefer to fast from lunch to lunch, on the same principle.

Give your body several weeks to adjust to regular fasting before you introduce any further stages. After four or five weeks, you will be ready to try a normal fast for the same twenty-four-hour period. Drink only water, but *plenty* of it.

After several months of adjusting to a normal fast, you could choose to move on to a thirty-six-hour fast: all three meals in a given day. It is a common mistake to try to "tank up" on extra calories before a fast, and an equally common error to eat a big meal after one. A fast should be broken gently with a light, non-fatty meal, generally of fruits and vegetables. Longer fasts need to be broken even more gradually. Foster offers specific guidelines on the dynamics of a longer fast but urges that beyond the thirty-six-hour variety, it is best to discern through prayer whether you are called to a fast of several days or more.

There is no reason to push yourself to heroic effort where fasting is concerned. If you feel tempted to do so, take a hard look at your motives. Has fasting become a source of pride in personal achievement? Are you competing with yourself to win a record? Are you trying to score points with God? "More" is not necessarily "better" in this matter. Perhaps you are called just to be faithful to the humble practice of a partial fast once a week. Do not underestimate what God can accomplish in you through the consistent offering of such a discipline.

Other Forms of Fasting

In a culture obsessed with consumption, I believe fasting needs to be considered in terms of its inner dynamic: *abstinence*. The concept of abstinence applies to more than alcohol and sex. It needs to be considered in relation to the whole of our affluent and addictive lifestyle. Our society voraciously consumes just about anything and everything: food, drink, sex, drugs, guns, cars, clothing, energy, gadgets, TV, radio, social media, online activity, gossip, fads, ideologies, programs, even work and leisure. Our intimate relationships have often suffered from this gluttonous consumer mentality: enjoy while useful and stimulating, discard when broken or no longer satisfying. The world of God's gifts has indeed become a world of mere objects to satisfy temporary and restless appetites, leaving in their wake enormous waste.

The point of abstinence is not the denial of all enjoyment in life; as professor and author Dallas Willard rightly points out,

St. Augustine once said that God is always trying to give good things to us, but our hands are too full to receive them. If our hands are full, they are full of the things to which we are addicted. And not only our hands, but also our hearts, minds, and attention are clogged with addiction. Our addictions fill up the spaces within us, spaces where grace might flow. . . . [T]he spiritual significance of addiction is not just that we lose freedom through attachment to things, . . . [but] that we try to fulfill our longing for God through objects of attachment.

Gerald May

"We dishonor God as much by fearing and avoiding pleasure as we do by dependence upon it or living for it."[8] The purpose of abstinence is to learn *rightly* to enjoy God's gifts. We need disciplines of abstinence because we have come to relate to food, drink, sex, money, recognition, and many other things in life not as lovely gifts to be enjoyed in moderation and gratitude but as objects of consumption to fill emotional voids. When what we consume is consuming us and what we possess is possessing us, the only way back to health and balance is to refrain from using those things that have control over us. "To give up anything that comes between ourselves and God"[9] is the core dynamic of self-denial.

What forms might this kind of "fasting" take in our lives? One possibility is to abstain from constant media stimulation. Choosing natural sounds or silence over incessant television and radio would be a pertinent form of fasting for many. For others, it might mean choosing to check personal email or social media sites only at chosen intervals, to resist the peer-pressured expectation of constant updating. What about abstaining from eating overpackaged and overprocessed foods or from throwing away all packaging in our disposable culture? The recycling movement is making only a dent in our mountains of landfill. If your mailbox is like mine, it frequently groans under the weight of mail-order catalogs, even in a world of online shopping. Millions of people wade daily through a glut of slick advertising, whether it comes to their doorstep or beckons from electronic screens. Many of us need to rest our credit cards and reclaim precious time by fasting from needless shopping sprees.

We might consider abstaining not only from lack of all physical exercise but also from fitness mania; not only from compulsive eating but also from compulsive dieting.[10] We have a tendency to fall off the path of moderation into extremes. We like to impress ourselves and others with "the big splash." It is a more difficult discipline to slowly change your eating habits and lose two pounds a week than to lose fifteen pounds quickly and swing back to former eating patterns. Part of fasting in this case is to relinquish the temporary excitement that comes with spectacular achievement. A counterweight to the desire for congratulation is abstaining from personal recognition. We can scarcely make a big splash if we practice anonymity in our charity or engage in our vocation without seeking to be honored.

What would it mean to fast from judging others or even from judging ourselves too harshly? Most of us are quick to prejudge people we barely know on the basis of external appearance, mannerisms, or a few statements taken out of context. Worse yet, we judge people on hearsay. Spiritually speaking, this is a dangerous habit. Often we are ashamed of our prejudgments (prejudices) when we actually get to know the person in question. To abstain from judging others in the secret places of our heart is a challenging discipline to learn and sustain.

Perhaps one of the most difficult forms of abstaining today is from overpacked schedules, for both ourselves and our children. When we become exhausted, depressed, and short-tempered, when we have little energy left for our friends or families, much less for ourselves, do we give more glory to God? Here, again, we clearly see our desperate need for reclaiming sabbath time. Indeed, honoring the boundaries of sabbath time may strengthen our spiritual muscles for other expressions of abstinence.

With so many ways to practice fasting through abstinence, we will need to make choices appropriate to our character and life circumstances. Behind every fitting choice of abstinence lies the question, What do I do to excess? What I do to excess reveals my inordinate desires, my compulsions, the attachments that have control over me. They are precisely the areas of my life that need the freeing lordship of Christ rather than my own abysmally ineffective efforts at control. Fasting is not primarily a discipline through which I gain greater control over my life but one through which *God* gains access to redirect and heal me in body, mind, and spirit.

Do you tend to say yes to too many things? Take some time to examine your motives for doing so. Is there something you are trying to prove? Someone you are trying to save or to impress? Is it God's will or yours you are following?

Review the various forms of fasting suggested in this section. Each one is a way of allowing the Spirit to bring your life under control. Select one in which you need to establish boundaries. Try it for a day. Then commit to a full week. Assess your experience in writing, or talk it through with a faithful friend.

Invitations to Explore

Keeping a Journal during a Fast

If the purpose of your fast is spiritual, your inner attitudes will be of greater significance than your physical reactions. Keeping a journal can help you focus on the spiritual dimensions of a fast. Answering some questions may help your journal-keeping process: How do I respond to hunger pangs? What feelings attend the experience of physical emptiness—panic, irritation, boredom, helplessness? How do I express these? Do I sense any inward cleansing, release, or freedom? Do I feel a need to draw the attention of others to what I am doing? Do I find myself attentive to God's presence in new ways? connected to others in new ways? What is God revealing to me through my responses?

The following excerpts are taken from the journal of a person who, as a spiritual discipline, committed himself to fast once a week for two years. It reveals the kind of growth that can occur through an extended practice of fasting for the sake of God. It is also a good example of the way a journal can be used to help record the movements of the mind and heart.

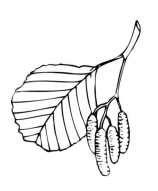

I felt it a great accomplishment to go a whole day without food. Congratulated myself on the fact that I found it so easy. Also, enjoyed the fact that I lost weight . . .

Began to see that the above was hardly the goal of fasting. Was helped in this by beginning to feel hunger . . .

Began to relate the food fast to other areas of my life where I was more compulsive. . . . to move out of the grip of necessity . . . I did not have to have a seat on the bus to be contented, or to be cool in the summer and warm when it was cold.

Continued to feel less at the mercy of my own desires—more detached. . . . Reflected more on Christ's suffering and the suffering of those who are hungry and have hungry babies . . .

Six months after beginning the fast discipline, I began to see why a two-year period had been suggested. The experience changes along the way. Hunger on fast days became acute, and the temptation to eat stronger. For the first time I was using the day to find God's will for my life. Began to think about what it meant to surrender one's life.

I now know that prayer and fasting must be intricately bound together. There is no other way, and yet that way is not yet combined in me.[11]

Recovering the Fast of Repentance

I have said little thus far concerning the role of fasting as an expression of repentance. Since fasting and repentance are so clearly joined in the Bible, recovering this dimension of a fast seems appropriate and important. John Calvin followed the biblical tradition of interpreting major disasters as divine messages. He urged that when war, famine, plague, or other natural calamities threaten a nation, "the whole people ought to accuse themselves and confess their guilt." He felt that regional threats obligated local pastors "to urge the church to fasting, in order that by supplication the Lord's wrath may be averted."[12] While Calvin's language may seem quaint, the impulse behind it may strike us as rather pertinent.

If ever there was a time when repentance was called for on a national and international scale, it is now. Personal and social sin abounds everywhere we look. World powers stand by while despots wreak havoc on their own populations. Ancient hatreds continue to fuel wars all over the globe. Racial and ethnic tensions threaten the cohesion of our communities. Levels of violence and addiction exceed all bounds. Family structures crumble, and children become both victims and perpetrators of abuse in their homes and schools. Our way of life places intolerable burdens on the resources of the earth, fouling the very elements we depend on for life.

Even a fraction of this woeful catalog should be enough to put us on our knees! Would not a time of corporate mourning and repentance be in order? Surely our religious leaders could gather and appoint a time of fasting and prayer for all believers. Yet if our leaders will not be so bold, we can take up the invitation to make sincere repentance a key in our personal fasting, and we can intercede on behalf of those who apparently see no need for a change of heart.

Springtime for the Soul

Perhaps we can now see how abstaining from food is connected to other forms of abstinence. Regular fasting at its most basic level may well be the most effective way to deal with all the appetites and compulsions that rule us. Why else would fasting be so heartily recommended by so many saints over so many years? Combined with prayer, it is a potent means of making ourselves available to the cleansing, restoring, empowering grace of God.

Abstinence, of course, is not the sum total of the Christian life. It simply creates enough space in us so that the Spirit can creatively use our talents and energies in the service of God's reign: "A proper abstinence actually breaks the hold of improper engagements so that the soul can be properly engaged by God."[13] Disciplines of *engagement* balance our practice of abstinence.

Fasting teaches temperance or self-control and therefore teaches moderation and restraint with regard to all our fundamental drives.
Dallas Willard

91

Most of the practices considered in this book are disciplines that call us to actively invite God's presence and engage God's purpose in deeper ways: worship, spiritual reading, prayer, self-examination, guidance, and hospitality. Yet coloring and enlivening their practice are aspects of abstinence: silence, solitude, secrecy, and sacrifice. The abstinence of fasting is integrally connected to the engagements of prayer and active service. Indeed, fasting from physical food can scarcely be experienced as spiritual until it is joined to the sense of feasting on God's gracious love and responding by loving others. Fasting prepares us for authentic service. Author Macrina Wiederkehr expresses this connection beautifully:

> Fasting is cleansing. It cleans out our bodies. It lays bare our souls. It leads us into the arms of that One for whom we hunger. In the Divine Arms we become less demanding and more like the One who holds us. Then we experience new hungers. We hunger and thirst for justice, for goodness and holiness. We hunger for what is right. We hunger to be saints.
>
> Most of us are not nearly hungry enough for the things that really matter. That's why it is so good for us to feel a gnawing in our guts. Then we remember why we are fasting. We remember all the peoples of the world who have no choice but to go to bed hungry. We remember how we waste and squander the goods of this world. We remember what poor stewards of the earth we have been. We remember that each of us is called to be bread for the world. Our lives are meant to nourish. Fasting can lead us to the core of our being and make us more nourishing for others.[14]

All forms of spiritual discipline help us to make more space for God in our lives. Fasting and prayer, the traditional disciplines of Lent, seem to be two of the most effective tools in clearing away our self-preoccupation so we can be more responsive to God's life in and through and around us. Perhaps we can think of it this way: fasting is a form of interior "spring cleaning." It involves real labor, but how satisfying and freeing it is to get rid of all that unnecessary stuff!

There is, finally, a light and joyful quality to the practice of fasting. Release, clarity, and freedom shine through the sometimes painful and often tedious process of stripping away what is false in us. Spiritually, the result is restoration to what the Orthodox call "the natural life," which is nothing other than the Christ life: "it is no longer I who live, but it is Christ who lives in me" (Gal. 2:20). May we come to discover more fully in our own experience this spring-time of the soul.

Notes to the Text

1. John Calvin, *Institutes of the Christian Religion*, ed. John T. McNeill, trans. Ford Lewis Battles (Philadelphia: Westminster Press, 1960), bk. 4, ch. 12, para. 15, p. 1242.

2. Benedicta Ward, ed., *The Sayings of the Desert Fathers* (Kalamazoo, MI: Cistercian Publications, 1975), 144.

3. Alexander Schmemann, *Great Lent* (Crestwood, NY: St. Vladimir's Seminary Press, 1974), 98.

4. Ibid., 94–95.

5. In this interpretation, I am indebted to insights from Alexander Schmemann's *For the Life of the World* (Crestwood, NY: St. Vladimir's Seminary Press, 1973) and to one of his foremost Protestant interpreters, Dr. V. Bruce Rigdon.

6. Schmemann, *Great Lent*, 97.

7. See Richard J. Foster's chapter on fasting in *Celebration of Discipline* (San Francisco: Harper & Row, 1988), 49.

8. Dallas Willard, *The Spirit of the Disciplines* (San Francisco: Harper & Row, 1988), 180.

9. W. R. Inge, *Goodness and Truth* (London: Mowbray, 1958), 76–77.

10. Eating disorders such as anorexia and bulimia are true physiological addictions and cannot simply be turned off at will. They require either professional help or a communal therapeutic structure such as a twelve-step program. The language of fasting can be used both to cover and to reinforce eating compulsions.

11. From Elizabeth O'Connor, *Search for Silence* (Waco, TX: Word Books, 1971), 103–4. Used by permission of author.

12. Calvin, *Institutes* bk. 4, ch. 12, para. 15–17, pp. 1242–43.

13. Willard, *The Spirit of the Disciplines*, 176.

14. Macrina Wiederkehr, *A Tree Full of Angels: Seeing the Holy in the Ordinary* (San Francisco: HarperSanFrancisco, 1991), 37.

Notes to the Sidebars

Dallas Willard, philosopher, professor, and author in Christian formation, 1935–2013. *The Spirit of the Disciplines: Understanding How God Changes Lives* (San Francisco: HarperSanFrancisco, 1988), 167.

James Earl Massey, dean emeritus of Anderson School of Theology, Indiana. *Spiritual Disciplines* (Grand Rapids, MI: Francis Asbury Press, 1985), 66.

Gerald May, psychiatrist, theologian, and senior fellow of Shalem Institute, Bethesda, Maryland, 1940–2005. *Addiction and Grace* (San Francisco: Harper & Row, 1988), 17, 92.

Dallas Willard, *The Spirit of the Disciplines*, 167.

CHAPTER 7

Of Conscience *and* Consciousness

Self-Examination, Confession, and Awareness

Search me, O God, and know my heart;
test me and know my thoughts.
See if there is any wicked way in me,
and lead me in the way everlasting.
Psalm 139:23–24

Psalm 139 is a beautiful expression of a profound truth: God is the searcher of every human heart, the One from whom no secrets are hidden. God examines and knows every aspect of our being in more intimate detail than we ourselves can see. This may inspire more than a few beads of sweat, or it may give us great comfort. Who is to say whether the verses that follow express an assurance of complete security in God's presence or the near panic of finding no escape from an omnipresent deity?

You hem me in, behind and before,
   and lay your hand upon me. . . .
Where can I go from your spirit?
   Or where can I flee from your presence?
           (Ps. 139:5, 7)

While the truth that we cannot escape God's all-seeing eye may weigh us down at times, it is finally the only remedy for our uneasiness. If we wish to hide from the penetrating gaze of holy love, it is because we know it falls on what is unholy and unloving within us. Only under God's steady gaze of love are we able to find the healing and restoration we so desperately need. When we feel "searched and known" by a gracious God, we are both moved and enabled to

Examination of the world without is never as personally painful as examination of the world within. . . . Yet when one is dedicated to the truth this pain seems relatively unimportant.
        M. Scott Peck

search our own hearts honestly. That is why scripture and Christian teaching urge us to examine ourselves and to confess what we find before God and others. Self-examination and confession do not call us to self-hatred or self-condemnation; they open the doors of our heart to cleansing, renewal, and peace.

Points of Departure

We need to know two basic truths if we wish to engage in self-examination as a healthy spiritual discipline. If we do not know these truths in an experiential way, self-examination will be either a superficial exercise or an invitation to despair.

The first truth is the most basic affirmation of our faith: *God loves us*. This is not a general rule to which you, personally, may be an exception. It is not a conditional rule that applies only when you are good, pure, and lovable. God's passionate and personal love for each and every human being expresses who God is. Unfailing love is the divine nature and the divine choice in relation to us. God loves us with an overwhelming love that none of our sins can erase. While we can grieve and disappoint this love, nothing we do or fail to do can alter its depth or reality. It is a gift, a given. We cannot control whether God loves us by efforts to gain this love or even to lose it. Since we neither deserve nor earn such love, God's fondest dream is that we will *receive* and *respond* to it.

The second truth is our human weakness and brokenness in relation to God. We are creatures damaged by the disorientation of sin. Sin means being "off target," like an arrow wrongly directed. Instead of being aimed toward God, we are aimed toward a distorted image of self. We are directed by self-centered desires, chained to unmet needs, compelled by illusions about who we are and what makes us acceptable or important. We strive to be in control of our lives. In the process, we manipulate those who seem to get in the way as well as those who appear to be stepping stones to our goals. Our state of misdirection makes us blind. Even if we think we believe in God, we try, in effect, to stand in God's place. As long as we are turned in on ourselves, we deny our essential dependence on God. We do not see how compulsively we try to manufacture our own security and meaning in life.

An important turning point in our spiritual life comes when we acknowledge both truths and admit that we can neither earn God's love nor achieve our own security and perfection. We cannot "fix"

Spend some time pondering these two basic truths. Do you find them easy or hard to accept? Why? If you find one easy to believe and the other hard, take a closer look at where your feelings are coming from.

ourselves or anyone else the way we want to. When we realize that grace lies at the center of life, we start to see in a new way. Turning to face God instead of self is the beginning of Good News, the beginning of personal and relational transformation. Scripture calls this turning "repentance." Facing toward God's tenaciously faithful love frees us to start being real. In the light of God's grace and mercy, we find the courage to look honestly at who we are. Bathed in God's love, we can see clearly and nondefensively all the destructive patterns of our false self: the facades we have hidden behind; the excuses we have relied on to avoid taking responsibility; our habits of deception and control; our failure to love God, others, or ourselves.

The epistle of James instructs the early Christian community, "confess your sins to one another, and pray for one another, so that you may be healed" (5:16). Confession unlocks a process of spiritual healing, opening us to forgiveness, cleansing, reconciliation, and renewal. But we cannot confess our sins unless we know what they are. This is where the art of self-examination comes into play.

Two basic forms of self-examination are described in this chapter. The first, "examination of conscience," is an explicitly penitential practice that helps us name and acknowledge our weaknesses. The second, "examination of consciousness," sharpens our awareness of both positive and negative aspects of our attitudes and behaviors. While related, each practice suggests a somewhat different focus and approach. Both can be daily disciplines, although examination of consciousness is probably easier to practice daily whereas examination of conscience is often recommended as a weekly preparation for common worship.

I want to be perfectly clear that self-examination is not an invitation to psychoanalysis, problem solving, self-lecturing, or ego-absorption. The whole point of self-examination is to become more *God-centered* by observing the moments when we are or are not so.

Examination of Conscience

An examination of conscience is a time when "a soul comes under the gaze of God and . . . is pierced to the quick and becomes conscious of the things that must be forgiven and put right before it can continue to love One whose care has been so constant."[1] In the history of the church, this form of self-examination has been considered an especially significant way to prepare for receiving the sacrament of Communion.

For those who are new to examination of conscience, it is helpful to begin with a "life review." This is an opportunity to look back through your life with a clear and impartial eye. The idea is to observe yourself as if from outside, objectively noting character traits, habits, attitudes, and tendencies across the years. Every effort should be made to put on neither the rose-colored glasses of naive optimism nor the gray-colored glasses of needless pessimism. There is no need to justify, explain, blame, judge, or excuse. You are simply observing yourself with as much detachment as you are capable of by God's grace. Of course you will not achieve perfect impartiality. This is just a beginning in honest self-assessment.

A process of this sort has been commended through many centuries of Christian practice. Not accidentally, it corresponds to the fourth step of the popular Twelve Step recovery programs. Twelve Step groups are among the few communities today that take seriously the need for rigorous and specific confession to God and to one another. They perceive real confession to be the ground for authentic reconciliation and transformed living patterns. While this understanding is rooted in biblical faith, many of our churches have abandoned serious confession, imagining that it reflects or reinforces a lack of self-esteem. Certainly people with low self-esteem can use confession to express feelings of lack of worth, but this is not the purpose of confession. It is precisely because we are worth so much in God's eyes, and ought so to value one another and ourselves, that we confess our shortcomings. We place our hope in God's forgiveness and renewal, trusting that changeable attitudes and behaviors do not indelibly define who we are. A true spirit of confession actually increases authentic self-acceptance and love.

Step Four of a Twelve Step program is to "make a fearless and searching moral inventory of ourselves." A "fearless inventory" will identify those personality traits, inclinations, attitudes, and behaviors that interfere with our truest good and the good of others (i.e., with God's will). We discover where and why our lives and relationships are out of order. The immediate effect of such rigorous truthfulness is self-knowledge. The larger purpose is to surrender our destructive, maladaptive life patterns to God so that we can become more fully the person God intends. This "step" offers a practical and concrete model for a life review.[2]

Before starting, several points need clarification. First, a process like this may take many days or even weeks to complete. You will discover very little about yourself if you try to rush it.

Self-examination is not morbid introspection or self-condemnation, but the honest, fearless confrontation of the self, and its abandonment to God in trust.

Kenneth Leech

Second, you can be sure that shining the light of truth into places until now left uninspected will elicit uncomfortable emotions such as fear, guilt, shame, and embarrassment. It is important to acknowledge these feelings and let them be real. At the same time, these feelings should not be allowed to control you or prevent self-examination.

Third, assume that you will not see all your character flaws right away. The self-protection of denial will be at work. You need to let go of the perfectionism by which you imagine you can figure out and fix yourself by sheer astuteness. In self-examination, we rely on the grace of God to give us insight into who we are and how we behave. God knows what we are ready to look at and when we need to do so.

Finally, you need to resist the temptation to focus attention on what others have done to you in the past. What others have done to you is their responsibility, not yours. Self-examination is an opportunity to discover the problematic parts of your own attitudes and choices.

The following process describes one way to do a life review.[3] The full benefit of this review comes with undertaking the process twice: once to identify personal weaknesses (the basic focus in examination of *conscience*) and once to identify personal strengths and learnings. Linked together, these two phases of the life review correspond well with the examination of *consciousness*. Because the first phase provides an excellent foundation for daily examination of conscience, I will focus primarily on the confessional phase of the life review in this section.

Life Review

Take several pieces of paper and write a single focus at the top of each, such as Fears, Resentments, Emotional Security, Material Security, Social Acceptance, Sexuality, and Faith. While there is a certain logic to the order as listed, you may treat the topics in any order you choose. Taking each theme in turn, go back to your earliest memories and gradually move forward in time. For example, identify your particular fears and resentments (people, circumstances, institutions) from childhood through to the present. Write them down. For each one, identify the effects and how you contributed to the problem. Use "I language," so as to describe your own feelings and experiences rather than blaming others. The following example of a resentment is offered to help you see the process more clearly. I have chosen a childhood experience because gaining greater understanding of experiences from the past can often help us see more clearly the behavior and attitude patterns in our adult life.

- *Resentment*: I am resentful of my elementary school classmates.

- *Cause*: I did not feel accepted socially when I entered fourth grade as a new student. I felt excluded from conversation and games because I was different.

- *Effects*: Hurt, withdrawal, loss of confidence, defensiveness, resentment, pattern of hiding real feelings, nursing pride, determination to prove myself, fear of rejection, self-pity.

- *My Contribution*: I didn't take any initiative to make friends, expected others to move first, and generally allowed myself to be "victimized."

When you look at your character weaknesses in relation to emotional and material security, a somewhat altered process may help. List by name the persons with whom you have recurring problems or who have deeply affected your sense of physical and emotional security. Note the feelings that attend each relationship and the cause of those feelings in your experience. But instead of naming the cause in terms of "what she or he did to me," name your basic needs or desires that were not met or the boundaries that were transgressed. Then consider the effects in your life. For example:

- *Person*: My spouse

- *Feelings*: Pain, shame, anger, depression, confusion

- *Cause*: Loss of self-respect, not feeling accepted, loss of love

- *Effects*: Tend to accept as true what others say about me; don't trust my own perceptions; feel helpless even when I could do something; sometimes take out my frustration on the kids

When you examine events or experiences that have affected your sense of material security, include financial issues. What are your attitudes toward money, and where do they come from? How do they affect your way of life now? Look at your way of relating to food, drink, clothing, and other material goods.

When you examine your sexuality, list specific behaviors and the attitudes that lie behind your actions. Include the effects in your life and the ways your behavior has affected others. With issues of social acceptance, consider the relationships you have had that were painful or unsatisfying. How are these experiences related to a desire for attractiveness, status, recognition, or achievement? What reactions do you typically have to painful social situations? Do you harm yourself or others by your responses?

An important part of a life review concerns your experiences and struggles in faith. Who is God for you? What is your God-image and how did it develop? Is your current image of God the same image you had as a child? Have you tried to manipulate or use God for your own agenda? What kind of relationship have you had with the church? Have you ever tried to use spiritual practices (prayer, Bible study, service) to make yourself perfect or to "fix" others? What feelings accompany these efforts? What are the effects on you and on others?

Remember that while the first phase of a life review is basically confessional, the process is not complete until you have taken time to observe your gifts and acknowledge your strengths as well. So when you have finished this inventory, go back through each category and ask what personal strengths you brought to the circumstances and relationships you identified. What positive character traits and attitudes have developed out of your life experience? What did you learn in each situation? List these in writing. Often negative traits are the reverse side of a positive trait you have not fully recognized or developed. It is important to realize that grace has been and continues to be at work in you even through the problematic parts of your life.

The most overlooked feature of genuine humility is the quiet acceptance of our strengths—those qualities God-given which are just as surely ours as our limitations and weaknesses.
Ronald V. Wells

You may find yourself confessing to God and seeking grace at many points in this process. However, once you have completed the entire review, you are ready to "confess your life" to God in prayer. You can say, in effect, "God, here are the patterns I see at work in my life. This is who I know myself to be and how I know myself to act. Yet you know more than I do. Bring me to greater clarity and understanding of myself. Let every true need in me be filled by you, every wound and defective response be healed and taken into your will. And thank you for these particular gifts and learnings that are part of my life journey. Strengthen them in me and help me share them with others."

The entire process of a life review is generally done only once. The first phase of that process gives us an opportunity to identify the flaws of character, attitude, belief, and response that typically permeate our personal histories. Becoming aware of these faults and their underlying causes puts us in a better position to keep an observant eye on ourselves through daily self-examination. I am speaking of self-examination now in its confessional sense (examination of conscience).

Daily Self-Examination

There are several ways to go about a daily practice of self-examination. For example, the Twelve Step program calls for a "daily inventory," in which you try to identify particular instances of general character weaknesses discovered in your life review. A specific list helps you examine your behavior; it might include traits such as selfishness, dishonesty, resentment, fear, jealousy, self-pity, greed, envy, and hatred. You are free to leave off traits that do not apply to you and to add traits that do. Pride, lust, impatience, procrastination, irresponsibility, judgmentalism, and lack of faith could be added. No doubt you will find your own relevant categories. An important part of this step is to name specific ways these faults surfaced in your behavior today and to indicate how you will make amends to anyone who might have been hurt by them.

Patterns for self-examination and confession in our Christian heritage are numerous. Historically, Eastern Orthodox Christians have used the Beatitudes as a liturgical aid to confession, while the Ten Commandments have more typically served that function in Roman Catholic tradition. Protestants have used both.[4] The classic pattern of "*Examen of Conscience*" in the Roman Catholic monastic tradition involves five steps: gratitude for graces given, prayer for the light of insight, particular and general self-examination, acts of sorrow and contrition, and the resolution to do better.

There is a balance in Christian tradition between private and corporate confession. The Puritans, who felt liberated from priestly confessionals, often used their private diaries to record highly introspective self-examinations before God. The intensely personal nature of these written disclosures was the primary reason so many journals were burned when their authors died. Yet Puritans joined every major branch of the church in stressing the necessity of common confession in public worship.

Try this exercise on two consecutive days. Reflect on your behaviors and attitudes in light of the Ten Commandments (Exod. 20:1–17) the first day. Do the same with the Beatitudes (Matt. 5:1–11) the next day. Does one approach help you to see yourself more clearly than the other? Why? Does one move you to a greater desire for holy living? Why?

Meeting with a Fellow Pilgrim

There is a kind of middle ground between purely private and purely corporate forms of confession. It is the age-old tradition of confessing to one particular brother or sister in faith. Before the rise of the professional priesthood, Christians confessed to each other and prayed for one another's healing. In the desert tradition of the fourth to sixth centuries, it was accepted practice to seek out a spiritually mature person—an "elder," or in more personal terms, a spiritual father or mother—who was more often than not a lay monk or hermit.[5] People unburdened their hearts to the elders in confession and sought from them assurance of God's forgiveness. Over time the practice of confession became formalized in church liturgy, and the role of confessor became identified with the ordained priesthood. But alongside such official confession, the less formal practice of meeting with a trusted friend or elder continued through the centuries. We can still seek out holy hearts among the people of God to listen to our deepest hurts and hopes.

Author Richard Foster describes a moving incident in his own life when he chose to meet with a trusted and faithful friend for this purpose.[6] He had sensed that something in his past was impeding the flow of God's grace and power in his ministry. So he divided his life into three periods: childhood, adolescence, and adulthood. On three consecutive days, he examined one of these periods before the gaze of God, asking the Lord to reveal to him anything that needed healing or forgiveness. In a state of silent prayer and meditation, he wrote down everything that surfaced in his memory without analyzing or judging it. Then he went to his chosen friend-confessor and read what he had written. His friend heard in silence, took the paper and shredded it into a waste basket, offered a brief word of absolution, then prayed for the healing of every hurt and sorrow of the past. Foster emerged from that experience with a new freedom. It was a profound turning point in his spiritual journey.

Other circumstances might call for a different process. For example, you may be perfectly aware of a particular sin that is eating away your peace of mind. If it is within your power to confess directly to a person you have wounded, pray for the courage and humility to do so. If you have no way to contact the offended party, seek out a friend in Christ whose faith, compassion, and confidentiality you trust. Perhaps you will simply tell your story and receive your friend's response. If the offense seems too painful to speak of, write it out and let your friend read it. There may be times when you cannot bring yourself to reveal a particularly shaming thought or act. Then you can ask for your friend's assistance: "I need your help. There is a sin that I cannot bring myself to confess."[7] Perhaps the friend can help you find a way to bring into the open whatever is terrorizing that dark corner of your soul. If not, seek out a pastor, priest, or experienced spiritual director for help.

Naturally you will not choose to share deeply personal confessions with someone you do not trust implicitly. Exercise discretion in your selection, and ask if your friend is willing to take on this role.

Have you ever confessed to a faithful friend? If so, what was this experience like? If not, can you think of anyone to whom you would be drawn to share a confession?

In some cases you may want the assurance of God's forgiveness through an ordained representative of the church. While I do not mean to deny the power of sacramental absolution from sin in corporate worship or the value of liturgical assurances of pardon, the power of face-to-face interaction can effect tremendous release.

I know one Protestant pastor who, in the absence of a theology that sanctions personal absolution, has created his own ritual. It occurs in the context of pastoral counseling and in the privacy of his study. In this simple rite, the person suffering guilt is marked with the sign of the cross on the forehead, reminded of his or her baptism, and assured of God's enduring love.

Don't be afraid to ask your pastor about the possibility of such a rite if your church tradition does not already include one.

Examination of Consciousness

So far, I have been speaking of the more explicitly confessional side of self-examination. But as noted earlier, the art of self-examination has a larger context than confession alone. Since "examination of conscience" has become associated with a penitential purpose, a different phrase has emerged to describe the broader focus of self-examination: "examination of consciousness."[8]

Examination of consciousness is a process of becoming aware of the contents of our consciousness so that we can respond before God in an appropriate way. It is more concerned with the level of our awareness than with particular character flaws and behavioral lapses. In this practice, we pay attention to both the good and the bad, observing our state of mind and heart during various events and interactions each day. The purpose is twofold: to notice where God's grace has been present in our day and to see where we have or have not responded to that grace.

What we call "consciousness" includes awareness of both external and internal realities. We are conscious of physical, sensory data: the places, people, events, sights, sounds, tastes, smells, and textures of life. We are also conscious of mental and emotional data: our thoughts, questions, beliefs, commitments, observations, feelings, and suspicions.

Examination of consciousness, then, will naturally include both external and internal data. When we reflect on what happened outwardly, we need to be aware of what was going on internally at the time. We are not automatically aware of our feelings, questions, or beliefs in the midst of a given encounter or event. Sometimes we can't quite articulate a question or conviction floating around inside us. Then when someone gives us the words or framework for understanding our actual questions or beliefs, it seems to be a genuine revelation! We may not know how we really feel about something until well after it happens; perhaps our feelings seemed like something else at the time. Noticing physical clues can help us become more fully aware of our "inner data." The turmoil in my stomach may tell me that I was feeling fear, not just surprise. The tension in my shoulders may indicate that I was angry as well as shocked. Questioning ourselves can help to clarify the nature of our feelings as well: Why was I feeling off balance in that conversation? Is my worry justified, or merely compulsive?

Finally, we are noticing what lies behind our feelings and reactions. What motivated my response? Was it basically fear, pride, or greed (self-preservation)? Was it genuine concern for another, love of creation, desire for God's will (self-giving)? Looking back over the thoughts, events, and interactions of the day, we come to the ultimate question: "Was it your love, God, that moved me?"[9] If we can say yes to that question with a clear conscience, self-examination will lead to gratitude for the grace of staying in touch with our living Source. If our answer is no, we will be led to confess our failure and seek the grace of forgiveness and renewed strength.

Behind this practice of self-examination lies a very basic assumption: we have made a choice to offer ourselves to God's service, and we have an active desire to live in God's presence, being led by the Holy Spirit each day. We examine our minds and hearts in order to see clearly where we have been led, when we have had a sense of God's presence, and where or when we have lost that connection. Questions can guide us: How has God been present to me through the people and situations I have encountered this day? Have I been aware of divine presence? Where have I been responding to the Spirit today? Where have I not responded? Why?

Invitations to Explore

Below you will find two simple processes of self-examination that may prove helpful in your daily spiritual practice. The first, "life-centered prayer," is a modern expression of examination of conscience. The second, "a daily practice with journal writing," is a contemporary form of examination of consciousness.

Life-Centered Prayer

Ben Campbell Johnson speaks of learning to "pray with our lives." He suggests a basic process to "integrate the life of prayer into the ordinary events and decisions of everyday life."[10]

- *Gather the day.* Identify the ten or twelve major events of your day, including prayer, particular conversations, meetings, meals, work, and other activities. List them.

- *Review the day.* Reflect upon each occurrence listed, without judging yourself, avoiding feelings, or making excuses. This is the actual substance of your daily life.

- *Give thanks for the day.* Thank God for each part of your day, for your life, and for God's presence in the midst of it.

- *Confess your sin.* Acknowledge your faults in thought, word, and deed toward God, your neighbor, and yourself (you might add the creation, too).

- *Seek the meaning of the events.* Reflect on the larger significance of each event in your life, asking yourself such questions as, What is God saying to me? What am I being called to do? How is this connected to the rest of my life? Write down what comes to mind.

A Daily Practice with Journal Writing

Author and spiritual director Tilden Edwards has described a basic form of daily examination developed by the Shalem Institute in Bethesda, Maryland. This practice emphasizes contemplative awareness and is not intended to be intense or analytical. It is short—only five to ten minutes: "a light, open glance at the day . . . with a desire for its fragments to be recollected in God."[11] I have adapted the process and suggest that you note down your observations in a journal. Keep these notes short and simple; even incomplete phrases are sufficient to capture the essence of your learnings. While this step adds a few more minutes to the process, it is well worth it for the record it gives you over time.

- Begin by relaxing your mind. Gently remind yourself of God's presence, and get in touch with your desire to be attentive to that presence during your day. You might offer a simple prayer that the graces of the day will be revealed to your consciousness.

- You need not try to find things; simply be "still and open, listening for what might rise from the day." When something surfaces, pay attention to the nature of the grace involved. How was God present? Let yourself feel and express gratitude for the gift.

- Then notice how you were present to God or others in the midst of that moment. If you observe that you were unaware of grace or unresponsive—perhaps holding the reins of ego control—you might breathe a simple prayer like "Lord, have mercy." Let yourself be aware of desire to respond differently another time.

- If you observe that you were responsive to, or at least conscious of, grace, simply "smile to God with thanksgiving."

- Allow something else from your day to rise into awareness; repeat the process. "Thus you are noticing both the hidden presence of God in the day and your own way of participating in, missing, or resisting that presence."

- When you have completed your observations, make note of any responses that seem significant to you. Have you seen something surprising? discovered a pattern in your way of being present to others? received a special sense of grace or gratitude today?

We can see that this is not necessarily a "confessional" process, although we are willing to look openly at ourselves for whatever may be revealed. When practiced daily, it offers a useful way to observe the movements of our heart over time.

Perhaps no other practices enable us to see so clearly where God's grace is present in the daily round of routine tasks and relationships or to see how we are responding to grace. Daily self-examination is closely allied to prayer. It is also a natural aid to the ongoing relationship of spiritual guidance I describe in chapter 8.

A True Spirit of Confession

The spirit of confession can be genuine or false. Genuine confession is marked by humility, while the counterfeit is riddled with anxiety and pride. Whenever we become fascinated by our sins or sucked into despair over our weaknesses, we may be sure that false humility is at work.

Teresa of Avila, a magnificent teacher on the subject of humility, warned her nuns:

> Now be also on your guard, daughters, against some types of humility given by the devil in which great disquiet is felt about the gravity of our sins. This disturbance can afflict in many ways even to the point of making one give up receiving Communion and practicing private prayer. These things are given up because the devil makes one feel unworthy. . . . The situation gets so bad that the soul thinks God has abandoned it because of what it is; it almost doubts [God's] mercy.[12]

Self-absorbed anxiety about sin is called *scrupulosity* in Christian tradition. It leads us to think obsessively about our faults, to wallow in guilt, to punish ourselves mentally. Beneath this self-condemnation lies a peculiar form of spiritual pride in which we give such weight to our sin that we imagine ourselves unredeemable: "I'm so awful even God can't forgive me!" Lack of confidence in God's grace can be an expression of pride as well as fear.

The only remedy, Teresa tells us, is to "stop thinking about your misery, insofar as possible, and turn your thoughts to the mercy of God, to how [God] loves us and suffered for us."[13] As soon as we see that our thoughts are revolving endlessly around our own sins, we need to lift our eyes to the One who showed us God's heart by forgiving human sin. When we can personally receive the love of God revealed in Christ, our focus shifts from sin to grace.

Authentic humility keeps us facing God. It teaches us to accept the fact that we will falter and fail. When we fall into temptation, humility prevents us from vicious self-recrimination and simply turns us back to God's love and help. Clear-eyed humility takes the place of wounded pride. Then the self-consuming flames of shame can become cleansing tears of sorrow, which turn into tears of gratitude before God's healing grace. That is why Teresa can say with full assurance, "Humility does not disturb or disquiet or agitate, however great it may be; it comes with peace, delight, and calm."[14]

Offered in this spirit, there is a certain lightness to self-examination. If we find ourselves attuned to grace, we are moved to gratitude for blessings already perceived. If we are out of tune with the Spirit, we seek the blessing of forgiveness, healing, and restored awareness of divine grace. There is no way to lose!

Self-examination is an occasion for spiritual refreshment, whatever we discover within ourselves at the time of review. Its purpose is always to bring us into greater intimacy with the Lover of our souls so that we can learn to walk more freely in God's path for us. Indeed, the practice of self-examination will blossom only out of a genuine desire to belong more completely to God and to love as God loves.

On our bad days we are affirmed as forgiven sinners; on our good days we are affirmed as blessed children.
Richard J. Hauser

The Fruits of Self-Examination

There are many benefits to daily self-examination. Exercised under the penetrating gaze and guiding grace of the Spirit, it leads to healthy self-awareness. Tradition tells us that knowledge of self and knowledge of God go hand in hand. We only know who we really are in relation to God, and knowledge of God leads us to perceive our true status. Since it belongs to the work of the Spirit to reveal us to ourselves, we are incapable of clear self-knowledge apart from grace. Examination of consciousness is a means to self-awareness in relation to God's love.

A result of increasing self-awareness is increasing truthfulness. Humility allows us to be real. We no longer have to put on a good face or a false front. There is no need to impress or to hide. We are not trying to protect or advance ourselves in God's eyes. Truthfulness gives us the freedom to let go of pretense and start living in simple honesty. This is one expression of Jesus' promise, "you will know the truth, and the truth will make you free" (John 8:32).

One of the most precious results of self-knowledge is greater compassion. The more clearly we see ourselves, the harder it becomes to judge the weaknesses and failures of others. We discover that we continually stumble on the path, even when we fervently desire to grow more Christlike and have committed ourselves to love and serve in his name. Self-examination helps us see the circumstances under which we fall into patterns of jealousy, rationalization, hostility, anxiety, self-defeating behaviors, and desire for prestige or control. We begin to see through the distorted motives of the human heart and understand from experience the attraction of evil.

As we perceive the realities of sin in ourselves, we can identify with the brokenness of others. Instead of condemning someone whose behavior is irritating or unacceptable, we may recall similar behavior in our own lives. This doesn't make the behavior more palatable, but it gives us fresh perspective on the wounds of the person behaving under compulsion. We learn to separate the unworthiness of a person's behavior from the worthiness of that person's being

A brother at Scetis committed a fault. A council was called to which Abba Moses was invited, but he refused to go to it. Then the priest sent someone to say to him, "Come, for everyone is waiting for you." So he got up and went. He took a leaking jug, filled it with water and carried it with him. The others came out to meet him and said to him, "What is this, Father?" The old man said to them, "My sins run out behind me, and I do not see them, and today I am coming to judge the errors of another." When they heard that they said no more to the brother but forgave him.
The Sayings of the Desert Fathers

as a child of God. We may even find ourselves praying for people we never imagined we could pray for!

Self-examination allows us to become people who are at peace with ourselves and who can therefore make peace with others. Compassion bears fruit in forgiveness. Without a sense of complicity in the common human condition of sin, it would be impossible to forgive others. As we see our weaknesses released and healed by a gracious God, we become capable of sharing the gift with others. God's freely offered love softens our hearts so that we can free others from the cords of our judgment. Such forgiveness is the ground of reconciliation and the beginning of all peacemaking.

There is much more to discover about the art of self-examination. With practice, examination of consciousness teaches us how to discern the movements of the Spirit in our heart. We begin to see more clearly what is of God and what is not. This art is called "discernment of spirits." It prepares us to make choices and life decisions that accord with God's intentions for us.[15] Guidance from a Christian who is experienced in this art can significantly help our growth in the practice of self-awareness and discernment of spirits. Chapter 8 will lead us into an exploration of the nature of spiritual guidance.

Notes to the Text

1. Douglas V. Steere, *On Beginning from Within* (New York: Harper & Brothers, 1943), 80.

2. Keith J. Miller's *A Hunger for Healing Workbook* (San Francisco: HarperSanFrancisco, 1992) is a helpful interpretation of Twelve Step programs as a model for Christian spiritual growth.

3. This material is adapted from pp. 49–72 of Keith J. Miller's *A Hunger for Healing Workbook* in the form of a highly condensed paraphrase of his Fourth Step with my own examples. I am much indebted to Mr. Miller for working out such a useful, concrete process of life review.

4. As recently as 1946, the *Presbyterian Book of Common Worship* included a "Service of Preparation for Holy Communion" that used the Beatitudes to help the faithful examine their hearts before receiving the Lord's Supper.

5. The term *monk* originally referred to both men and women. See Parker J. Palmer, "Borne Again: The Monastic Way to Church Renewal," *Weavings* 9, no. 1:12.

6. See Richard J. Foster, *Celebration of Discipline: The Path to Spiritual Growth* (San Francisco: Harper & Row, 1988), 149–50.

7. Ibid., 154.

8. I make this distinction for clarification. In historical terms, "examination of conscience" has often included awareness of the graced moments of our lives along with our miserable failings. The practice of *Examen* outlined by Saint Ignatius (sixteenth-century founder of the Jesuit order) included discerning "consolations" and "desolations." *Consolation* refers to that state in which we experience the presence and grace of God, and it calls for gratitude. *Desolation* represents the opposite state, and it calls for confession. Richard Baxter, the seventeenth-century English Puritan, also describes how self-examination leads to knowledge of a grace-filled or grace-less state of heart.

9. Tad Dunne, *Spiritual Mentoring* (San Francisco: Harper & Row, 1991), 101. See especially chapter 5 for a more complete discussion of the art of noticing what is in us.

10. These quotes and the following paraphrase of process are taken from Ben Campbell Johnson's *Invitation to Pray* (Decatur, GA: CTS Press, 1992), 18–22.

11. This quote and all quotations in the process that follows are from Tilden Edwards, *Living in the Presence: Disciplines for the Spiritual Heart* (San Francisco: Harper & Row, 1987), 84.

12. *The Collected Works of St. Teresa of Avila*, Vol. II, trans. Kieran Kavanaugh and Otilio Rodriguez (Washington, DC: Institute of Carmelite Studies, 1980), 189.

13. Ibid., 190.

14. Ibid., 189.

15. For further reading on this subject, see Tad Dunne, *Spiritual Mentoring* (San Francisco: Harper & Row, 1991); Margaret Guenther, *Holy Listening* (Boston: Cowley Publications, 1992), Jeannette Bakke, *Holy Invitations* (Ada, MI: Baker Books, 2000), and Timothy Jones, *Finding a Spiritual Friend* (Nashville: Upper Room Books, 1998).

Notes to the Sidebars

M. Scott Peck, psychiatrist and author. 1936–2005. *The Road Less Traveled: A New Psychology of Love, Traditional Values and Spiritual Growth* (New York: Touchstone Books, Simon & Schuster, 1978), 52.

Kenneth Leech, Anglican priest, author, and lecturer. *True Prayer: An Invitation to Christian Spirituality* (San Francisco: Harper & Row, 1980), 135.

Ronald V. Wells, minister, professor, and seminar leader. *Spiritual Disciplines for Everyday Living* (Schenectady, NY: Character Research Press, 1982), 97.

Richard J. Hauser, Jesuit professor of Theology, Creighton University. *Moving in the Spirit: Becoming a Contemplative in Action* (New York: Paulist Press, 1986), 55.

In *The Sayings of the Desert Fathers,* The Alphabetical Collection, trans. Benedicta Ward (Kalamazoo, MI: Cistercian Publications, 1975), 117.

CHAPTER 8

Companions on the Journey

The Gift of Spiritual Direction

Spiritual direction is the act of paying attention to God, calling attention to God, being attentive to God in a person or circumstances or situation. . . . It notices the Invisibilities in and beneath and around the Visibilities. It listens for the Silences between the spoken Sounds.

Eugene H. Peterson

"I am starting to realize that God is only real to me in my head. I believe in God, and sometimes I think about God, but I don't know if I've ever really experienced God. I'm not very aware of God most of the time. I'd like to be, but I'm not sure how to make it happen. I guess I'd like to talk to someone who knows God from experience."

"My life feels off-center right now. I think I'm spending too much time working. But I get itchy if I'm not doing something productive. I know I don't pray enough and sometimes I feel guilty about it. But my prayers don't seem to get results, so I've pretty much given up. Maybe I'm not praying right. I wonder if I could find a person with a real prayer life to talk to."

"I'm in transition right now. Everything seems to be changing. All the things I thought were settled are shifting. I feel that maybe God is asking me to consider something new, but I'm not sure what. I want very much to know what God's will for me is. This is the question I keep wrestling with. But I'm pretty confused. I don't know how to "read the signals" when my life is in so much flux. I'd like to be clear about what God wants for me. I wish there was someone who could help me discern God's will."

"God has taught me a lot over the years. I know from experience the power of prayer. Sometimes I've kept a journal that has been tremendously helpful in my spiritual growth. But I'm too sporadic about my spiritual disciplines, even though I know how fruitful they are. I'd like to covenant with someone else who's been on the journey, just to encourage me and make me more accountable."

Do any of these voices echo part of your experience? They are representative of many people in our culture, including our churches. For different reasons, each expresses a desire to have a companion on the journey of faith—a fellow Christian who can speak to his or her condition. Perhaps that condition is a desire to know the reality of God from personal experience. Perhaps it is the hunger to trust a God who is all too real but frightening. It may simply be a desire to live more faithfully and compassionately in God's world or a yearning to grow into deeper intimacy with the Lover of human souls.

Have you ever felt a need for a person who could occasionally offer guidance, support, or creative challenge in your faith journey? If so, your desire joins you with unnumbered ranks of seekers and believers across the centuries who have sought "spiritual direction."

Spiritual Direction in the Christian Tradition

Spiritual direction, classically understood, is essentially the relationship of a teacher and learner in the area of practicing the spiritual life. Every faith tradition in the world has teacher-learner relationships. Spiritual teachers have various names: prophets, priests, rabbis, roshis, gurus, elders, mentors. They are people who give visible evidence of a certain maturity or level of mastery on a particular spiritual path. Learners also have different names: followers, disciples, novices, and apprentices. They are people who are drawn to inner growth yet often find themselves stumbling or wandering in confusion when they attempt to walk a spiritual path alone.

Jesus, like prophets and rabbis before him, gathered disciples and taught them daily, both publicly and privately. His example is the cornerstone of spiritual guidance in the Christian tradition. It is a deeply personal pattern of relationship. What Jesus taught had significance because of who he was. He embodied what he taught. In its early phases, the relationship with his disciples reflected certain characteristics of a parent-child or master-servant relationship, but without authoritarian qualities. As it progressed, the relationship developed traits of a more mutual friendship (see John 15:12–17; 21:15–17).

The apostle Paul was a strong teacher and mentor to the fledgling churches he established. He called himself a "father through the gospel" to his Corinthian congregation (1 Cor. 4:15) and saw himself as a mother "in labor" to bring forth Christ in the balky Galatian church (Gal. 4:19). We have noted that between the fourth and sixth centuries, Christians flocked to the deserts of Egypt and Arabia to consult on personal spiritual matters with the elder monks of the desert. These monks firmly established the deep-rooted tradition of "spiritual fathers and mothers" in the church. They offered advice, words of wisdom, parables, personal examples of Christian life, and sometimes simple silence as means of direction. Through the centuries, spiritual direction has been provided by priests, monks, ministers, and elders in the church. Protestants have typically called it "pastoral counsel" or "spiritual consultation" and have often given it in small groups or families rather than individually.

But in Christianity, spiritual guidance is not the sole preserve of those who have a special call or training to carry on the tradition. It can be offered by any layperson seen to be mature enough in faith to offer guidance to others. The Christian church trusts that the Holy Spirit is active within the community of believers. The grace of the Spirit is given to all Christians, not only to its ministers and priests. Professed vows and ordination are no guarantee of spiritual maturity! Different graces are given to different people according to God's wisdom. Some laypersons are more gifted in spiritual guidance than many clergy. This has been so since the time of the early church.

Very few have ever been true "masters" of the Christian spiritual life, and those who come closest would never claim the title. A spiritual guide need only be one who has traveled some distance along the path of the Christian life. A guide should be knowledgeable about the markers that lead forward on this path as well as familiar with the pitfalls, detours, trials, and temptations along its course. Such a person will reflect something of the character of Christ as a result of following in his way. A Christian who gives no evidence of humility, wisdom, compassion, or the ability to speak truth in love will not likely be sought out as a spiritual guide.

Spiritual directors themselves participate in a dimension of childlikeness: they sit with the person, listening and responding to movements of truth that come from beyond their management and possession.

Tilden Edwards

What Does a Spiritual Director Do?

From a Christian perspective, spiritual direction is the guidance one believer offers another to help that person "grow up in every way . . . into Christ" (Eph. 4:15). From a broader perspective, a spiritual guide is someone who can help us see and name our own experience of God. Each of us needs to grow out of secondhand faith to knowledge of the way the Spirit works in our own lives, to recognize the daily tracings of divine grace and respond to them. At times, spiritual guides may teach, admonish, or confront us firmly in love to hold us accountable for our attitudes and behaviors. Far more often, spiritual directors act as companions, encouraging and supporting us, praying for us, listening to us, and occasionally sharing learning from their life journeys.

Spiritual guides have certain responsibilities. The list that follows describes what spiritual directors typically do:

So what does the spiritual director teach? In the simplest and also most profound terms, the spiritual director is simultaneously a learner and a teacher of discernment. What is happening? Where is God in this person's life? What is the story? Where does this person's story fit in our common Christian story?

Margaret Guenther

1. *A spiritual guide listens to us.* When we need someone to hear our life story in terms of faith, a spiritual guide offers hospitable space for us to speak and be heard. Often we do not fully know our thoughts or experiences, our questions or unresolved issues. We do not know until we have had a chance to put them into words before an attentive and receptive ear. A spiritual director can "listen us into clarity," helping us articulate our thoughts, feelings, questions, and experiences in relation to God.

2. *A spiritual guide helps us to notice things.* God's presence and the ways of the Spirit are not generally self-evident to us. They are subtle and unobtrusive, often hidden in the midst of ordinary events and interactions. It takes practice to see the grace of God in everyday life. A spiritual mentor can help us pay attention to signs of grace, to listen for God's "still small voice" in our daily encounters and experiences. A guide can also direct our attention to the dynamics of the heart so that we become more aware of how God speaks to us through it

3. *A spiritual guide helps us respond to God with greater freedom.* When we begin to notice God's presence, guidance, provision, and challenge in our daily lives, we are faced with choices. How shall we respond? The choice is not always easy. God's presence and provision are comforting, naturally eliciting gratitude and praise. But God also faces us with the darker realities in our lives, calling us to genuine change. It is hard to let go of old habits and ways of being. Out of these encounters, God calls us to a new sense of purpose and mission in life. A spiritual director can encourage us toward fuller freedom to respond to God in loving obedience.

4. *A spiritual guide points us to practical disciplines of spiritual growth.* Without the help of particular practices it is difficult to become

more aware of, and responsive to, God's activity in our lives. Most of us could use guidance on ways of prayer that attune us to God's presence. We may need suggestions for spiritual reading, tips on keeping a journal, or reminders about the nature of authentic humility in self-examination. Perhaps we need someone who has practiced fasting to help us stay on track with our efforts. A spiritual companion can suggest various practices to us as they seem appropriate and help us discern when or whether to change them. A guide can also help keep us accountable for the disciplines we commit ourselves to.

Why is it harder to face a person to whom you have broken a promise than to face God?

Ben Campbell Johnson

5. *A spiritual guide will love us and pray for us.* This is probably the most important function of a companion in Christian faith. The love of a spiritual director for the one directed is always mediated by the love of Christ. It is *agape* love. The ongoing expression of that love is faithful prayer, both within and beyond meeting times. If this is in effect, many inadequacies in a guide can be covered by grace. If it is not present, even virtuoso technique can scarcely make up for it!

Styles of Spiritual Direction

There are a variety of patterns in spiritual direction, some quite formal and others much less so. When novices went out to the desert to receive initial training in the Christian life from the elders, the relationship to a spiritual father or mother was one of absolute obedience. The spiritual father or mother had authority second only to scripture. But it was an authority based on the authenticity of the elder's spiritual life, an authority grounded in love, an authority conferred by novices who were free to leave at any time. The elders had the gift of reading the human heart and could offer unique words of counsel based on their discernment. This form of spiritual direction is a rarity in the modern world.

In Roman Catholic seminaries, students for the priesthood are required to have a spiritual director. Often the entire faculty is required to provide this direction. There is little choice in the matter, as students are assigned to faculty members. It is an institutional expression of spiritual direction that takes little account of personal gifts or desires. It does, however, reflect the understanding that anyone on a seminary faculty will have sufficient experience with spiritual direction to be able to offer it to a student in the formative phase of preparation for the priesthood. This represents a formal arrangement where the lines of authority are very clear.

Protestants are, for the most part, more comfortable in patterns of relationship without authoritarian overtones. It is still common for the guidance relationship to be "one-way," that is, focused on the spiritual growth of the one seeking guidance. Again, voluntary authority is given to the guide by the guided. But it is based on qualities observed in the spiritual guide that are respected by the one who wishes to grow in faith. Essentially, this means that the person seeking guidance trusts the director to be attuned to the presence and movement of the Holy Spirit rather than to mere personal wisdom.

Even in this kind of relationship, there is variation in form. For example, two Christians who are essentially peers and who respect each other's ability to attend to God may choose to enter a mutual relationship of guidance. In one meeting, one acts as the director and the other receives guidance; in their next meeting, they reverse roles. If they meet for a more extended time, they might even exchange roles during the same meeting.[1] This sort of mutuality expresses well a Protestant emphasis on the "priesthood of all believers." But it may not satisfy those who seek someone they perceive to be "more advanced" on the spiritual journey.

Finally, there are very informal patterns of spiritual guidance that are distinctly mutual and nonprofessional. Some prefer to call these "spiritual friendships." Many of us probably have relationships of this sort already, without thinking of them as forms of spiritual guidance. Prayer partners are basically spiritual friends. Often, small covenanted groups in a church provide us with spiritual friends. You may simply have a friend you enjoy talking with about spiritual matters or someone you turn to for comfort and assurance in times of perplexity and doubt.

While these are natural and wonderful gifts, it is possible to become more intentional about spiritual friendship. You might choose to develop a friendship you already have by deciding to meet regularly for spiritual conversation and prayer. You might recognize that you have a friend or acquaintance you would like to propose this idea to. It is basically a commitment to travel together on the path of faith.

Getting Started with Spiritual Direction

If you think you would benefit from a spiritual companion, the first step is to clarify in your own mind why you want such a relationship. What do you hope to gain from this process? I remember my first experience with spiritual direction in seminary. I had heard about the practice from Roman Catholic friends, and since I was interested in the spiritual life, I thought it was something I should try. The Cenacle sister I met with was a compassionate and experienced director, but I had no clear ideas about what I wanted from direction. Since I had not identified any spiritual issues that might have moved me to seek guidance—only curiosity—I experienced little benefit from our meetings and quit after only three or four sessions. I was not ready for spiritual direction until two years later.

Once you are clear about your reasons for wanting a spiritual mentor, ask yourself what kind of person you would be most comfortable working with. Does it matter to you whether your guide is a man or woman? Are you looking for someone older than yourself? Is it important to you that the person shares your own faith tradition or denomination? How far would you be willing to travel to meet with this person? Most important, what personal qualities are you looking for?

The following personal qualities have become my central criteria for people from whom I seek spiritual guidance. I commend them as general guidelines:

1. *Look for Christians with a certain maturity of faith.* I want a spiritual mentor to have a wide-ranging experience of life and faith; to be practiced in a life of prayer; to be familiar with the scriptures and some of the spiritual classics; to be knowledgeable about the ways of the human heart; and to have an eye for discerning the "footprints of God."

2. *Look for people who know they are not perfect.* I look for someone who knows human suffering and frailty from personal experience; who is honest about her or his limitations and not afraid to be vulnerable. Humility and compassion for the weaknesses of others are important marks in her or his life. I want a guide whose faith is strong through flexibility rather than rigidity, whose wisdom is practical and salted with humor.

3. *Seek out people who are patient and attentive listeners.* I need a guide who is not easily shocked, who can hear all kinds of feelings and acknowledge the human reality of all kinds of behaviors without condemnation. I want a guide who can listen to God as well as to me, who is attuned to the promptings of the Spirit when we meet.

The greatest spiritual guides have been men and women of prayer and quiet, people possessed by an inner stillness of soul, people who are able to guide others because of their own closeness to God.
Kenneth Leech

Take five minutes to think through the qualities and characteristics of a person you would seek out as a spiritual guide. Write them down.

119

4. *Look for people who invite trust.* I want someone who will hold confidences so that I can speak freely. I also need to trust my spiritual companion to speak honestly to me about my condition when I am avoiding something I need to face.

5. *Look for mentors who place their trust in the grace of God.* God is the true director of every spiritual encounter. I am not looking for professional competence or confidence in one's own ability apart from the work of the Spirit. I seek someone who is willing to stand before God with me as a forgiven sinner and whose love and prayer for me is rooted in Christ.

Once you have clarity about the kind of person you are seeking as a spiritual companion, the place to begin is with prayer. Ask God to show you the right person for you to work with. Even if you already have someone in mind, pray for clarity and confirmation. If you have no idea who might be a spiritual guide for you, ask God to reveal someone to you as you are inwardly ready. The Spirit may bring a name, image, or clue into your consciousness in prayer. The Spirit may also act through the suggestion of another person of faith. Seek out recommendations from those you trust.

Start thinking about the people you know. Is there anyone with whom you are already acquainted and to whom you feel drawn? If so, bring him or her before God in prayer with complete openness and expectancy. Pay attention to the sense you have of this person in prayer and to the feelings that surface. If you feel uncomfortable or awkward about asking someone in your circle of personal acquaintances to take on this role in your life, attend to the reason. Maybe the person is too close to be objective with you. Perhaps you value your relationship as it is. Maybe it is a professional relationship that would make intimate disclosures uncomfortable or inappropriate. Perhaps the person is too busy or lives too far away.

When you bring a request of this sort before God, be prepared for the unexpected. You may be led to someone you don't know or to someone quite unlike yourself. You may well be led to one who does not see him- or herself as a spiritual guide at all. If your initial query is met with resistance because a person feels unprepared for the task, do not lose heart. People who have genuine spiritual gifts are usually humble, ordinary folk who are deeply conscious of their own spiritual struggles and failures. They may be shocked that anyone would consider asking them to act as a spiritual mentor. Yet that sense of inadequacy may be one of the authentic marks of

The great Director of Souls is the Holy Spirit.

　　　　　　Dom Columba Marmion

My first spiritual director didn't know he was a spiritual director. He had never so much as heard the term spiritual director, and neither had I. But our mutual ignorance of terminology did not prevent the work.

　　　　　　Eugene H. Peterson

a spiritual guide. You can always ask the person to consider your request in prayer and to be open to the possibility that God is calling you together by the Spirit.

It is important that you have a sense of "rightness" about asking a particular person for spiritual guidance. When you receive a willing response, arrange for an initial meeting to explore the possibilities. Talk about your desire for companionship and direction on your faith journey. Indicate why you are seeking guidance at this time. Tell the person that you feel called to explore guidance with him or her in particular. Discuss your hopes and expectations for a spiritual direction relationship. If the person agrees to work with you, set a limited number of meetings (perhaps over a three-month period) in which to establish and test your relationship. This is a time to get more fully acquainted and to pray for signs of confirmation that God is calling you together in this work before further commitment.

Meeting with a Spiritual Director

When you meet for your first session of spiritual direction, several matters must be decided. What type of relationship do you want? What will be the frequency and length of your meetings? How will you structure each meeting? What kind of evaluation process will you build into your relationship?

The first thing to do is to clarify your mutual hopes and expectations. What does each of you want to receive or offer in this relationship? What does each of you see as the object or goal of your time together? What style of spiritual direction will this be? Is it to be clearly focused on helping *you* relate more fully and freely to God, or is this to be a more mutual friendship?

Next, agree on an overall meeting rhythm and time frame. Will you meet every two weeks? once a month? Take your schedules into consideration, especially if either of you travels frequently. Spiritual direction will bear little fruit if it is not a serious commitment. It will need to take priority over other things at times. Once you have decided on frequency, ask how much time you will give to each meeting. If you meet every week or two, forty-five minutes to an hour may be sufficient. If you meet once a month, an hour to an hour and a half may seem a minimum. I know spiritual companions who live far apart and meet only a few times a year. They spend several days together when they meet and keep in touch between meetings with regular letters, emails, and phone calls.

Another practical decision is how to use the meeting time itself. Be clear about your intentions so as not to waste time that could be focused on your purpose for meeting. You might decide, for example, to give five minutes to small talk (weather, traffic, minor news) as a transition from the immediate experiences of the day into spiritual guidance. It is helpful to begin spiritual direction with several minutes of silence. This allows you both to "center down," clear the surface chatter of the mind, and become aware of divine presence. The silence can be broken by a simple prayer, offered by one or both of you in turn. As the one seeking guidance, you would then begin to share experiences, reflections, and questions with your companion. Your guide in turn would respond with questions, insights, stories, suggestions, or shared experiences. The session might be closed with prayer again. If you offer the opening prayer, you might want your guide to conclude with prayer, or vice versa. In more mutual situations, you might prefer to share both prayer times.

Finally, decide how many times to meet before evaluating your relationship. I recommend committing to at least six meetings for a fair test of how well you work together. The final session will be an opportunity to look frankly at how you experience your relationship and whether it fits your goals and expectations. If it does, you may choose to renew your commitment for another period of time. If not, you can choose whether to clarify your expectations and restructure your time together or to end the relationship. It should be understood from the outset that either person can terminate the covenant if it is not working well or seems unhealthy in any respect.

Any of these initial decisions about the structure and format of your meeting may change over time as the relationship develops. You may need to explore various options before you discover what works best for the two of you. Some people need more flexible and creative patterns in spiritual guidance than others.

Many years ago, I met with a woman spiritual friend one day each month at a convent in the mountains. At first we devised a structured schedule in which each of us had equal time to raise our own issues while the other listened and responded. But sticking to this time line became artificial. As we came to know one another more deeply and to trust the movement of the Spirit between us, we began to give each other whatever time seemed needful. On some days, only one of us acted as guide to the other. Over time, we tried to balance our respective roles as spiritual mentors to each other. This flexibility evolved gradually and naturally. The one arena we always shared in a completely mutual manner was our spoken prayer time, which flowed spontaneously back and forth between us until it came of its own accord to silence. This relationship was the most mutual spiritual companionship I have ever known.

What Do You Talk About in Spiritual Direction?

Some of us have never known a relationship in which we felt comfortable talking about God. Perhaps we grew up in a family where faith was as private as sex, an intimate matter one never put public words to. Perhaps religion was a sore topic for our parents or no topic at all because it was considered fantasy. Maybe we grew up in a church that rigidly forced certain doctrines upon us, and we never felt free to ask our real questions for fear of being ridiculed, harangued, or rejected. Perhaps God simply seemed so awesome that we had trouble saying anything particular about the mystery.

A spiritual companion is someone with whom we can find the freedom and trust to begin exploring who God is in our lives. What do I actually believe about God? Who is God for me? How does God seem to work in my life? How does God relate to my family, my work, my life in the world? How can I be more aware of God's presence and activity in my daily life? How am I called to respond? These are some of the questions and issues you can expect to explore in a spiritual guidance relationship.

Sometimes we have clear ideas about God and how God acts in our lives. Maybe a transition or impending crisis motivates us to seek spiritual direction. In cases such as these, we are likely to talk more about events and relationships and how God is or is not felt to be present in them. Spiritual guidance is not the same as psychological counseling. Psychological therapies tend to focus on self-image, relationships, or work issues in a problem-solving way. Most do so without reference to God, sometimes even in pastoral counseling! Spiritual direction always keeps God in the picture. Your relationship with God is really the heart of spiritual guidance, whatever else you may be dealing with in life.

Here is a sample dialogue of the kind of conversation that might occur when Pat starts coming to Eleanor for spiritual guidance:

PAT: I feel like I don't know how to pray anymore. I used to pray a lot, and it was very easy. You know, it just came

The primary relationship in spiritual friendship is between God and the friend, not between the friends themselves.

Tilden Edwards

123

naturally. But for some reason I'm having trouble now.
. . . It bothers me. I want to feel close to God.

ELEANOR: Tell me more about your prayer when it came naturally.

PAT: Well, I just talked to God about anything that was on my mind. I talked things out with him as if he were in the room with me, like any other person. That made it easy.

ELEANOR: (*nodding*) So God seemed to be like any other person. Has that changed in some way?

PAT: I think maybe . . . I'm not sure. Sometimes I get really confused about how to think about God. Last month our preacher was saying that the ancient Jews wouldn't even name God because he was beyond all our thoughts or concepts or images. And then I started thinking about that catechism I learned in Junior High School: "God is a Spirit, infinite, eternal, unchanging. . . ." I'm beginning to think that I've had a really childish picture of God all these years . . . like some wise old half-ghost who could float through solid objects. I bet this sounds really dumb!

ELEANOR: It doesn't sound dumb. It sounds as if your image of God is changing.

PAT: I guess it is. But I'm not sure I want it to change! Thinking of God as a person made it easy to pray. Now God feels somehow more . . . removed from my life. A God that's like some disembodied spirit just seems so distant. I don't know how to pray to this kind of God.

ELEANOR: What happens when you try?

PAT: Well, I just have this feeling of trying to get my thoughts way out there somewhere, wherever God is . . . and then I think, well, God knows everything already, so why should I be praying anyway?

ELEANOR: What do you associate with the word *spirit*?

PAT: (*long pause*) I guess it makes me think of something insubstantial, gauzy, not quite real. . . . Oh! . . . Maybe that's it. I feel like God isn't real anymore!

You can see that by attentive listening and a few probing questions, Eleanor has enabled Pat to come to a moment of self-discovery in her prayer life. Pat had not realized that her image of "spirit" translated into "unreality" in her mind. This is the immediate source of difficulty in her prayer life. Eleanor might point Pat toward some other ways of understanding *spirit*, perhaps by reflecting on pertinent scripture passages. They can also explore how Pat experienced the reality of God in her life before her image started changing and where the reality of God is revealing itself to her even now, through the change.

Problems and Potentials in Spiritual Companionship

If you are new to spiritual direction, expect to encounter some of the ups and downs of any close relationship. Remember that in and through this companion, you are dealing with the most intimate and mysterious of all relationships—the one you have with God. There may be relational bumps connected to God, your director, or both!

Sometimes you will feel dissatisfied or irritated with your spiritual mentor. Perhaps you will feel your mentor is either not giving you sufficient direction or is being too directive. If you feel this way, you should discuss it openly. There may be good reasons for the approach that bothers you. Your guide may want you to discover something on your own rather than pointing it out to you, or your guide may sense that you need firm directives to counteract certain personal traits that prevent you from responding freely to God. Or maybe your mentor needs clarification from you on an approach that would be more helpful. If you talk it through, your distress can be part of your learning process.

Sometimes negative feelings toward a spiritual director are really displaced feelings of fear, anxiety, or anger toward God. A sensitive guide can help us see when this is the case. Growing in relationship with God is not easy. We have many defenses against the changes God invites into our lives. Writer Flannery O'Connor warns, "All human nature vigorously resists grace, because grace changes us and change is painful."[2]

Sometimes personality conflicts emerge in spiritual guidance. If these are recognized and dealt with constructively, they can be part of the spiritual growth God brings out of such relationships. A person with a different personality can give us perspectives we would never see on our own. People with opposite characteristics often complement each other wonderfully, each stretching the other to new points of view.

However, it may be that your director really doesn't understand your spiritual journey sufficiently to be of help to you. If you feel that a guide is imposing a personal path that doesn't fit you and discussion of the matter is no help, then the relationship is not right for you.

There are seasons in all relationships. Some will be short, intense but fruitful. Others will be long-term commitments that evolve slowly and change shape as they grow. There may come a time in the best of spiritual companionships when the guide has offered all she or he can. Then it is time for this particular relationship to end, even though you may continue your friendship by other means.

Finally, it is important to speak of the sexual dimension of spiritual guidance. If you choose to work with someone to whom you could become sexually attracted, there is always the possibility of attraction turning into attachment. If you sense that this movement is taking place, it needs to be brought into the open and talked through. If the dynamic cannot be changed by frank discussion, terminate the relationship. There are absolutely no circumstances in which it is appropriate for sexual behavior to take place within spiritual direction. The boundaries appropriate to your purpose need to be respected.

Testing a Spiritual Companionship

The first several months of a new relationship are the best time to test it. You need to be sure you are comfortable with your mentor or you will not feel free to share the deeper issues and concerns of your life in God. Pay attention to your level of trust. Does it deepen quickly over your first several meetings, or is something holding you back? Nagging concerns in the back of your mind are important indicators. Resist the temptation to dismiss them, and examine each one in the light of reason and prayer. Is there something that bothers you about this person? Pay attention to your intuitions. "Gut-level" feelings can often alert us to problem areas long before they come to conscious clarity.

The following questions may help you evaluate your relationship with a spiritual director:

- Is this relationship helping me to grow in my way of understanding and relating to God? Is it helping me to connect my life and my faith?

- When I am with my guide, am I thinking mostly about my life in relation to God and the spiritual dimension of my other relationships? (If you are thinking mostly about your guide, something is wrong.)

- Am I quite comfortable with my guide? Do I expect to be able to open up more and more freely, or is something disturbing me?

I felt a large roominess in his company—a spiritual roominess, room to move around, room to be free. He didn't hem me in with questions; he didn't suffocate me with "concern."
Eugene H. Peterson

Use common sense when you are testing out a person's ethical sensibilities. It helps if the spiritual guide you are considering or evaluating comes with unreserved recommendations from people you know and trust.

The Value of Spiritual Guidance

There may be times in your life when a spiritual guide is invaluable to you and times when you do not need such a relationship. Sometimes the general teaching and preaching of the church is sufficient to our needs. Sometimes we find the direction we are seeking from books. Teresa of Avila acknowledged centuries ago that when we cannot find a living Christian to guide us we may rely on good spiritual books. The authors of spiritual classics, whether ancient or modern, are often excellent guides.

Small groups in the church—Bible study groups, experiential learning classes, or covenant groups—serve to direct and support us in our spiritual journeys. Para-church groups such as Twelve Step programs, Marriage Encounter, and Cursillo (Protestant adaptations include Walk to Emmaus and Tres Dias) have been life-changing for many thousands. Small groups are more accessible to many people than individual spiritual guidance and should be openly explored. They can be fine sources of guidance.

Still, as the voices that opened this chapter remind us, there are times when what we really yearn for is one other person who can give us concentrated time and attention. We may need someone with more experience or simply someone with an outsider's objective perspective on the spiritual concerns we struggle with. The fruits of such a companionship in faith can be tremendous. We can come to name God's grace in our lives and to understand our own experiences of faith. New ways of praying and offering our lives in service to God can be explored. We can find ourselves personally affirmed and loved even when we confess our deepest needs and vulnerabilities. We are supported in our practice of spiritual disciplines and held accountable to a flesh-and-blood human being. This is how one man described the benefits of his spiritual mentoring:

> I have discovered personal support for my journey. Not only have I been accepted, affirmed, appreciated, and given words of assurance about God's work in my life, but I have known the incalculable support of prayer from a man who knows me and who cares about God's work in my life. I no longer feel alone in my struggle.[3]

Spiritual companionship in the Christian life is a precious grace. Our journeys are not meant to be utterly solitary. Trying to be faithful to God can be a lonely and trying path. We need others, and we grow best in community. Four centuries ago, Saint John of the Cross stated this truth eloquently yet simply: "God has so ordained things that we grow in faith only through the frail instrumentality of one another."[4] May we find joy in being such instruments for one another!

Notes to the Text

1. For a personal illustration of this kind of mutual guidance relationship, see Ben Campbell Johnson's fine little book, *To Pray God's Will: Continuing the Journey* (Philadelphia: Westminster Press, 1987), chap. 5.

2. Sally Fitzgerald, ed., *The Letters of Flannery O'Connor—The Habit of Being* (New York: Vintage Books, 1980), 308.

3. Johnson, *To Pray God's Will*, 90.

4. Cited without source reference in editor's introduction, *Weavings* 2, no. 4 (July–August 1987): 3.

Notes to the Epigraph and Sidebars

Eugene H. Peterson, Presbyterian pastor, author, former professor of Spiritual Theology at Regent College, Vancouver, B.C. Epigraph from *Under the Unpredictable Plant: An Exploration of Vocational Holiness* (Grand Rapids, MI: Wm. B. Eerdmans Publishing Co., 1992), 181.

Tilden Edwards, Senior Fellow and co-founder of Shalem Institute for Spiritual Formation, Bethesda, Maryland. *Spiritual Friend: Reclaiming the Gift of Spiritual Direction* (New York: Paulist Press, 1980), 86.

Margaret Guenther, Episcopal priest, emeritus professor at General Theological Seminary, New York City. *Holy Listening: The Art of Spiritual Direction* (Boston: Cowley Publications, 1992), 43.

Ben Campbell Johnson, author, interfaith dialogue promoter, former professor at Columbia Theological Seminary, Decatur, Georgia. *To Pray God's Will: Continuing the Journey* (Philadelphia: Westminster Press, 1987), 89.

Kenneth Leech, Anglican priest, author, and lecturer. *True Prayer: An Invitation to Christian Spirituality* (San Francisco: Harper & Row, 1980), 50.

Dom Columba Marmion, Benedictine abbot of Meredsous, 1858–1923. Quoted in Kenneth Leech, *Soul Friend: The Practice of Christian Spirituality* (San Francisco: Harper & Row, 1977), 73.

Eugene H. Peterson, *Under the Unpredictable Plant*, 183

Tilden Edwards, *Spiritual Friend*, 110.

Eugene H. Peterson, *Under the Unpredictable Plant*, 186.

CHAPTER 9

Entertaining Angels Unawares

The Spirit of Hospitality

Come, you that are blessed by my Father, inherit the kingdom prepared for you . . . ; for I was hungry and you gave me food, I was thirsty and you gave me something to drink, I was a stranger and you welcomed me.

Matthew 25:34–35

I had just graduated from college three months before. My mother had earned a precious sabbatical, and we were taking the trip of a lifetime, starting in Scotland. On this particular day, we had left Edinburgh to venture into the Scottish countryside. The legendary Highlands were carpeted in heather and chill mist. By the time our bus arrived in the isolated town where we would spend the night, darkness had fallen and it was pouring rain. The bed-and-breakfast we had arranged to stay in was already full. With no access to a telephone, we were simply given the name of another house to try. A cab dropped us in front of a home with no lights on. It was late and cold. Our legs and suitcases were dripping by the time we reached the door.

A pleasant but surprised couple answered our knock. When we asked for accommodations, they explained apologetically that they already had a boarder for the night. Our faces must have fallen as low as our spirits. Where would we go at this hour in such a downpour, in a tiny hamlet that seemed to have folded up for the night? They told us to wait inside the door. We heard muffled voices consulting. A few moments later, we were being ushered, with quiet smiles, into a cozy and pleasant room. Grateful and relieved beyond telling, we didn't ask questions. We sank, exhausted, into deep sleep in a comfortable double bed.

Next morning, the woman prepared a sumptuous Scottish breakfast for us: fruit juice, eggs, kippers, toast, butter, jam, and tea. It was not until we were packed and ready to leave that we discovered the extent of our hosts' generosity. With guest quarters already occupied, this couple had given us their own bedroom. They had slept in the living room.

The experience is etched in my memory. This couple cheerfully sacrificed their comfort to meet our need. Not a hint of sullenness or resignation shadowed the act. It was a simple, straightforward expression of hospitality—the first of many such experiences on that trip. When I came down with a fever in Italy, the woman whose pension we stayed in brought my mother a large bowl of expensive fruits to help me regain my health. It was a gift from the heart. On more than one occasion we received extraordinary generosity from total strangers.

What are your most vivid memories of receiving hospitality? of offering it?

It has been my experience that those of modest means are often the most willing to share what they have. A friend once recounted a trip to Mexico during which her group attended a village church for worship. Afterward, they were besieged with invitations to village homes for the Sunday meal. My friend knew that several families had pooled their meager resources to put on a feast. They cooked the one chicken they had and insisted that their guests take the best portions. My friend felt a mixture of wonder, gratitude, guilt, and humility. Her hosts offered what they had with joy and festivity. She received the meal as an act of pure generosity and fellowship.

Hospitality in Jewish and Christian Tradition

It is hard for us to comprehend, but hospitality in the ancient Near East was originally offered to complete strangers. People who appeared from the unknown might bear gifts or might be enemies. Because travel was a dangerous venture, codes of hospitality were strict. If a sworn enemy showed up at your doorstep asking for food and shelter, you were bound to supply his request, along with protection and safe passage as long as he was on your land. All sorts of people had to travel at times through "enemy territory," which meant that hospitality to strangers was a matter of mutual survival. It was a kind of social covenant, an implied commitment to transcend human differences in order to meet common human needs.

It is not surprising, then, that hospitality was a hallmark of virtue for ancient Jews and Christians. Yet in scripture, hospitality reflects a larger reality than human survival codes. It mysteriously links us to

God as well as to one another. Abraham and Sarah's hospitality to the three angels at Mamre unseals God's promise of a son in their old age (Gen. 18:1–10). The angels are representatives of God's own presence. In a phrase echoing their story, the author of Hebrews urges, "Do not neglect to show hospitality to strangers, for thereby some have entertained angels unawares" (13:2, RSV). Hospitality in biblical times was understood to be a way of meeting and receiving holy presence. Although providing hospitality was risky, it was a risk taken in faith. After all, the stranger just might be an angel—a messenger of God!

For Christians, the risk was seen as an opportunity to meet a singular stranger, the Risen Christ. Jesus made it clear that whatever kindness or neglect we show to "one of the least" of his brothers or sisters, we do to him. "Oft, oft, oft goes the Christ in the stranger's guise," says an old Celtic rune. Christian hospitality finds classic expression in the Rule of Saint Benedict: "All guests to the monastery should be welcomed as Christ, because He will say, 'I was a stranger, and you took me in.'"[1]

Professor of mission and evangelism Mortimer Arias tells us that the remarkable explosion of Christianity in the first century was due not only to proclamation of the gospel but also to the extraordinary quality of Christian hospitality. It evidently so impressed one Roman emperor that he commanded his provincial governors to begin practicing hospitality like that of the Christians, if they wanted their empire to grow and remain civil. The quality of mutual respect and love in those early Christian communities must have created hospitable space for very different kinds of people to enter and find a spiritual home. Arias calls that attractive character of early Christianity "centripetal mission" or "evangelization by hospitality."[2] There was, for many, something irresistibly enticing about a community that *saw* Christ "in friend and stranger." Those outside the circle were drawn in like leaf tendrils to light.

Can you name an incident in your life where you felt you met Christ in the guise of a stranger?

The Essence of Hospitality

Hospitality means receiving the other, from the heart, into my own dwelling place. It entails providing for the need, comfort, and delight of the other with all the openness, respect, freedom, tenderness, and joy that love itself embodies.

This is how I like to describe the nature of hospitality. The *other* can be literally anyone apart from ourselves. Ancient practices of

What is the essence of hospitality for you? Write down your own definition. What do you think the most important ingredients of hospitality are? Take a few minutes to note your response.

hospitality had particular application to strangers and enemies. This is a challenging notion for us today but one that deserves our attention. Who are the "strangers" and "enemies" in our midst: immigrants? addicts? the mentally ill? people who differ from us in ethnic origin, religious conviction, or political affiliation? Do adolescents in general, or our own teenagers in particular, feel at times like complete strangers to us?

Our "dwelling place" may be physical—a room, apartment, or house. It may also be a metaphor for mental and emotional "space." We can invite others into an inner world of thoughts and feelings, sharing gifts of heart and mind. Gracious inner space gives others room to play, question, and converse; room to be heard and understood; room to reveal themselves as they choose.

Hospitality is essentially an expression of love. It is a movement to include the guest in the very best of what we have received and can therefore offer. It is the act of sharing *who we are* as well as *what we have*. Thus, hospitality of heart lies beneath every hospitable act. The classic elements of hospitality offered to guests are food and drink, shelter and rest, protection and care, enjoyment and peace. These paired categories cover a basic range of physical, emotional, and spiritual needs. They reveal that hospitality is concerned with the total well-being of the guest.

In offering shelter, nourishment, rest, and enjoyment to our guests, we often discover that they gift us with their presence. The relationship of host and guest is one of mutuality; "the very root of the word 'hospitality' . . . *hospes* means both host and guest."[3] The uncanny sense of receiving more than we give applies to many situations. I once telephoned an acquaintance who was dying from cancer, wanting to offer what solace I could. The conversation completely reversed my expectations of who was ministering to whom. I received a powerful witness to resurrection faith from a man who was full of joy and amply prepared to face his Maker.

God's Hospitality to Us: Gift and Grace

Hospitality begins with God. Because we have a supremely hospitable God, in whose image and likeness we are made, we are capable of reflecting hospitality back to God, to others, to the earth, and even to ourselves. Hospitality to strangers does not come easily to us. Until we are deeply rooted in the experience of God's grace, we have neither the living example nor the strength of commitment to live hospitably in a hostile world. Whatever form our hospitality may take, it is already a response to God.

God's first great act of hospitality to us is the Creation itself. "In the beginning" God made a home, a dwelling place for creatures of the Divine Hand. And what a home it is! Expanding on imagery from Genesis 2, we may envision it as a garden of delight, filled with every conceivable provision: food, shelter, beauty, and peace. All is gift—given to us for nourishment and joy and given into our care to tend with gratitude.

The most basic image of God's hospitality in creation is food. It is no accident that sharing food is the primary expression of hospitality in human culture. Theologian Alexander Schmemann notes that "centuries of secularism have failed to transform eating into something strictly utilitarian. Food is still treated with reverence. A meal is still a rite—the last 'natural sacrament' of family and friendship."[4]

In Orthodox theology, the physical matter of creation was to have been, for human beings, a means of spiritual grace and communion with God. We were to respond in thanksgiving and blessing. Yet on the heels of the Creation came the Fall. The intended communion between God and human beings through creation was lost. What went wrong?

One could say that we chose to receive gifts of hospitality without thanking or even acknowledging the Host. We tried to provide for ourselves rather than to receive provision from God. We even made every effort to become Host of the universe in God's place! It was a tragic breach of relationship—an undisguised denial and rejection of divine love.

But God's love did not leave us in our self-imposed exile. For Christians, the second great act of divine hospitality is the Incarnation: "The Word became flesh and dwelt among us" (John 1:14 RSV). It is a rather inconceivable thing that God should come among us *in person* to forgive, reconcile, and restore human creatures to the communion God intends. In fact, the apprehension of God-in-Christ was so momentous to the early Christians that Paul could describe the mystery only as *New Creation*. The *first* Creation and the *new* Creation provide us with a framework for comprehending the immensity of divine hospitality to us.

God-in-Christ enters "enemy territory," a society of people so immersed in rebellion and delusion that they no longer recognize or acknowledge him. Into such an estranged world the Holy One can come only as stranger—one unrecognized, unsought, and unloved by most of those to whom he came.

The Creator God has spread out for our delight a banquet . . . of rivers and lakes, of rain and sunshine, of rich earth and of amazing flowers, of handsome trees and of dancing fishes, of contemplative animals and of whistling winds, of dry and wet seasons, of cold and hot climates . . . and so are we, blessings ourselves, invited to the banquet.

Matthew Fox

Why would God—the Holy, Righteous, and Pure—choose to enter the messy circumstances of our perverse and distorted humanity? Evidently the divine eye sees through a different lens than we expect. It is not that God doesn't perceive with crystal clarity the terrible travesty of our sin. But God seems to see even the greatest evils of which we are capable as mortal wounds. God sees the ugliness of our sin with the eyes of the Great Physician who yearns to heal. God feels the tragic consequences of our alienation with the heart of the Good Shepherd who suffers compassion.

How do you experience God as a "stranger" in your life? in the life of our culture?

If we can discern motives for God becoming human, they are to be likened to the monastic practice in the Middle Ages of hospitality to travelers and wayfarers that developed into caring for the sick. Modern hospitals and hospices embody the legacy of these earlier Christian ministries. Like the merciful Samaritan of Jesus' parable, God steps into our situation and stoops to tend the deadly wound of our sin. "Those who are well have no need of a physician, but those who are sick," says Jesus to the Pharisees. "For I have come to call not the righteous but sinners" (Matt. 9:12, 13).

The lengths to which God will go to heal us are fully revealed on the cross. A costly divine forgiveness lies at the heart of New Creation hospitality. Jesus' arms stretched on the beam—extended to release our sin, to receive all in love, to invite us to new life—are the very image of God's unaccountably gracious hospitality to us. On the cross, Jesus lives out his own parable of the father whose open arms gladly receive back a wayward child. Recall how the father in that story throws a lavish feast to celebrate his son's restoration to the family! Such a heart represents the essence of divine hospitality. In Baptism, God opens the door to the family house and says, "Welcome home, my child!" In the Eucharist, God brings us to the dinner table and cries, "Eat! Eat! I made this feast especially for you!"

How do you experience the hospitality of God? of Christ? of the Spirit?

God-in-Christ has received us into his own dwelling place, where we find in plenty all we have need of—forgiveness, healing, reconciliation, comfort, peace, joy, communion—abundant life for body and soul. Could there be any hospitality to match that of the Host of Heaven?

Our Hospitality to God: Receptivity and Response

To speak of our hospitality to such a God is humbling, for no response seems adequate. It is not in our power to make "adequate" responses. God asks only that we offer whatever love and gratitude we have in us. In the upside-down order of grace, the more we empty out our love to God the more we are filled with it.

Our first act of hospitality to God is to *receive* what God gives. How distressing for God to offer grace so freely, only to have us refuse or ignore it! We have devised many excuses for closing the door on divine love. We allow ourselves to become distracted and preoccupied, so we remain unaware of the value of God's gifts. We decide that we are unworthy to receive anything from God, so we refuse the gift. We convince ourselves that we must first prove worthy of receiving something, so we spend our days trying to *earn* what can only be *received*. It takes genuine humility to receive God's gifts. This simple truth is illustrated in the following story from the desert wisdom tradition:

Can you identify some ways in which you "close the door" on God's gifts to you? Do you find it hard to receive gifts from others? Hard to give gifts? Why?

> Once some of the elders came to Scete, and Abba John the Dwarf was with them. And when they were dining, one of the priests, a very great old man, got up to give each one a little cup of water to drink, and no one would take it from him except John the Dwarf. The others were surprised, and afterwards they asked him: How is it that you, the least of all, have presumed to accept the services of this great old man? He replied: Well, when I get up to give people a drink of water, I am happy if they all take it; and for that reason on this occasion I took the drink, that he might be rewarded, and not feel sad because nobody accepted the cup from him. And at this all admired his discretion.[5]

When we become willing to receive from God, we naturally express the hospitality of gratitude. Adoration, thanks, and blessing are the most fitting ways to receive the Holy One hospitably into our inner "dwelling place." Every expression of trust, praise, and joy delights our God. Gratitude expands our hearts, creating more space for God and others.

What is the place of gratitude in your own spiritual journey right now?

We offer hospitality to God when we make ourselves consciously present to the Divine Presence and listen for what the Spirit is communicating. The story of Jesus with Martha and Mary (Luke 10:38–42) offers a striking illustration. We usually think of Martha as the one who offers hospitality to Jesus and his disciples. Does she not invite them into her home and busy herself with much serving? We tend to assume that Mary "does nothing but sit" and listen passively to a charismatic Jesus. We have imagined that the story pits service against prayer, action against contemplation.

But Mary *chooses* to sit and listen to Jesus. In doing so, she lays aside the traditional role her culture and sister expect of her. Is her choice not also an act of service to Jesus? He came to preach a message, to proclaim God's reign, to invite conversion of life. Jesus yearned for people who would hear his words. Mary chooses to receive the gift of Jesus' presence with her own presence, to receive his message with her hearing. Is it possible that Jesus experienced Mary's listening as a deeper act of hospitality than the provision of food and drink?

Listening attentively to the great Other is a service of hospitality. God has a deep and passionate desire for us to listen for the divine word. This word is our life-source, our means of communion with One whose love we are destined to share. God wants fellowship with us! Every means by which we allow ourselves to be present, to listen, and to be encountered by the Holy One is a form of hospitality.

What kinds of hospitality do you offer directly to God? What would you like to be able to offer?

Finally, however, listening implies obedience. The hospitality of attentiveness remains stillborn unless joined by the hospitality of acting in accord with what is heard. To *do* the will of God is the ultimate expression of receiving the Holy Other into the inner sanctuary of our hearts and the larger temple of our lives. Hospitality to God is finally expressed in our intentions and actions toward every creature God loves. We are not permitted to separate our love for God from our love for others.

Our Hospitality to One Another: Compassion and Community

Our love for one another is a direct expression of our love for God: "those who do not love a brother or sister whom they have seen, cannot love God whom they have not seen" (1 John 4:20). One of our more persistent problems is that we do not *see* one another as sisters or brothers, much less love one another as such.

An ancient Rabbi once asked his pupils how they could tell when the night had ended and the day was on its way back. "Could it be," asked one student, "when you can see an animal in the distance and tell whether it is a sheep or a dog?" "No," answered the Rabbi. "Could it be," asked another, "when you look at a tree in the distance and tell whether it is a fig tree or a peach tree?" "No," said the Rabbi. "Well, then what is it?" his pupils demanded. "It is when you look on the face of any [person] and can see . . . your brother [or sister]. Because if you cannot do this, then no matter what time it is, it is still night."[6]

What does it take to see in *every* other person a sister or brother? If we cannot truly accept our weaknesses as well as our gifts, we will be unable to love others in their brokenness and giftedness.

Once again we are speaking of humility. A humble heart is hospitable. It accepts people as they are—a mix of familiar and unfamiliar, good and bad. Acceptance leaves others free to be themselves in our dwelling places. It does not require them to be like us. Our guest may be friend or total stranger, cognitively impaired or emotionally estranged, different in race, faith, social circumstance, or political persuasion. Hospitality means giving all guests the freedom to reveal themselves as they choose. A guest should not need to fear personal attack, rejection, or conversion efforts on the part of the host. *Freedom* is the medium of human exchange in true hospitality.

I recall an occasion when my family, en route to Florida for vacation, was invited to stay overnight with acquaintances. It was at the height of the Vietnam war, a war my college-age brothers were strongly opposed to. During the course of dinner conversation with our host family, the subject of the war arose. When my brothers rather naively voiced their sentiments, the table fellowship immediately palled. Clearly our hosts disapproved of my brothers' views. Their capacity to make us feel welcome as guests was affected by this difference. The gracious home with all its amenities was no longer hospitable space.

The practice of hospitality cannot depend on shared views or values. When we impose or imply such conditions, we are offering entertainment rather than Christian hospitality. We must learn to value the strangeness of the stranger, as community-building consultant Parker Palmer points out:

> Hospitality means letting the stranger remain a stranger while offering hospitality nonetheless. It means honoring the fact that strangers already have a relationship—rooted in our common humanity—without having to build one on intimate interpersonal knowledge, without having to become friends.[7]

This perspective goes against the grain of North American culture. We tend to pride ourselves on being friendly and on making friends easily. We also tend to see the world as divided into two camps: friends or enemies. If others do not conform to our norms of friendship, we may find ourselves uncertain of how to navigate the relationship. Perhaps the idea of the stranger is so threatening that we can scarcely conceive of any value in strangeness. Yet the very unfamiliarity of the stranger is a means through which we gain new perspective on our too-familiar lives. One who is different can shake us loose from stereotypes and false convictions. We need to preserve room for the stranger in our hospitality.

Sometimes we experience the shock of encountering a hidden side in someone we have known for years. Changes in attitude and behavior can make strangers out of spouses or close friends. It is most disorienting to find someone with whom we live or work becoming a personal enemy. Practicing hospitality with our nearest and dearest can at times be as challenging as with complete strangers!

I have spoken of the risk involved in offering hospitality to strangers. There is also risk in refusing hospitality. We may miss God's gift. Had they not invited the stranger to enter their lodging and sup with them, Cleopas and his friend (Luke 24:13–49) would have missed recognizing their traveling companion as the risen Christ!

> *[P]eople do not enter our lives to be coerced or manipulated, but to enrich us by their differences, and to be graciously received in the name of Christ.*
> *Elizabeth Canham*

> *Benedict says, "Be here; find Christ in the restless teenager, demanding parent, insensitive employer, dull preacher, lukewarm congregation." . . . create a hospitable space for whoever and whatever God sends into [your] lives now.*
> *Elizabeth Canham*

Invitations to Explore

Practicing hospitality of heart has implications for every common dimension of our lives. It affects our homes, workplaces, neighborhoods, schools, churches, and ways of being public citizens. A few possibilities are sketched below; I encourage you to add your own creative reflections.

Hospitality at Home

There is a very real sense in which hospitality "begins at home." Family relationships are the first place to put the art of Christian hospitality into practice. Children are not personal possessions but sojourners in our homes. They belong to God, who entrusts them to our care through their growing years. Providing safety and love are essential to the internal hospitality of family life. Yet security is balanced by allowing increased freedom over time, appropriate to each child's capacity and level of development.

Parents provide a hospitable home by being genuinely present to their children—available to listen, affirm, guide, and correct. Taking time to listen and talk to one another is one of the most important expressions of hospitality in home life, especially in an age when time is at a premium. It requires self-sacrifice on the part of adults to make this a priority. One of the best ways to ensure family time is to protect the dinner hour several days of each week.

Are children free to learn from their mistakes in your home? Parents can be clear that certain behaviors are not acceptable (physical aggression, lying, stealing, cheating) while making it equally clear that each child is loved and accepted as a person. Making distinctions between the person who chooses and the behavior chosen is important. When our children make poor choices, we can let them know that we trust them to be capable of better ones. Hospitality leaves room for change and growth.

How do you respond when your children's aptitudes and values differ from yours? You love classical music and your teenager lives for hard rock; you're an outdoor enthusiast and your child prefers the company of books. Parents who affirm each child's unique personality and gifts offer hospitable space to little ones who seem at times like strangers in our homes. Since children in the same family can be vastly different from one another, parental affirmation of diversity also helps children accept the differences between themselves.

Family life involves the daily interactions of people with different desires and agendas living in common space. Conflicts inevitably occur. Learning to forgive the daily scrapes and bruises that result from bumping up against one another's interests is a central expression of hospitality. Forgiveness is a direct sharing of God's hospitality to us. It frees us from the bondage of resentment and desire for retribution. It frees us from anxiety and constraint. Forgiveness opens the door to renewed care and concern for one another, clearing a path for healed and healthy relationships.[8]

Playing with children is an expression of hospitality, for it offers the gifts of delight and joy. From making up stories to camping ventures, play is important to the child in all of us. We need times of sheer fun and silliness, times for a little "divine madness" to liven us with levity. Laughter, imagination, and play enlarge the soul.

When adult relationships in a home embody presence, acceptance, affirmation, forgiveness, and playfulness, there is plenty of room for children, friends, and strangers to enter comfortably into family life. By contrast, when these adult relationships are marked by self-interest, controlling behavior, unresolved conflict, and anxiety, very little hospitality can be offered to anyone—inside or outside the family.

The quality of hospitality within family relationships profoundly impacts the hospitality offered to those outside who enter the home. My husband and I used to visit friends who seemed to enjoy triggering each other's sensitivities in our presence. Each tried to gain our sympathy against the spouse. As friends and guests, it was a most uncomfortable position to be placed in. There was no room for us to be ourselves or, in truth, to be with them. There was room only to take sides in a chronic power struggle.

Author Wendy Wright suggests that families can express the original vision of hospitality to strangers in a variety of ways. One way is through adoption, especially of hard-to-place children who have siblings, disabilities, or mixed racial background. Another might be sheltering a homeless couple, a pregnant teen, or a young person estranged from his or her family. It can be an act of hospitality to take in a foreign student or a foster child for a period of time.[9] Such expressions of hospitality will involve particular challenges and should not be undertaken lightly or simply to appear noble. Each family needs to decide, under the leading of the Spirit, what forms of hospitality are appropriate to its circumstances.

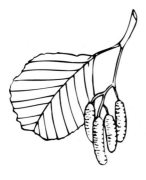

Hospitality in the Workplace

A central expression of hospitality at work is listening openly to others' ideas, concerns, and critiques. Hospitality means being receptive to good ideas, whether they come from a mail clerk or a senior vice president.

If you have an office door, leave it open at regular intervals. Indicate your willingness to welcome others into your work space. It signals that you value the thoughts and questions of your coworkers. You will doubtless need time for work when you are not available to others as well. Keep a balance.

Is the physical ambiance of your workplace inviting or sterile? Consider what you might do to make it more welcoming. Good lighting and functional equipment are important. Is your furniture comfortable and invitingly arranged? Small touches such as plants and pictures add pleasure for the eye and heart.

Honoring appropriate boundaries in common work areas is an act of hospitality. Do not enter another person's work space too often or without good reason. In work areas without separate rooms, avoid loud or prolonged conversation. Be courteous in your language; even humor can be used to mock or exclude certain people.

In meetings, actively encourage (but do not force) the participation of those who are more reticent. If you tend to talk willingly or you hold a position of authority, deliberately withhold your speech in order to leave room for others to speak.

If you are a supervisor or manager, you have more power to make the workplace hospitable. Aim to create an organization that allows employees to grow both personally and professionally. Be sure people have access to the information they need to do their jobs. Build an environment of trust and credibility rather than of fear and suspicion. Keep in touch with your employees, offering encouragement, appropriate praise, and constructive suggestions. Be careful not to overload your employees with meetings and committees; give them sufficient time to do the work for which they will be held accountable.

Hospitality in the Neighborhood

In typical neighborhoods today, residents might know only their immediate neighbors; the rest are virtual strangers. Work patterns, frequent moves, fear of the unknown, and individualism all contribute to our increasing isolation from one another. How can we help make our neighborhoods more welcoming places?

Make the effort to become acquainted with your neighbors. Neighbors who trust one another can offer many small courtesies that make residential areas safer and more hospitable. You need not be close friends to watch someone's apartment or home or to feed pets when a neighbor is away.

Take time to listen to a lonely neighbor. Many older people live alone or with a spouse who needs sustained care. To be able to unburden anxiety or relieve boredom through conversation is a real help. There are a few "stay-at-home moms" in my neighborhood who crave adult company while caring for small children. When I am especially busy, it is a real discipline for me simply to offer the hospitality of ten minutes of attentive listening.

Single parents feel the burden of working and raising children alone. You might offer to watch the kids for an evening, freeing your single neighbor to do necessary errands or enjoy a movie without having to pay a sitter.

If you like to organize, throw a block party to help people on your street get acquainted. Invite everyone to cook up their favorite dish

When a street is cordoned off, refreshments provided, music and games offered by the neighbors to each other, and people are given an excuse to mingle for a few hours on a summer evening, then the street takes on new and more hospitable meaning. Do it often enough and that street becomes a place where people pass each other with warm memories and hopeful expectations rather than unawareness and suspicion.

Parker J. Palmer

to share, or set up grills in a central yard for a big cookout. Plan games for the kids and get parents involved in supervising them.

Parker Palmer suggests canvassing the neighborhood for "a 'catalog' of personal skills and resources."[10] Are there people on your street with special skills or hobbies they would be willing to share with neighbors, either freely or in exchange for a different talent? Someone might want to share carpentry skills with a person who could take care of a mending pile. Others might be happy to change the oil in your car for the love of being a "grease monkey." When people are willing to share their talents and services with neighbors for the sheer joy of it, hospitality has taken root in the neighborhood!

Hospitality in Our Churches

Of all places, Christian churches ought to be supremely hospitable. As the body of Christ, the church is called to reflect the hospitality God has shown us in Jesus. Is your church a hospitable community? Here are some questions to help you evaluate.

How does your church welcome visitors and newcomers? Does your congregation convey the spirit of an open, receptive community or a closed, social clique?

How does your church make its own members welcome? Are every person's gifts honored in the community? How are weaker members of the "family" supported and encouraged? How does the community respond to those who depart in some way from social norms or expectations and who may therefore struggle to find a community of love and acceptance: people with physical handicaps or learning disabilities; gay, lesbian, or transgendered individuals; the families of someone incarcerated; those who suffer from mental illness?

How constructively does your church deal with conflict? As with families, every church has its share of discord. Because we differ from one another in temperament, personality, upbringing, and conviction, we will come to loggerheads over certain decisions. How much room is there for theological disagreement in your church? Do people feel free to express their deepest convictions without fear of being personally attacked or rejected? Hospitality does not require us to agree with one another; it requires that we offer free space for speaking and listening.

Is your listening to one another encompassed by a deeper listening to God? In the church, our trusting invitation to receive the clarity of the Spirit is the best container for our hospitality to other people's beliefs and interpretations.

Does your church see intercessory prayer as a form of hospitality to others? When we intercede for others in prayer, we welcome them into our inmost sanctuary of compassion. We participate in the spacious hospitality of God's grace for each person. Since hospitality has a special place for the stranger, praying for our enemies (inside or outside the church) is a most fitting expression of the heart's hospitality.

How does your faith community receive its pastors? Your pastoral leaders need your love, encouragement, and prayer as much as you need theirs. Many priests and ministers feel isolated, embattled, overwhelmed, and inadequate. They feel they never have enough time to meet all the demands of church life, let alone respond adequately to family or personal needs. Guilt over lack of a personal prayer life is common.

Here are a few simple acts of hospitality you could offer to the leaders we invest with great expectations and responsibilities. Listen to your pastors. Find out what a typical work week is like. Ask if they take regular days off. Do they have sufficient time for personal spiritual nurture to sustain the service of their ministry? Ask what kind of support you can offer that would enable them to continue growing in vital spiritual lives. Then give them the support they need. Pray for your church leaders, during worship and through the week. Invite your pastor (and family) to your home occasionally for enjoyment and fellowship.

Finally, how does your church offer hospitality to those who may never enter its sanctuary? Do you provide overnight facilities to the homeless? meals for the hungry? prison visitation or support for the families of prisoners? a home for new refugees? What we do for the least, we do for our Lord.

Does your church practice the "passing of the peace"? If so, is it understood as an occasion to share the peace of Christ that enables us to transcend differences and be reconciled to one another in love?

When pastor André Trocmé was once asked why he inspired an entire French village to risk giving shelter to Jews during World War II, he replied simply, "I could not bear to be separated from Jesus."

Civic Hospitality

Hospitality in our larger social communities finds expression in the structures of human society and governance. Are the basic resources of our common life—homes, schools, medical care, and recreation— widely available? Perhaps we need to work for zoning regulations in our neighborhoods that ensure housing options for people of various income levels. We can work for clean, safe parks that are located within walking distance of various neighborhoods. Community programs in sports, recreation, and arts that encourage healthy child and family activity are an important form of civic hospitality.

How hospitable are our schools? Do we need to work for alternative ways of funding schools to ensure more equitable distribution of educational resources? How hospitable is our educational process? Highly competitive classrooms create a hostile and intimidating learning environment for most students. In such settings, "knowledge" is often an external commodity to be digested like lunch, and "learning" is little more than conforming to a teacher's expectations. Hospitable education allows students to discover and express the understandings they already have. It encourages learners to connect their life experiences with larger questions, issues, and perspectives. Teachers can welcome students into classrooms where they are given freedom to explore and express their growing understandings in safety and peace.[11]

Many U.S. citizens are not registered to vote, especially those who are recent immigrants or who are poor and undereducated. Can we ensure that all who are eligible to vote are registered and have the basic information necessary to make informed choices? Are voting sites accessible to the whole community?

Does your town have a "welcome wagon"? These organizations are effective in orienting newcomers to the resources and services of the community. They also encourage new residents to become active in areas of public concern that interest them.

Our discussion of hospitality would not be complete without including the natural world. Many other creatures, upon whom we depend more than we know, inhabit this planet with us. The results of our exploitation of nature have never been so grievously apparent. If hospitality means receiving the *other* into our own dwelling place with freedom, respect, and joy—if it means welcoming strangers in our midst and providing for their need, comfort, and delight—then what does it mean with respect to God's other creatures? How can we be hospitable to the inhabitants of the earth whose dwelling places we are rapidly crowding out and despoiling? We must give serious attention to this question if we wish to be hospitable to God, who created all living things and a world sufficient in provision for every kind.

Rooted and Grounded in Love

Do some aspects of civic hospitality sound more like "social justice" than "hospitality"? Hospitality to the stranger is, in truth, a way of "doing justice." The biblical meaning of justice is simply "right relationships" with one another. Showing kindness to the wayfarer, supporting the widow and orphan, taking in the homeless poor, and offering hospitality to strangers—these were expressions of just relations with the neighbor in scripture. They remain so today, even in a more complex society.

We are no doubt afraid of some forms of hospitality. They seem naive and unrealistic in a society that has become violent and dangerous. Certain expressions of hospitality are more risky than others. We need to make choices based on what we believe God is calling us to do for the sake of Christ and the world God so loves.

Our hospitality is rooted and grounded in God's hospitality to us in Christ. Until we know this love deep in the core of our hearts, we will have neither courage nor trust to share hospitality with others in more than superficial ways. Christian hospitality is a risk taken in faith. It is an act of sacrificial joy offered in the full light of the risen Christ, a light that transforms our perspective on everything.

As we learn to receive God's hospitality to us, we will become more hospitable to God, to one another, and to our fellow creatures. This will make us a different kind of community. Others will see something enticing in us. Perhaps they will even say "See how they love one another!"

Notes to the Text

1. *The Rule of St. Benedict*, trans. Anthony C. Meisel and M. L. Mastro (Garden City, NY: Image Books, 1975), 89. See chap. 53 for Benedict's vision of receiving Christ in the guest.

2. Mortimer Arias, "Centripetal Mission or Evangelization by Hospitality," *Missiology: An International Review* 10, no. 1 (1982): 69-81.

3. Parker J. Palmer, *The Company of Strangers: Christians and the Renewal of America's Public Life* (New York: Crossroad, 1986), 69.

4. Alexander Schmemann, *For the Life of the World: Sacraments and Orthodoxy* (Crestwood, NY: St. Vladimir's Seminary Press, 1973), 16.

5. Thomas Merton, *The Wisdom of the Desert* (New York: New Directions, 1960), 70.

6. Printed in "Social Concerns Newsletter from the Passionists," Union City, NJ. You can find this story online at http://www.spiritualityandpractice.com/books/excerpts.php?id=22854. The source referenced there is "Peacemaking: Day by Day," a booklet published by Pax Christi, 1990.

7. Palmer, *Company of Strangers*, 68.

8. Forgiveness is a thorny topic in family life, and more complex than a single paragraph can describe. For example, where there is no recognition of fault and no serious repentance, forgiveness on the part of the offended party is not likely to open the relationship for healing. For more on this important subject, see *Forgiving Your Family* by Kathleen Fischer (Nashville: Upper Room Books, 2005). I also have two published books on the general subject: *The Way of Forgiveness*, Companions in Christ, participant book (Nashville: Upper Room Books, 2002); and *Forgiveness: A Lenten Study* (Louisville, KY: Westminster John Knox Press, 2014).

9. See Wendy M. Wright, *Sacred Dwelling: A Spirituality of Family Life* (New York: Crossroad, 1989), 60. Motives become important here. Some people have taken in foreign students for the summer in order to exploit their labor, and some parents take in foster children in order to receive state funding. These are closer to expressions of hostility than hospitality.

10. Palmer, *Company of Strangers*, 151.

11. Clearly this refers to the ambiance of learning created by the teacher's own attitudes and manner. If the external reality of a school is dominated by violence and security issues, the possibility of real education is the first casualty. For an excellent discussion of hospitable teaching, see Parker J. Palmer, *To Know as We Are Known* (San Francisco: Harper & Row, 1983), and his landmark book, *The Courage to Teach* (San Francisco: Jossey-Bass, 1998, 2007). See also Henri J. M. Nouwen, *Reaching Out* (New York: Doubleday & Co., 1975), 58–63.

Notes to the Sidebars

Matthew Fox, iconoclastic Dominican scholar turned Episcopal priest, originator of "Creation Spirituality." *Original Blessing* (Santa Fe, NM: Bear & Company, 1983), 112–13.

Elizabeth Canham, Episcopal priest, retreat leader, spiritual director, and author. "A School for the Lord's Service," in *Weavings* 9, no. 1 (January–February 1994): 13.

Elizabeth Canham, "A School for the Lord's Service," 15.

Parker J. Palmer, Quaker author, educator, activist, senior partner and founder of the Center for Courage & Renewal. *The Company of Strangers: Christians and the Renewal of America's Public Life* (New York: Crossroad, 1986), 145.

CHAPTER 10

Putting It All Together

❧

Developing a Rule of Life

We make no progress because we have not squarely taken our own measure, we do not persevere in the work we begin, and want to acquire virtue without effort.

Abba Dorotheos of Gaza

Certain kinds of plants need support in order to grow properly. Tomatoes need stakes, and beans must attach themselves to suspended strings. Creeping vines like clematis and wisteria will grow on any structure they can find. Rambling roses take kindly to garden walls, archways, and trellises. Without support, these plants would collapse in a heap on the ground. Their blossoms would not have the space and sun they need to flourish, and their fruits would rot in contact with the soil. We would be unable to enjoy their beauty and sustenance.

When it comes to spiritual growth, human beings are much like these plants. We need structure and support. Otherwise our spirituality grows only in a confused and disorderly way. The fruit of the Spirit in us gets tangled and is susceptible to corruption, and the beauty of our lives is diminished. We need structure in order to have enough space, air, and light to flourish. Structure gives us the freedom to grow as we are meant to.

There is a name in Christian tradition for the kind of structure that supports our spiritual growth. It is called a *rule of life*. Without a rule of life, very little of what you have been reading and exploring in this book will prove to be of lasting value to you. This final chapter is an opportunity for you to begin putting together what you have learned. It is time to make some choices concerning the spiritual practices you feel called to engage in.

It is unlikely that we will deepen our relationship with God in a casual or haphazard manner. There will be a need for some intentional commitment and some reorganization in our own lives.

William O. Paulsell

149

What Is a Rule of Life?

A rule of life is a pattern of spiritual disciplines that provides structure and direction for growth in holiness. When we speak of *patterns* in our life, we mean attitudes, behaviors, or elements that are routine, repeated, regular. Indeed, the Latin term for "rule" is *regula*, from which our words *regular* and *regulate* derive. A rule of life is not meant to be highly restrictive, although it certainly asks for genuine commitment. It is meant to help us establish a rhythm of daily living, a basic order within which new freedoms can grow. A rule of life, like a trellis, curbs our tendency to wander and supports our frail efforts to grow spiritually.

To shift the metaphor, a personal rule is a way of ordering our lives to catch the wind of grace. As our spiritual practices open us over and over to the expansive flow of God's loving guidance, we find ourselves drawn into a holistic sense of life—an integrated orientation toward God including our deeper attention; attuned senses; lens of perception; choice of attitudes; and habits of thought, speech, and action. We choose particular disciplines to help us reframe the whole of our lives around God, the true center of all. One of my dear mentors, Rueben Job, recounts how his family once experienced the great Northern Lights. Vacationing on a remote island in the North Woods, they discovered that the best way to see these lights was to lie flat on their backs on the dock. Rueben points out that spiritual disciplines are simply ways we position ourselves to see divine beauty and grace more clearly, so we might respond fullheartedly.[1]

Throughout Christian history, those who have been serious about maturing in the spiritual life have embraced discipline. Remember that *discipline* means training and practice. Author William Paulsell notes that while we tend to resist the whole idea of discipline, we have to admit that it allows us to make the most of our God-given gifts:

Athletes, musicians, writers, scientists, and others progress in their fields because they are well-disciplined people. Unfortunately, there is a tendency to think that in matters of faith we should pray, meditate, and engage in other spiritual disciplines only when we feel like it.[2]

The desert elder who wisely diagnosed our spiritual condition in the epigraph of this chapter understood the ancient human predicament. We do not know our own measure—neither our true capabilities nor limitations. We do not persevere in our spiritual practices until they yield their full fruits. Children of a quick-fix culture, we want "virtue without effort," transformation without labor, life without death. Our prayers are like intermittent geysers. Our desire for God runs hot then cold. Divided in our loyalties, we become diluted in spirit. We need a clear center and unapologetic priorities to grow spiritually. What is at stake is the reach of our spiritual maturity, the depth of our human integrity, the authenticity of our Christian character.

After all, the purpose of a rule of life is to help us grow into wholeness and holiness. God calls us to be holy as God is holy, to grow into greater intimacy with the One we are created to resemble: "Beloved, we are God's children now; what we will be has not yet been revealed. What we do know is this: when he is revealed, we will be like him, for we will see him as he is" (1 John 3:2). A rule of life allows us to cultivate and deepen this growing likeness.

Yet this gradual transformation into the full image and likeness of God does not happen automatically. It is not a process of natural growth, like that of a sapling into a mature tree. Rather, it is a process that requires the death of much that seems natural to us in order to allow a deeper mystery of our life in God to rise up. Maturation in faith is like the metamorphosis of a caterpillar into a moth. The caterpillar must yield up the life it knows and submit to the mystery of interior transformation. It emerges from this process transfigured, with wings that give it freedom to fly. It is naturally attracted to light, although still vulnerable to ruin if deceived by artificial light. A rule of life gives us a way to enter the lifelong process of personal transformation. Its disciplines help us to shed the familiar but constricting "old self" and allow our "new self" in Christ to be formed—the true self that is naturally attracted to the light of God.

We have to find a central focus that pulls together the scattered fragments and shredded fringes of life as we must live it. . . . We skip from thing to thing and are drawn in many directions of pleasure and grief.

Dallas Willard

Examples of Personal Rules

Christian tradition is filled with examples of both corporate and personal rules of life. Perhaps the best known of all corporate rules is that of Saint Benedict, attractive and practical because of its moderate tone and commonsense wisdom. The Rule of Saint Benedict describes both inward attitudes and outward practices to guide monks in their common life.[3]

Personal rules are formulated by individuals to help them receive and express more fully the gifts of the Spirit. They are very diverse, reflecting the needs and spiritual aspirations of those who devise them. Some focus more on developing inner attitudes, values, and habits such as humility, charity, faith, and gentleness. Others emphasize specific practices such as prayer, fasting, and self-examination. These, of course, are meant to lead us toward the inner attitudes mentioned as well as to their outward expression in human community.

When Pope John XXIII was a seminary student, he included the following elements in his rule:

- Fifteen minutes of silent prayer upon rising in the morning

- Fifteen minutes of spiritual reading

- Before bed, a general examination of conscience followed by confession; then identifying issues for the next morning's prayer

- Arranging the hours of the day to make this rule possible; setting aside specific time for prayer, study, recreation, and sleep

- Making a habit of turning the mind to God in prayer[4]

A very different style of rule was developed by Catherine de Hueck Doherty, the Russian baroness who founded Madonna House in Ontario, Canada. Drawing on the Russian hermit tradition, she recommends a monthly retreat into silence and solitude for a twenty-four-hour period. A hermitage (*poustinia* in Russian) is a simple cottage isolated from human traffic that allows for fasting, prayer, and immersion in scripture.[5]

Dorothy Day, who began a ministry called "houses of hospitality" for the poor in New York, had another kind of personal rule. She received the Eucharist daily, read the Bible daily, and kept a journal that was, for her, a form of prayer. She saw Christ in the faces of the poor.[6]

Martin Luther King Jr. developed a rule to guide the nonviolent protests of the civil rights movement. His rule emphasized the spiritual principles and inner attitudes undergirding one's actions, although it also included specific practices, such as meditation, prayer, and service. Every demonstrator had to agree to this rule:

1. Meditate daily on the teachings and life of Jesus.
2. Remember always that the nonviolent movement in Birmingham seeks justice and reconciliation, not victory.
3. Walk and talk in the manner of love, for God is love.
4. Pray daily to be used by God in order that all might be free.
5. Sacrifice personal wishes in order that all might be free.

6. Observe with both friend and foe the ordinary rules of courtesy.
7. Seek to perform regular service for others and the world.
8. Refrain from violence of fist, tongue, or heart.
9. Strive to be in good spiritual and bodily health.
10. Follow the directions of the movement and the captains of a demonstration.[7]

It should be clear from these few examples that there can be great latitude in a personal rule of life. Your rule will be tailor-made—unique to your personality, circumstances, and needs—yet in harmony with the basic historic practices of Christian life and faith through the centuries. Developing a personal rule is therefore a matter of discernment.

It can be helpful to see the variety of rules that communities and individuals have devised over time. Yet we cannot live another's life, and, no matter how excellent, another's life will not fit us. If we try to imitate another too closely, we are merely role-playing. For example, I have come to see the "mid-life crisis" as a crisis of authenticity. We are deciding if we have the courage to come out from behind the smoke-screen of our socially cultivated *persona* and be who we really are, or perhaps more aptly, *to become real* by God's grace. Regardless of life stage or age, a rule of life allows us to take responsibility for becoming our truest self, rooted in Christ who embodies our full humanity.

If you want to devise a personal rule of life, you can follow three basic steps: (1) Take a faith-illumined inventory of your life as it stands. (2) Prayerfully discern what will help you grow toward a deeper communion with God, others, and your true self. (3) Make realistic choices about disciplines you can actually commit to.

A Faith-Illumined Inventory

Grace comes to us in ways uniquely suited to who and where we are. Therefore we need to pay close attention to our current contexts. One of my colleagues calls this "taking a faith-illumined inventory."[8] Ask: What are my actual life circumstances and commitments? These are key to how your rule of life will be most naturally and effectively structured.

Start with your primary relationships. Are you married? If so, you have made vows before God and a whole community to live in a certain manner with your spouse. You have promised fidelity in marriage, growth in mutual love, and commitment to encourage, support, and care for each other in good times and bad. This is no small matter in a personal rule of life. The way you live out your marriage vows is a crucial dimension of your rule.

Do you have children? It has been observed that raising children is an automatic invitation to asceticism! You have had to learn, perhaps with irritating frequency, to release your own agenda for the sake of a child's need. You have let go your own dreams in order to make space for your children's dreams. You have sacrificed sleep and given away your youth in the wear and tear of caring for little ones. You have anguished over parenting adolescents in varying stages of the teen journey. Yet giving your children a solid foundation in life—the security of love, the clarity of healthy boundaries, affirmation of their gifts, encouragement for their hopes, and the example of a lived faith they may choose to share—is surely integral to your rule of life!

Do you care for aging parents? In our rapidly aging society, increasing numbers of adults find themselves caring for their elders, often alongside continuing support for young adult children. It is a delicate matter, finding the balance between honoring our parents' roles in our lives and taking responsibility for those matters they can no longer manage. Learning how to support and care for our elders physically and emotionally often requires genuine discernment and can become a significant spiritual practice in itself, as I will expand on shortly.

Do you consider your work a vocation, that is, a calling from God? The same basic principle applies. What does a life of integrity, respect, care, and creativity look like in relation to your coworkers, supervisors, employees, or clients? Even with work that is clearly not a calling, it is important to ask such questions. A deeply held intention to live your life with authenticity and care will permeate every kind of work—whether vocation or avocation, paid or unpaid, public or private.

As you can see, your actual commitments and responsibilities are key dimensions of your rule. They constitute the shape of your personal mission in the world at this time. In truth you already have a rule of life, whether or not you have recognized it as such. The deeper question is how you choose to live out these relationships and tasks.

We identify the particular gifts, sufferings, circumstances, vocational activities, and above all, relationships that are given to us by Providence. These, in turn, define the essential elements of our mission from God in this world, our responsibilities toward God, ourselves, and others.

William Wilson

Take a few moments to list what you consider essential in your current life commitments and responsibilities. Note down choices you have already made in terms of how you wish to live out your primary relationships and tasks. Recognize this as the basic scaffolding of your rule of life.

Discerning What We Need to Grow

Recalling that union with God is the goal of the spiritual life, we move to a process of discerning what will enable us to grow into deeper communion. A few key factors ask for consideration here: (1) the spiritual gifts and faith values that shape Christian character, such as love, mercy, justice, truthfulness, kindness, and perseverance; (2) the personality traits and preferences that help us notice how we derive our energy and what our natural physical-emotional rhythms teach us; (3) the particular circumstances and seasons of our lives that present both opportunity and limitation in relation to spiritual practices.

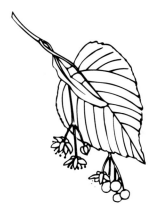

What kind of person do you want to become by practicing a rule of life? Think about the spiritual gifts and values that have most profoundly shaped your life. In which of these do you especially want to mature as you face your current relationships and tasks? What biblical texts best express for you these characteristics? As you note your responses, you will be clarifying an image of who you hope to become by grace.

Now factor in your personal traits and inclinations. Do you tend to be energetic or mellow, artistic or practical? Do you have limited physical or emotional energy that could impact how you engage your disciplines? At what time of day do you experience peak energy? Some of us wake up perky and vigorous at five in the morning, others are wide-eyed at midnight, and still others find their best energy midday. If we truly honor God and value our spiritual growth, we will give a portion of our best energies to the work of the Spirit.

Alongside these traits, ponder your innate personality preferences. What follows is derived from the basic typology of the Myers-Briggs Type Indicator (MBTI), with which many faith communities are now familiar.[9] Your natural preferences sketch a personality profile that can help you assess spiritual practices that suit you. If you do not already know your "personality type," explore the four contrasts described in the following paragraphs, and make a few notes on where you see your own preferences reflected.

1. Are you introverted or extroverted, that is, do you receive your primary energy from time alone or from fellowship with others? Introverts take readily to solitude and silence, tending to be drawn toward disciplines such as contemplative prayer and self-examination. Since extroverts find nurture in community, they are more likely to be attracted to communal expressions of worship or to acts of service and hospitality that suit an interactive personality.

2. Are you more attuned to the outer world of the senses or to the inner world of meaning? A sensing type of person

generally needs more physical embodiment in spiritual practice, perhaps using candles, icons, or prayer beads in personal worship or taking a prayerful stroll outdoors. Those attuned to the inner world of meaning will be nurtured by metaphor and attracted to pondering symbolic meanings in sacred texts, poetry, art forms, or the created order.

3. Do you relate to life largely through reason or feeling? Those more oriented to the process of rational thought need study and reflection. One dear friend who exemplifies this preference finds his deepest devotion emerging through the careful reading of weighty theologians. Many people are more oriented to their feelings and tend to see life through the lens of emotion. They seek inspiration and heartfelt relationship in spiritual practices such as singing hymns and songs; listening to inspirational speakers; or engaging in service that connects strongly with the needs, sorrows, and joys of others.

4. Do you like clear structure and regular habits or prefer spontaneity and variation? This final pair of preferences has particular impact on shaping a rule of life. If you tend toward clear structure and predictable, orderly patterns, you may have less trouble maintaining a rule of life than those who prefer to "go with the flow." It is challenging for those who love spontaneity to set regular patterns in any spiritual practice. I speak from personal experience—a dubious authority for one who teaches others about spiritual practice! Yet it is possible to create a workable rule even without the natural inclination to follow schedules.

Life Seasons and Circumstances:
An Evolving Rule of Life

As we consider how our life stages both limit and open opportunity for various practices, I hope it may be helpful to share the evolution of my own rule to illustrate how a pattern of practices naturally changes with our seasons and circumstances.

We have noted that a personal rule has as much to do with the frame of mind carried into our daily activities as with particular exercises of faith. My rule has changed significantly over the years in this regard. Early in my ministry of spiritual formation, I practiced more time-specific disciplines: silent retreats, spiritual reading, scriptural meditation, journaling, partial fasting, and evening prayers with my husband. My circumstances gave me freedom to deepen these practices; I was self-employed and enjoyed the flexibility of designing my own schedule. When I took on a full-time commuting job, my rule needed substantial reshaping. I began to practice a version of what the monastic tradition calls "vigilance over thoughts." For me this meant cultivating greater self-awareness throughout the day, including particular intentions: aiming to see God's image in every person and refraining from hasty judgments, practicing gratitude in advance and expressing thanks with real anticipation of blessing, looking for grace and humor in situations that seemed devoid of them. These aspects of my rule challenged me to grow into new habits of mind and heart.

Amid this shift in personal practices, I discovered an essay by Robert Morris that beautifully conveyed the nature of the change I was experiencing in my rule. Morris admitted that his life seemed too episodic and unpredictable to implement a steady prayer life. But one day, behind schedule and rushing, he stubbed his toe on the stairs and uttered a frustrated curse—"O God!"—along with a colorful expletive. He recognized that by invoking God's name he was, in fact, praying. And as he took several conscious breaths, he found the impulse to curse transforming into the desire for blessing. Pondering that experience, Morris recognized that his "search for a daily prayer discipline had finally found the place to set up practice"—right in the midst of daily frustrations! He began to see life's unpredictable turns as the occasion for spiritual practice and the spirit we bring to each circumstance as part of our daily offering to God.[10]

What forcibly struck me was this: Morris had moved from a *time-based* to a *situation-based* model of spiritual practice. I now had a framework for naming the shift that had been occurring in my life. Let me caution, however, against imagining that we can plunge directly into lasting changes of perception and attitude without at least periodic immersion in time-based spiritual practices. The habits formed through time-based practice come directly into play in our daily circumstances.

By the time I left full-time work and returned to self-employment, family circumstances were entirely different from my early phase of freedom. My husband and I had been caring for one or both of our elderly mothers in our home for seven years, and I would continue in the care of my mother-in-law four years more. My ability

We use specific rules and practice certain disciplines in order to come to the point where the very experiences of our daily life are the means and the place of our consummate union with God. . . . Ultimately our rule should yield and blend into the spontaneous flow of our life.

William Wilson

157

to reclaim longer periods of prayer, reflection, and journaling were intermittent at best. Moreover, my energies were sapped by the constantly increasing demands of one whose capacities were slowly diminishing. I soon realized that caring for my mother-in-law *was* my primary spiritual practice. The way I chose to be present to her—to exercise patience with her needs, to listen through her confusion, to be gentle in her care—these were the daily disciplines required of me in this phase of life. Learning to truly love in the midst of her anxiety, impatience, and deafness was perhaps the most challenging spiritual practice I have known. I cannot claim to have passed the test consistently. At times her care carried me quite effectively out of my self-absorption, and at times I succumbed to my own pity party.

As these circumstances grew more demanding and my state of physical and mental exhaustion increased, I clung to breath prayers drawn from sacred texts, including the following, that describe with great practical beauty what new life in Christ looks like:

- "As God's chosen ones, holy and beloved, clothe yourselves with compassion, kindness, humility, meekness, and patience. Bear with one another." (Col. 3:12–13a)

- The fruit of the Spirit is love, joy, peace, patience, kindness, generosity, faithfulness, gentleness, and self-control. (Gal. 5:22–23a)

- Be glad in the Lord! Let your gentleness show; the Lord is near. Don't be anxious at anything. Pray and give thanks. The peace of God will keep your hearts and minds safe in Christ Jesus. Focus your thoughts on what is excellent and admirable. All that is true, holy, just, pure, lovely, and worthy of praise. Practice these things. The God of peace will be with you. (Phil. 4:4–9 CEB, adaptation)

My breath prayers were but short portions of these texts. The adapted passage from Philippians, however, still greets me in full daily, fixed at the edge of my computer screen on a sticky note.

The Principle of Stretch and Balance

We are generally attracted to spiritual practices that seem natural to our personality. Such disciplines will likely engage our energies with greater consistency and satisfaction They offer the best path forward when getting started with a rule, especially if we have little spiritual discipline at present. Over the long haul, however, they may not be the practices that stretch us toward deeper growth or bring greater balance into our lives.

The Christian spiritual life expresses our entire being, since the Spirit is concerned with every dimension of humanity. Perhaps precisely because you are an introvert, God is calling you to open yourself to a community spiritual practice. When it is too easy to sink comfortably into private reflection, you may need to develop the relational side of your spirituality. Or precisely because you are an extrovert, God is inviting you to look inward, perhaps to pay attention to the motives or needs behind your desire to interact with others.

The Rule of Saint Benedict takes balance in human life seriously. Times of common and private prayer are balanced. The daily rhythm of monastic life balances exercise for spirit, mind, and body through prayer, study, and manual labor. We need to consider this wisdom as we choose disciplines to help structure our lives. Each of us needs balance between personal and corporate practices as well as between practices that help us look to our own hearts and those that help us forget ourselves in meeting the needs of others. By the grace of the Spirit, these disciplines work together to sustain our wholeness.

What helps you bring greater balance to your life? What kinds of choices do you already make, for example to balance work and play or personal time and family time? What activities help you to feel more whole?

God calls us to grow by drawing us beyond our comfort zones, stretching us to develop the non-dominant side of our personality. We are capable of using the dominant parts of us—those in which we feel confident and secure—to judge, control, and manipulate both others and ourselves. If I am a thinking type, I may bury my feelings or devalue them in relation to my rationality. If I am a feeling type, I may be tempted to dismiss my rational thoughts as a mere "head-trip." We need to learn that all facets of human personality are part of our psychological makeup, however recessive they may be. Balancing the comfortable fit and the challenging stretch will allow the Spirit to bring us to a more complete integration of identity.

Making Choices

If you are like me, you will by this time either be very excited by all these possibilities for spiritual growth, or you will feel overwhelmed. Some of us are tempted to think we should do everything, all at once! But of course this is humanly impossible, even for monks or solitaries who have intentionally devoted their entire lives to the practice of spiritual disciplines. As people who live in a world of families and work commitments, we must choose what seems most central and what is genuinely feasible for us. How do we go about making such choices, especially when so many seem good?

The first thing to do is pay close attention to what you feel most attracted to. Go back over the chapter headings in this book. Look at the "Invitations to Explore" sections in chapters 2, 3, 6, 7, and 9 and the practical suggestions in each chapter. Are there certain suggestions you feel especially drawn to? Is there anything that seems to "have your name on it"? Write down what comes to mind.

Next, ask yourself why you are attracted to a given discipline. Does it seem suited to your personality? Does it represent an area of growth you feel in need of at this point in your life? Does it promise a measure of balance in your life you do not currently enjoy? Are you simply attracted inwardly for reasons that are not apparent at the moment?

Look closely also at the practices described in this book that do *not* appeal to you or that may even repel you. Bring the matter into your prayer. Why do you feel such resistance to this particular discipline? Does God have anything to say to you about it? A strong negative reaction to a practice such as fasting or self-examination may reveal that you are resisting paying attention to a part of your life in need of healing. Ask God to show you what spiritual disciplines you need in your life right now. You may be surprised by the response!

To summarize, there are three basic categories of questions to reflect on in choosing disciplines for your rule of life:

- What am I deeply attracted to or repelled by, and why?

- Where do I feel God calling me to balance or stretch my spirit?

- What practices best fit my circumstances or season of life?

When you ask what practices to take up, you need to ask also what to let go. Creating space for new disciplines involves displacing other things. Think of what you give attention to that doesn't deserve your full energies: clothes, gadgets, too much daily news or social media. Letting go aspects of your life that can interfere with spiritual growth is the "ascetic" approach to rearranging your priorities.

As you let go of less important matters, you make room for the life God wants to give you. When choosing among spiritual practices, the ultimate questions are these: What gives you abundant life? What opens you more fully to the mystery of grace? What draws you into greater intimacy with the Lover of your soul? Listening to the answers that surface in your depths is the "mystic" approach to rearranging your priorities.

With some measure of clarity about these questions, you can then ask what is truly realistic to commit to. This is a matter of honoring personal limitations. Don't get carried away by your enthusiasm for changing habits. In the spiritual life, less is often more. Far better to commit to a single practice and stick with it than to take on five and quit altogether because you cannot keep up. Many of us set ourselves up for such failure every January first! The spiritual life is not a heroic achievement; it is a matter of gradual growth in faithfulness. Realistic commitment is an expression of trust and humility. The Spirit can work great transformation in you through just a few steady practices over time. Nurture the roots of a few healthy plants and observe how the garden grows.

Please understand that even with a very modest rule of life, you can expect to trip up often. Don't be too distressed by this. You are learning to walk in a particular way, just like a toddler. You will fall often, so just get up and start again. An observant person once noted that "falling in the water does not drown us. It is staying there that does it."[11] You will frequently fall back into your busy life and ordinary attitudes. On the one hand, if you give up all effort at spiritual practice you risk drowning in a flood of worldly pursuits; on the other hand, if you insist on judging and punishing yourself for skipping your practice, you will simply slow your progress. Allow yourself the grace of starting fresh each day with renewed commitment.

Abba Poemen said about Abba Pior that every day he made a fresh beginning.

Abba Poemen

Keeping Ourselves Accountable

Once you have decided on a rule of life that challenges you realistically, write it down in the simplest possible terms. Include the choices you have identified for living out relational commitments to spouses, children, elders, and colleagues. Make sure you have some measure of balance between time-based and situation-based practices. Honor both who you are now and who you hope to become by grace. Remember, this is not an eternal stone-carved document, only one that is practical at this time in your life. Place a copy of your rule where you can review it frequently, preferably near where you most often pray.

Choose at least one person you love and trust to share your rule with. Ask that person to pray for you and help hold you accountable to your practice. If you have a spiritual friend or decide to seek a spiritual director, this would be the natural person with whom to share your rule. A prayer partner, friend in faith, or small group seeking spiritual growth together could also serve in this role. Spouses and other family members should know enough of your rule to encourage your practice or at least not interfere with it needlessly. The better part of wisdom suggests that you *not* expect your spouse to be the primary person holding you accountable in your spiritual life.

When you become serious about developing spiritually, it is important to seek support from your faith community. The Christian life is dangerous terrain to travel alone. We are simply not designed to make it on our own and will find only loneliness and illusion if we insist on forging a solitary path. History is littered with the spiritual bones of aspiring Lone Rangers. It is easy to lose heart when our disciplines become boring, difficult, or do not produce the results we expected. Because we are novices, our perceptions are limited and inadequate. Moreover, we are quite capable of manipulating any spiritual discipline for our own ends rather than offering it to God as a means of transforming grace.

We need the wider community of faith to help us stay on track. That community comes to us through corporate worship, study, and service and through the grace of individuals whose experience and wisdom can guide our own. The body of Christ is given to us for mutual encouragement, support, clarity, and love. To receive that gift in all humility is an experience of grace. Indeed, the last word in practicing a rule of life is to seek divine grace in the whole of it and in every part. Grace is finally the key to all spiritual progress!

Concluding Thoughts

I trust it is very clear by now that the spiritual life in Christian practice is a joint intention. It joins the personal and the corporate: our individual disciplines need to be practiced in the context of a community of believers if they are to glorify Christ. It joins the inner and the outer: the disciplines that search and speak to our own hearts must be balanced by disciplines that engage us in self-forgetful service to others if they are to bear fruit in God's kingdom.

Finally, the Christian spiritual life joins the divine intent for us with our own intent to love and serve God more completely. Our desire to know the Lover of Souls intimately is far outweighed by a divine passion to draw us into the eternal, tender embrace of holy love that is our created destiny. Because our God is patient and faithful, we can offer our stumbling, inconsistent efforts at spiritual practice and know they will be accepted. As long as our desire is true and we are willing to persist despite many stalls, detours, and breakdowns, God's grace will strengthen us to persevere. The goal is infinitely worth all the effort, confusion, and pain along the path:

> For this slight momentary affliction is preparing us for an eternal weight of glory beyond all measure, because we look not at what can be seen but at what cannot be seen; for what can be seen is temporary, but what cannot be seen is eternal. (2 Cor. 4:17–18)

It is my prayer that you will have found something in these pages to encourage and guide your spiritual quest. The practices described are means of grace, paths to the food and drink we crave in our inmost being. God can use them to nourish us. Together they offer a true soul feast. Since you cannot indulge in a feast all at once, only in courses and over time, I trust you will choose and savor each food for the unique nourishment and delight it can give. Resist the temptation to be greedy at this table. Its bounty will not be depleted by many hungry seekers. Indeed, the more children at this table, the greater the abundance of supply. God's economy is not based on scarcity. The richest sources of spiritual nurture are permanently set upon the table of our lives. While it would be folly to ignore or refuse them, there is no need to rush or grab. Take and receive as you have need. Enjoy each to the full.

> Oh, taste and see that the LORD is good!
> Happy are those who take refuge in God![12]

O, Begin! Fix some part of every day for private exercises. . . . Whether you like it or not, read and pray daily. It is for your life; there is no other way: else you will be a trifler all your days. . . . Do justice to your own soul; give it time and means to grow. Do not starve yourself any longer.

John Wesley

Notes to the Text

1. I first heard Rueben offer this illustration when we cotaught a week of the Academy for Spiritual Formation, circa 1990. Used by permission.

2. William O. Paulsell, "Ways of Prayer: Designing a Personal Rule," *Weavings* 2, no. 5 (November–December 1987): 40.

3. See *The Rule of St. Benedict*, trans. Anthony C. Meisel and M. L. Mastro (Garden City, NY: Image Books, 1975).

4. Adapted from William O. Paulsell, "Ways of Prayer: Designing a Personal Rule," *Weavings* 2, no. 5 (November–December 1987): 41–42. Paulsell cites the pope's *Journal of a Soul* (selected diary entries) as a useful resource for those serious about formulating a personal rule.

5. See Catherine de Hueck Doherty, *Poustinia: Encountering God in Silence, Solitude, and Prayer*, Madonna House Classics, vol. 1 (Combermere, ON, Canada: Madonna House Publications, 2012).

6. Adapted from William O. Paulsell, "Ways of Prayer: Designing a Personal Rule," *Weavings* 2, no. 5 (November–December 1987): 42. You can find out more about Dorothy Day at http://www.catholicworker.org. A new book about her, titled *Dorothy Day for Armchair Theologians*, is now available through Westminster John Knox Press (2014).

7. William O. Paulsell, "Ways of Prayer: Designing a Personal Rule," 43. In his book *Rules for Prayer* (Mahwah, NJ: Paulist Press, 1993), Paulsell adapted these "Ten Commandments" from Martin Luther King Jr., *Why We Can't Wait* (New York: Signet Books, 1964), 69.

8. "Faith-illumined inventory" is a phrase I picked up in a workshop led by Fr. William Wilson, a former Trappist Cistercian monk who is now a married Anglican priest with children. He treats this idea, using the simpler phrase "a faithful inventory," in a brief chapter on rule of life in his book *Four Essentials: Classical Disciplines of Christian Spirituality* (Birmingham, AL: Spiritual Life Ministry Foundation, 2004).

9. The Myers-Briggs Type Indicator (MBTI) is now so widely known that most readers will be familiar with their own four-letter "personality type." For the sake of those unfamiliar with it, I have chosen to use standard MBTI words for temperament contrasts that are easily understood, such as Thinking and Feeling, and to substitute common language for words whose meaning is more opaque, such as Judging and Perceiving (all without caps to discourage turning them into hard or permanent categories). A helpful resource for the application of MBTI to spiritual practices is David Keirsey and Marilyn Bates, *Please Understand Me: Character and Temperament Types* (Del Mar, CA: Prometheus Nemesis, 1984). Keirsey wrote a greatly expanded version, *Please Understand Me II* (1998), which many consider even more useful.

10. See "The Second Breath" in *Weavings* 13, no. 2 (March–April 1998), an article that informs several of the paragraphs following.

11. From Douglas Steere, *Dimensions of Prayer*, 28.

12. Psalm 34:8 as adapted in *Psalms for Praise and Worship: A Complete Liturgical Psalter*, eds. John C. Holbert, S. T. Kimbrough Jr., and Carlton R. Young (Nashville: Abingdon, 1992), 57.

Notes to the Sidebars

Dorotheos of Gaza, sixth-century Palestinian monk. Epigraph from *Dorotheo of Gaza: Discourses and Sayings*, trans. with introduction by Eric P. Wheeler (Kalamazoo, MI: Cistercian Publications, 1977), 194.

William O. Paulsell, former dean of Lexington Theological Seminary and Disciples of Christ minister. "Ways of Prayer: Designing a Personal Rule of Life," in *Weavings* 2, no. 5 (November–December 1987): 44.

Dallas Willard, from foreword to Trevor Hudson, *The Serenity Prayer* (Nashville: Upper Room Books, 2012), 9.

William Wilson, former Trappist monk, now married Anglican priest and bishop. From *Four Essentials: Classical Disciplines of Christian Spirituality* (Birmingham, AL: Spiritual Life Ministry Foundation, 2004), 120.

William Wilson, Ibid., 121.

Abba Poemen, elder of the Egyptian desert in Scetis circa fourth–fifth centuries. From *Desert Wisdom* by Yushi Nomura (Garden City, NY: Doubleday & Company, Inc., 1982), 1.

John Wesley, Anglican clergyman, evangelist, and founder of Methodism, 1703–1791. From letter to a lay preacher, cited in Umphrey Lee, *John Wesley and Modern Religion* (Nashville: Cokesbury Press, 1936), 107–8.

Group Study Guide

The following questions for reflection and suggested exercises are intended to help small groups or classes work through the material in each chapter. The book can be used for a ten–twelve session study in one of several ways: (1) Work through each of the ten chapters in turn. (2) Begin your study with a gathering for personal acquaintance and group sharing around the introduction, assigned in advance; then work through the ten chapters. (3) Assign the introduction and first chapter's reading in advance of your first meeting; then add a meeting at the end to evaluate your group process and plan how to follow up on areas of key interest. (4) As you work through each chapter, give two sessions to chapter 3, one on prayer as communication and one on prayer as communion. By combining elements of these suggestions you can use the book over twelve meetings or more.

There are likely more questions and exercises listed under each chapter than can be adequately explored in any given group or class session. You will need to select the suggestions that seem most appropriate to your group. Pay attention to what parts of your discussion are most animated and the kind of sharing that elicits the most intense interest. These may suggest what your group would like to follow up with in further study or experiential activity.

Chapter 1: Hunger and Thirst for the Spirit

1. What indications of spiritual hunger and thirst do you perceive in our time? What do you see as the reasons for this hunger? Take time to share, as you choose, your own stories of spiritual yearning.

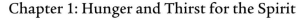

2. Discuss the terms *piety*, *devotion*, and *spirituality*. How do you respond to each of these words? What associations, positive or negative, do they hold? Look together at the following definitions of spirituality from contemporary writers:

> Spirituality is our self-transcendent capacity as human beings to recognize and to participate in God's creative and redemptive activity in all creation.[1]

> A spirituality is a walking in freedom according to the Spirit of love and life. This walking has its point of departure in an encounter with the Lord.[2]

> Spirituality is the pattern by which we shape our lives in response to our experience of God as a very real presence in and around us. . . . To be spiritual is to take seriously our consciousness of God's presence and to live in such a way that the presence of God is central in all that we do.[3]

How do you respond to these definitions? How would each of you define spirituality for yourself? What makes any given spirituality distinctively Christian?

3. Talk about *discipline* and your personal associations with this term. Why is discipline important? What are its limits? How do you respond to the idea of spiritual disciplines?

4. Look together at the exercises under "Tradition" on page 13. What does the word *tradition* evoke? Do you think there is a difference between tradition and convention? If so, how would you characterize the difference?

5. Take time to identify and reflect on the reservations or anxieties you may feel about exploring the spiritual life more deeply. All feelings, both of attraction and resistance, are important to acknowledge. They do not need to be resolved, only noted and appreciated.

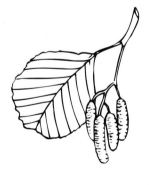

Chapter 2: Chewing the Bread of the Word

1. What is your typical way of reading? What kind of reading do you approach in an "informational mode" and what kind in a "formational mode"?

2. Discuss your understanding of the nature of scripture. In what sense is it God's Word? How do you respond to the

metaphor of the lake on page 19? Does the reverse perspective of iconography make sense to you as a description of the way God's Word works on us?

3. Talk about *Lectio Divina* and its phases. Do some stages seem more familiar or comfortable than others? Which parts do you think you might need encouragement and support for? Did any of you try out the process after reading this chapter? What did you discover?

4. Are there other kinds of written materials that you naturally read and respond to in a way similar to *Lectio Divina*? What types of spiritual reading beyond scripture are you attracted to (devotional reading, fiction, poetry)? Share with one another the books or sources that have been especially helpful in deepening your spiritual life.

Chapter 3: Communication and Communion with God

1. Begin by sharing with the group your perceptions of what prayer is. For instance, how would you define it? What is most central about your own understanding and practice of prayer?

2. Discuss communication in prayer. Share with one another how you try to listen to God and how you sometimes "hear" God. Are there certain avenues through which you seem more receptive to God's communication?

3. Talk about honesty in prayer. Did you grow up with certain assumptions or unspoken rules about what was "allowable" to say to God? How do you respond to the Psalms as a vehicle of honest emotion in prayer?

4. Share your beliefs and uncertainties concerning intercessory prayer. What experiences with petition and intercession have led you to pray as you do now? Take a look together at the various ways of describing what happens when we pray (see "Views of Intercessory Prayer," page 37). Which best express your understanding, and why?

5. Did anyone explore a new way of engaging in communicative prayer (imaging intercession, writing or paraphrasing a psalm, journaling a conversation from scripture; see pages 41–43)? If so, share your experience to whatever extent you are comfortable in doing so.

6. Have you ever considered prayer as a form of communion? Can you trust that God enjoys your company? Do you find yourself attracted or resistant to contemplative prayer?

7. Discuss impediments to your prayer. What distracts you outwardly and inwardly? How do you cope with these blocks and interruptions?

8. The relationship of prayer is essentially one of transformation. How do you feel about the possibility of being changed by God in the relationship of prayer? What do you want changed? What do you not want changed?

9. If anyone explored a contemplative prayer path (prayer of presence, prayers of the heart, Centering Prayer; see pages 45–48), share what you experienced, to whatever extent you are comfortable. Arrange to have one member of your group lead the rest in a prayer of presence (see page 45) as a closing exercise. Whoever leads this should be sure to allow spacious pauses for people to enter into the experience.

Chapter 4: Gathered in the Spirit

1. Does Kierkegaard's "theater of worship" shift your notion of what worship is? Do you think it is important for people of faith to gather for worship? Why or why not?

2. Share with one another your overall experiences of corporate worship. In what ways does it feed you? What do you yearn for that you do not experience?

3. Did you try the self-examination suggested on pages 65–66, or any other ideas for enlivening worship from this chapter? What effect, if any, did this exercise have on your experience of public worship?

4. It is often a mystery what moves us at any given time. Are there aspects of worship that frequently move you to a sense of divine presence? Does the Word more often come alive for you through music, prayer, preaching, silence, or sacrament?

5. Music expresses an intuitive, sensory, and affective side of our being. What is the role of sacred music in your worship experience? What are some of your favorite hymns and songs? What makes them special? Are there songs or hymns you just can't bear? Why?

6. Out of the crucible of African American slavery came the rich tradition of "spirituals" that speak of the unquenchable faith enabling people to not only endure but transcend pain with praise. What are your favorite spirituals? Take a look in the index of several recent hymnals to see what spirituals are included. Are you surprised at how many of our most popular hymns are spirituals? Sing one or two as a group and talk about what they have come to mean to you.

7. How do you experience the sacraments in worship? What does Holy Communion mean to you? Has its significance changed for you over time? Do you yearn for "something more" in sacramental life? If so, can you name it?

8. "Rituals, like stories, emerge from and speak to our intuitive, emotional consciousness. . . . When worship becomes too intellectual or wordy, it loses its depth and significance."[1] What do you think about this statement? What role does ritual play in your spiritual life? What about silence?

9. What is your feeling about postures and gestures appropriate to worship? Would you like more freedom of movement in worship, or are you comfortable with things as they are? What would give you the freedom to use different gestures?

10. What kinds of visual or sensory aids do you find conducive to worship (candlelight, symbols, banners, pictures, icons, fragrance, sounds, etc.)? How important is it to you to include the senses in worship? What suggestions are you comfortable with?

Chapter 5: Reclaiming Sabbath Time

1. Discuss the concept of healthy boundaries and life-giving borders in our activity level. What has happened to the natural rhythms that once supported personal and communal well-being? Do you think it is possible to restore a rhythm of sabbath time in our culture? If so, how?

2. Share ideas about how we might rest from our technological connectivity and how we could creatively help our children and grandchildren to value such rest periods.

3. How do you respond to the suggestion that the qualities of sabbath time come first in our lives as a spiritual principle (see page 71)? What difference would it make in your life

to think of evening as the beginning of God's day? Is this idea liberating or anxiety-inducing? What would it take to reframe our lives from the conventional secular rhythm to the sacred rhythm of life described on page 72?

4. Discuss what makes it so difficult to rest in our culture. Did you reflect on Psalm 127:2 (see page 73), and if so, what message or invitation did you find in it? How is trust in God related to sabbath time in your experience?

5. How many of you feel guilty when you take time out to relax? Is it difficult to give yourself permission to keep sabbath? Why or why not? To what extent is "people pleasing" involved in guilt over taking adequate rest or recreation? Whose expectations are you usually trying to meet when you refuse rest?

6. Have someone in the group read Psalm 23. Share where you hear the invitation to sabbath time in this psalm. How often, and under what circumstances, do you allow yourself to lie down in green pastures, be led beside still waters, and allow your soul to be restored? Where are your "green pastures"— those places, relationships, or activities that offer you true spiritual nourishment?

7. Take five minutes to fill in the following open-ended sentences:

   - I enjoy life most when . . .
   - I am most at peace . . .
   - I am aware of God's presence . . .

   Ask: What do my responses tell me about the kind of sabbath time I most need? Follow up with: What prevents me from taking it? Share your responses.

8. Think broadly together about what nurtures a balanced, healthy, joyful life. Gather from the group favorite self-care practices. Make a list; ask someone to type it up and distribute it.

9. Try this exercise: List some of your current activities and commitments. Then sift your priorities by asking (1) what do I *not really need* to do (that someone else could do as well), and (2) what do I *need not* to do (I don't have the knowledge/gifts; it's not the right time; it would overwhelm me). Based on responses, have everyone choose one thing on their list to let go of. Form pairs to support each other's choices with prayer and encouragement.

Chapter 6: The Practice of Self-Emptying

1. What images are associated with fasting for you? What are your reactions to the idea of fasting as a spiritual discipline? Discuss especially any anxieties or reservations you have.

2. How does your group respond to the notion of Lenten fasting as a spiritual springtime? In what ways do you believe that limits are life-giving? Explore how closely this idea relates to the chapter on sabbath time. See how many examples of this principle you can think of in life.

3. Does anyone in your group have experience with regular fasting? Invite people to share whatever experiences they have had, whether for physical, moral, political, or spiritual reasons. Do you think the motive behind a fast affects your experience of it?

4. Discuss the concept of abstinence in relation to our North American consumer culture. Reflect together on the margin quote by Gerald May on page 88.

5. Look at the alternative forms of "fasting" suggested on pages 88–89. Which of these seems most significant to you? Let your group brainstorm ideas to add to the list. How do you understand the relationship between food fasting and other forms of fasting?

6. Commit to try the exercise in practicing one form of fasting for a week, described in the lower margin of page 89. Find a prayer partner in your group to encourage and support your practice until your next meeting.

7. What do you think of the connection between fasting and repentance? Do you feel drawn in any way to take up the invitation in this section (see page 91)? How would you go about it?

Chapter 7: Of Conscience and Consciousness

1. Talk through your feelings about confession. What histories do you have with this word? How has it been used or misused in your families and churches? Why do you think that serious and specific confession has fallen into such disuse?

2. Take a look at the two basic truths described under "Points of Departure" (pages 96–97) and the exercise highlighted on pages 99–101. Talk about your responses.

3. Does anyone in your group have experience with regular self-examination? If so, perhaps that person would be willing to share in general terms how the practice is helpful.

4. Did anyone in your group try out the suggested exercise in the margin of page 102? If so, share reflections on that process. In general, how do you feel about the idea of using the Ten Commandments or the Beatitudes as an aid to self-examination?

5. Have you ever confessed a serious weakness to a trusted friend? How does this idea strike you? Talk about the natural fears and embarrassments that tend to prevent us from taking such a step. Whom do you trust with your sins or failings?

6. Clarify with one another the differences between "examination of conscience" and "examination of consciousness" as you understand them. Do you find one pattern more attractive than the other?

7. Did you try one of the two practices described under "Invitations to Explore" on pages 105–7? If so, share your experience of the process (do not share content unless you so choose).

8. Discuss the section on a true spirit of confession. What keeps self-examination healthy? What distinguishes genuine from false humility?

Chapter 8: Companions on the Journey

1. Have you ever felt, or do you currently feel, a need for companionship on your faith journey? Who has been a companion for you in the past? Is there someone who serves this role now, formally or informally?

2. Do you remember as a child finding the hidden objects in line drawings? Learning to see the hidden grace of God in daily life is something like this game. What kinds of circumstances or people help you to notice the hidden workings of God?

3. As you look through the key elements of spiritual direction on pages 116–17, which do you respond to most deeply?

4. Discuss the various styles of spiritual direction. Which do you feel more comfortable with?

5. What criteria would be most important to you in seeking a spiritual guide? What kind of personality, gifts, or traits would you look for? Make a group list.

6. How do you respond to the sample conversation of spiritual guidance on pages 123–24? Can you imagine yourself talking with someone about your prayer life or your images of God in this way?

Chapter 9: Entertaining Angels Unawares

1. Share with others your most vivid experience of receiving hospitality. Then share your most satisfying experience of offering hospitality.
2. What seem to you to be the most essential ingredients of hospitality? What is the difference between hospitality and entertainment?
3. Have you ever felt you met Christ in a complete stranger? Talk about the idea of offering hospitality to strangers. What is attractive and what is frightening about it?
4. Share incidents in your life in which the expected role of host and guest, giver and receiver, were reversed. Were you comfortable with the reversal? What did you learn?
5. Share with one another your experiences of God's hospitality to you.
6. Talk about how you offer hospitality to God. How well are you able to receive divine love, to listen to the Spirit, to respond to what you hear?
7. Who are the strangers and enemies in our lives today? What would offering them hospitality look like? What would make it possible to do so, in your estimation?
8. Discuss the practical ideas for hospitality at home, church, workplace, and in the civic arena. Which of these seem most important? most practical? What ideas can your group contribute?

Chapter 10: Putting It All Together

1. At your final meeting take time at the beginning to share with one another what has been most significant for you in the course of this study.
2. Discuss the place of structure in our lives. Why do we need it? How much do we need? When does it get in the way, and when does it facilitate the way?

3. Talk about the differences you see between natural growth and spiritual transformation (see page 151). How do you understand the purpose of a rule of life?

4. Look through the "Examples of Personal Rules" section. Which of those described are most attractive to you and why? How might they inform the way you would want to structure your own rule?

5. Were you surprised to learn that you already have a rule of life by virtue of your relational and work commitments? What kind of clarity have you discovered about the way you wish to live out these commitments? Share thoughts about your *de facto* rule of life and how to become more intentional about it.

6. Did you find the distinction between time-based and situation-based practices helpful? In what ways can you relate the changing circumstances in your life to the author's description of her evolving rule of life over time?

7. The following is a process that will take at least half an hour. Pair up with another person in the group whom you trust and respect. Reflect on any decision you may have made concerning the practices you need or desire in your life at this time. Share your thinking and discernment with each other. Discuss especially your responses to the three questions under Making Choices on page 160. Talk about how your priorities, personality, and circumstances affect realistic choices. Let your partner reflect affirmations or questions back to you. Reverse roles. Ask each other to pray for continued guidance, discernment, and strength of commitment. Promise support and encouragement to each other in specific ways beyond this meeting time: for example, schedule brief notes, telephone calls, prayer, or periodic meetings.

8. Take a little time to express your gratitude to one another for the time, insight, and support shared in this group over the period of your study. End with prayer, song, or both!

Notes to the Study Guide

1. Suzanne Johnson, *Christian Spiritual Formation in Church and Classroom* (Nashville: Abingdon Press, 1989), 22.

2. Gustavo Gutierrez, *We Drink from Our Own Wells* (Maryknoll, NY: Orbis Books, 2003), 35.

3. Howard L. Rice, *Reformed Spirituality* (Louisville, KY: Westminster John Knox Press, 1991), 45–46.

4. John H. Westerhoff, *Bringing Up Children in the Christian Faith* (San Francisco: HarperSanFrancisco, 1980).

Made in United States
North Haven, CT
20 January 2022